# Mobile-First Journalism

D0190536

Media publishers produce news for a full range of smart devices – including smartphones, tablets and watches. Combining theory and practice, *Mobile-First Journalism* examines how audiences view, share and engage with journalism on internet-connected devices and through social media platforms.

The book examines the interlinked relationship between mobile technology, social media and apps, covering the entire news production process – from generating ideas for visual multimedia news content, to skills in verification and newsgathering, and outputting interactive content on websites, apps and social media platforms. These skills are underpinned with a consideration of ethical and legal concerns involving fake news, online trolling and the economics of mobile journalism.

Topics include:

- understanding how mobile devices, social media platforms and apps are interlinked;
- making journalistic content more engaging and interactive;
- advice on how successful news publishers have developed mobile and social media strategies;
- adopting an approach that is entrepreneurial and user-centred;
- expert interviews with journalists, academics and software developers;
- learning key skills to launch and develop news websites, apps and social media outputs.

*Mobile-First Journalism* is essential reading for journalism students and media professionals and of interest to those studying on courses in social and new media.

**Steve Hill** is Course Leader of the MA in Multimedia Journalism at Westminster University, London. Previously, he lectured at Southampton Solent University, UK, and has a background in technology journalism. His books include *Online Journalism: The Essential Guide* (with Dr Paul Lashmar, 2013).

**Paul Bradshaw** is Course Leader for both the MA Multiplatform and Mobile Journalism and the MA in Data Journalism at Birmingham City University, UK. He also works as a consulting data journalist with the BBC England Data Unit. His books include the *Magazine Editing* (with John Morrish, 2011), *Snapchat for Journalists* (2016) and *Online Journalism Handbook* (2018).

# Mobile-First Journalism

Producing News for Social and
Interactive Media

**Steve Hill and Paul Bradshaw**

Routledge
Taylor & Francis Group

LONDON AND NEW YORK

First published 2019
by Routledge
2 Park Square, Milton Park, Abingdon, Oxon OX14 4RN

and by Routledge
711 Third Avenue, New York, NY 10017

*Routledge is an imprint of the Taylor & Francis Group, an informa business*

*British Library Cataloguing-in-Publication Data*
A catalogue record for this book is available from the British Library

*Library of Congress Cataloging-in-Publication Data*
Names: Hill, Steve (Lecturer in journalism), author. |
Bradshaw, Paul (Data journalist) author.
Title: Mobile-first journalism : producing news for social and
interactive media / Steve Hill and Paul Bradshaw.
Description: London ; New York : Routledge, 2019. | Includes index.
Identifiers: LCCN 2018019287 | ISBN 9781138289307 (hardback : alk. paper) |
ISBN 9781138289314 (pbk. : alk. paper) | ISBN 9781315267210 (ebook)
Subjects: LCSH: Online journalism. |
Journalism–Technological innovations. | Digital media.
Classification: LCC PN4784.O62 H545 2019 | DDC 070.4–dc23
LC record available at https://lccn.loc.gov/2018019287

ISBN: 978-1-138-28930-7 (hbk)
ISBN: 978-1-138-28931-4 (pbk)
ISBN: 978-1-315-26721-0 (ebk)

Typeset in Goudy
by Out of House Publishing

# Contents

# Figures

# Tables

# Preface

When we began researching this textbook, resources on mobile journalism were focused almost entirely on one aspect – how reporters record video content using smartphones. There was lots of material about framing techniques and which company manufactures the best microphone or tripod, but not a lot else.

This book aims to correct things. The impact of mobile and social media on journalism is massive. Tech analyst Ben Evans wasn't exaggerating when he proclaimed in 2016 that mobile is 'eating the world'. The audience (our users) view and engage with journalism content on a range of smart devices manufactured by tech giants such as Apple, Samsung and Amazon. Today a few social media companies, led by Facebook, dominate the distribution of news. Many media companies worry about power being put in the hands of so few large tech companies.

Mobile has leapfrogged print newspapers, desktop computers and traditional radio as the main way we stay informed about the world. Only TV news is more popular in the UK. As we will see later in this book, Google's Android software is the most popular operating system (OS) in the world, overtaking computers running Windows. Mobile and social media continue to have a radical and transformative impact on journalism. So we had no choice but to write this textbook!

This book isn't just about shooting video on mobile, although this is a core skill. We start by outlining a definition of mobile and social media journalism which is much broader than that contained in other textbooks. Our users view and engage with journalism content on a full range of devices and platforms. Some devices are mature technologies – such as iPhone and iPad. We encourage an experimental approach to newer smart devices and social platforms. We focus on newsgathering, production, output and design and take an approach to journalism that is user-centred – i.e. we focus on the audience throughout. In doing so, we look at the interlinked relationship between mobile devices, social media, news websites and apps.

The book has four core principles:

1) Mobile and social media are two sides of the same coin

Mobile and social media grew up together. Smartphones, tablets, smartwatches and even Amazon Alexa devices are social tools. We may use them to communicate with friends and often personalise them through the selection of apps and their appearance. Social media predate smartphone technology (and even the birth of the World Wide Web), but the success of the likes of Facebook, Instagram, Snapchat, Twitter and WhatsApp has been shaped by the availability of smart devices.

2) Adopting an approach that is mobile first and user-centred

Media companies have had to adapt to technology change. In the late 1990s they adapted the print user experience to desktop. Back then, we spoke about a publishing strategy that was web first where 'newspapers' broke their stories on the internet before print. The iPhone launched in 2007. It took time, but creating interactive content for mobile is now commonplace. Mobile and social is at the heart of the newsgathering process, although there are often subtle differences in strategies between media companies across Europe.

Media companies may claim to be user first, i.e. they accept that audiences consume and interact with journalism in the format and on a device and platform that is the most convenient at any given moment – whether that is a phone, TV or an internet of things (IoT) device. As journalists, being user-centred means we too must be highly adaptable to changes in technology.

3) Coding for journalists

Learning a little about coding makes journalists more employable. We discuss the concept of the code-friendly journalist. The aim is to understand how app developers, data visualisers and designs work within large media organisations.

4) Understanding the economic challenge

Generating revenue from online content remains challenging, to put it mildly. In fact this may be the biggest understatement you'll read in this book! We look at how content is monetised, i.e. how it generates revenue. There are risks in allowing distribution of content to be put in the hands of a few, relatively unregulated (compared to news organisations), social media giants. We consider whether social media companies need to do more to invest in journalism and reduce the amount of fake news and trolling of users on their platforms.

So now you know the aims of the book, let's get cracking.

# Acknowledgements

**From Paul:** Thanks to my students on both the MA in Multiplatform and Mobile Journalism and the MA in Data Journalism at Birmingham City University, who are always bringing me new examples of social storytelling and exploring new journalism techniques. Maria Crosas Batista, Carmen Aguilar Garcia, Jane Haynes, Zoe Head, Jonny Jacobsen, Barbara Maseda, Lea Nakache, Anna Noble, Victoria Oliveres, Carla Pedret, Michael Smith and Wan Ulfa Nur Zuhra are just some that did so while I was writing this book. Thanks also to my colleagues at the university whose knowledge and experience across a range of platforms I continually drew on, and those in the industry whose conversations helped whether they knew it or not: Caelainn Barr, Martin Belam, Emily Bell, Inger-Lise Bore, Bob Calver, Alberto Cairo, Sam Coley, Faye Davies, Ross Hawkes, Jon Hickman, Sarah Jones, Diane Kemp, Nick Moreton, Siobhan Mullen, Nic Newman, Rasmus Nielsen and Caroline Officer all deserve particular mention. To Steve for allowing me to co-author the book, and Kitty Imbert at Routledge for shepherding it through. Most of all, as always, to my family, who make it all fun.

**From Steve:** Many thanks to: my co-author Paul for joining me on this project. His website, OnlineJournalismBlog.com, remains the most influential resource for online journalism education in the UK and beyond. Everyone at Routledge who worked on this book, particularly Kitty Imbert and our former commissioning editor, Niall Kennedy. The photographers and illustrators who granted permission to use their work. Thanks to Matt Cooke, Matthias Guenther, Dina Rickman and Aidan White for agreeing to be interviewed. All the staff and students in the journalism department at Westminster University. Thanks to Dr Mercedes Bunz, Jim McClellan, Dave Gilbert and Deborah Vogel for their support, interesting chats and for being wonderful colleagues. My friend Mary Hogarth (Bournemouth University) for support and advice on book writing over many, many, years and my tech journalist friend Ken Young. Most of all, a big thank you to my mum and dad – Brenda and Malcolm. This textbook is dedicated to Tina and to her father Mr Rennie Tan (1942 to 2017).

# Introduction

## Mobile and social media journalism – past, present and future

The mood around mobile and social has changed dramatically in 2018. To those working in the field, it can sometimes feel like being caught in the crossfire of a battle. Fake news, Russian trolls, concerns over filter bubbles and hoaxes, censorship, algorithms and profit warnings have all shown that the path to mobile-first publishing is going to be anything but an easy one.

Like any new territory, the mobile landscape is being fought over fiercely. Step back from the crossfire and you will see that different actors are fighting over different things, in different ways: and there isn't just one battle, but three.

The commercial battle first erupted in 2013 when audience figures on news websites began to show some unusual changes: mobile visitors were starting to outnumber those on desktop. At first this was just happening at weekends, but things accelerated quickly: within the space of a year mobile-driven activity dominated every day of the week.

News organisations concerned with delivering those audiences to their advertisers had to adapt more quickly than they anticipated to a mobile-first strategy. The pioneering online publisher BuzzFeed went further than most: in 2014 it began hiring for a new BuzzFeed Distributed division, producing what would come to be known as 'native content' – journalism which existed primarily on social platforms rather than on the publisher's website. Others followed suit, with some businesses built entirely on Facebook.

Other publishers began producing video in square ratio so that it would work on a vertical screen, invested in teams dedicated to chat and social platforms, and hired partnership managers to collaborate with their new 'frenemies' – the web giants that news organisations' advertisers were fleeing to, but whom they were still increasingly reliant on to distribute their news. They looked to move into this new territory with journalists who could speak the language of social media, telling stories in different ways.

Meanwhile, another battle had opened on a second front – and this one was political. For as long as social media existed, there had been a cat-and-mouse game between protestors communicating via social media and authorities clamping down on the platforms being used: such was the case during the 2007 Myanmar protests, the Iranian elections during 2009 (when the US State Department famously asked Twitter to postpone updating its network so that its service would continue uninterrupted) and the events of the Arab Spring.

But in 2016 that information war entered Western consciousness too, and in new forms, as evidence surfaced of Russian attempts to interfere in the US election. Donald Trump was to regularly use the phrase 'fake news' to discredit critical news coverage in his own country, but it was fake news as a political tactic by foreign agents, alongside the use of 'troll factories' and fake accounts, that would come to public prominence.

Social platforms have been on the defensive ever since. Facebook performed a significant U-turn when it announced it would be taking steps to protect election integrity. Twitter identified and closed down 2,752 profiles believed to have been run by Russia's Internet Research Agency – many of which had been quoted in the UK media as if they were real people (Hern, Duncan and Bengtsson 2017). Then it closed down another 200,000 the following year. And Tumblr refused to comment when BuzzFeed reported that it was also being used by Russian trolls.

This information war could prove to be the most significant for modern journalists: by turning our territory into a battlefield it risks turning us all into war reporters by default: verification skills are no longer the preserve of the hard-bitten hack; information security is everyone's concern when news media are a target for state hackers.

But it is the third battle which is most easily missed: a battle of culture. If there was an opening shot that was fired here, it may well be 2016's open letter to Mark Zuckerberg from the editor-in-chief of the Norwegian newspaper *Aftenposten*, Espen Egil Hansen. In it, he responded to a demand from Facebook that the newspaper take down an iconic Vietnam war photograph by Nick Ut from its Facebook page. 'Dear Mark,' he wrote. 'You are the world's most powerful editor … I think you are abusing your power, and I find it hard to believe that you have thought it through thoroughly.'

These shots have continued to ring out from all corners. In early 2018 conservatives reacted angrily when Twitter froze or deleted thousands of accounts that it suspected of being bots, just weeks after the company had been accused of 'shadow banning' conservative accounts by downgrading certain tweets. And social media companies have been accused of not censoring *enough*, as trolls use their platforms to target prominent female figures – including journalists – or incite hatred based on ethnicity and sexuality.

The cultural war affects journalism in particular because is a fight to be heard, and a battle for relevance. It is a battle that takes place within news organisations too: while some editors and producers struggle to maintain a system where news organisations still control both the news agenda and its distribution, many news consumers already live in a world where agendas are set – via algorithms – by a combination of friends, family, strangers and editors; and where news does not begin and end at fixed times and spaces.

The cultural war is also a format war: the traditional inverted pyramid of newspaper storytelling has been overtaken by a proliferation of other shapes: engaging with a modern audience means engaging with new formats too, from the rise of visual journalism, live coverage and livestreaming, to GIFs, emojis and memes. Those who only speak in the language of the past risk losing the battle for the future.

Of course amidst all this fighting it can be easy to forget about the original promise of social and mobile – the opportunity to bring a wider range of voices into journalism, and tell stories that would otherwise be left untold; to report from places and times that a traditional news crew could never reach; and engage audiences who would otherwise be disconnected from our reporting.

These promises remain as important as ever in 2018. And as the battles over money, power and culture come to a head, it is important to remember this: retreating to the old ways is not an option. We need to move forward. This book should prove a useful map to this exciting new territory.

## Reference

Hern, A., Duncan, P. and Bengtsson, H. (2017) Russian 'troll army' tweets cited more than 80 times in UK media, *Guardian*. Available at www.theguardian.com/media/2017/nov/20/russian-troll-army-tweets-cited-more-than-80-times-in-uk-media

# 1  Understanding the user

**This chapter will cover:**

- The relationship business
- What is social media?
- Status in the community
- Isn't all news social?
- Smartphone addiction
- Mobile and social media – two sides of the same coin
- Personalised, portable, social and always on
- Mapping the mobile and social media landscape
- Mobile wars
- Technology and identity

## Introduction

Journalists have a responsibility to serve their audience. Talk to any newspaper or magazine editor and they will be able to list the average age, gender, social class and typical occupation of their readers. Traditionally, this information is gathered using reader surveys or audience focus groups.

If magazines have 'readers', then mobile websites and apps have 'users'. Analytics software is used to collect data on a website's most popular stories, page views, location of the user and the social media sites that generate the most traffic, etc. Google Analytics (analytics.google.com), which is free, is one of the most popular tools for monitoring news websites.

Throughout this book we encourage you to have a user-centred approach to your journalism, which takes into account the interactive nature of mobile and social media output. Having people view your content (a measurement known as 'reach' on social media) is one thing, but a user interaction with content is better. 'Engagement' is used to measure the number of shares, comments or other interactions with our journalism content on social media. We can also measure 'dwell time' – the time spent viewing an article online.

This data allow us to build up a picture of the user and the content they find useful.

This chapter seeks to understand how modern users not just view, but engage and interact with digital content. People do all kinds of things on their mobile devices and much of it *isn't* related to journalism at all. Mobile games, rather than media brands, dominate the Apple Store and Google Play top ten charts. Two classic examples of addictive and popular mobile games are Candy Crush and the augmented reality game Pokémon Go.

We use the term 'user' rather than 'audience' in this chapter. The term audience is problematic as it suggests passivity, i.e. a group of people passively watching TV in their living rooms. It is a model of media that presents the audience as the 'child' and we, the journalist, as a 'parent' who is 'teaching' the children what they need to know about the world. In fact the classic advice for feature writers is often 'show, don't tell' – we should allow the reader to experience the story through action, words, thoughts, senses rather than summarising the facts of the story.

Many theorists have outlined this changing producer–user relationship. Academic Jay Rosen (2006) coined the phrase 'the people formerly known as the audience' over ten years ago. Henry Jenkins (2008) described user participation as being an integral part of what he referred to as 'the new economy'. The ideal media consumer was 'active, emotionally engaged, and social networked', according to Jenkins.

Clay Shirky (2008) said mass media is shaped like a megaphone – content is 'broadcast' from a centralised location to a large audience made up of passive receivers of content. A radio show or article in a print newspaper cannot be changed, altered or interacted with by the audience. Social media and mobile technology encourages far more interactive modes of communication. Users switch between creating their own content (photos, videos, etc) and publishing it. They share gossip with their friends and consume content created by mainstream media brands, such as the BBC and CNN, all in a single day.

- **Mass media content – viewed by 'audiences'**
- **Digital content – engagement and interaction by 'users'**

A shift has taken place from a 'focus on individual intelligence, where expertise and authority are located in individuals and institutions, to a focus on collective intelligence where expertise and authority are distributed and networked' (Hermida, 2012).

We have moved from information scarcity in the pre-web days to information oversupply. The fact that social media are global, forever changing and allow anyone to publish, makes understanding them problematic. Journalists today are 'sense-makers' – explaining the importance of events to users who are being bombarded by information, much of it of dubious quality.

## The relationship business

Facebook has always known it is in the user-relationship business, not the content creation business. It aims to connect people, e.g. groups of friends together or users with advertisers. Facebook doesn't create much content itself. It likes to leave that bit to its users or content providers. Social media companies often claim to be merely platforms for others people's content, rather than media publishers.

### The journalism business

If you want to annoy a journalist, refer to the news, features and packages she or he produces as 'content'. Most journalists pride themselves on the fact they will try to 'break' stories and influence the public debate. The word 'content' suggests they are creating stories solely to fill a space online or to generate advertising revenue, hence the quality of the content really doesn't matter.

In 1994 the *Daily Telegraph* was the first UK national newspaper to launch a website – the Electronic Telegraph. Like many newspaper sites back then, it was little more than text and images from one platform – the printed paper – shoved onto to another platform – the web.

The *Telegraph* is in the journalism business – it invests in news production, employs professional journalists and seeks to 'break' exclusive stories. It embodies public sphere journalism much like the BBC, *Guardian* and *The Times*. But traditional media – print and broadcast – must also realise that they are now in the online relationship business and must engage at a much deeper level with their users.

Jeff Jarvis, the journalist and academic, has criticised traditional media companies for focusing on counting audiences rather than developing deeper relationships with the communities of interests they serve.

Print publishers cherish their lists of subscribers – the names, addresses and bank details of people who have the publication delivered to their homes. Subscribers are, by definition, the most loyal readers of a publication. Instead of picking up the magazine in a newsagent one month, but perhaps not the next – subscribers get the magazine delivered every week or month.

In fact looking at magazines in pure business terms, the subscriber list, along with a strong brand, are the two most valuable things a print publisher possesses. Sadly over the last 20 years, once loyal readers have become increasingly disloyal. They have cut their magazine subscriptions and have moved to accessing content for free online. But for decades the levels of engagement with print readers has rarely gone beyond collecting names, addresses and bank details.

### The relationship business

Clay Shirky (2008) said mass media is shaped conceptually like a megaphone – where content is 'broadcast' from a central point. Social media look very different. Social media are 'horizontal media' where information is shared person-to-person in a model that appears 'flat' and 'networked'. Journalists and media brands are no longer the centre of attention. With this networked model, journalism content mixes freely with gossip and personal updates. Once the main producer of content to a loyal audience, journalists have been side-lined on social media.

The internet was never *just* a technology. It always had a social dimension. People sent email (electronic mail) before the invention of the World Wide Web. Ray Tomlinson is commonly thought to have sent the first email in 1971. The World Wide Web, invented by Sir Tim Berners-Lee, arrived much later in the 1990s.

The post-millennium saw the rapid rise and fall of a series of social media sites. Those with long memories may recall social platforms such as Friendster (launched in 2002), MySpace (2003) and Bebo (2005). One platform that rose to fame and has yet to fall is 'TheFacebook', as it was known at launch. Created by Mark Zuckerberg from a dorm room at Harvard in 2004, it incorporated social technology such as email, message boards, direct messaging and group chat into one single platform. What separates Facebook from the social media failures is its focus on the user experience and keeping things simple. This is something we will return to throughout this book.

While traditional media companies like the Telegraph have relationships with their audiences of sorts, it is nothing compared to the vast amounts of user data the social media players collect. This means they can target adverts at specific demographics, based on things like age, gender, location in the world, etc.

As we mentioned at the start of this section, Facebook insists it is *not* a content publisher. It is a platform that hosts other people's content and it produces none, or very little, itself.

Journalism is expensive to produce and various external bodies regulate media publishers. In contrast, technology companies work within a lighter regulatory environment. Producing quality journalism can be a lot of hassle and so the tech giants often don't wish to be involved.

However, traditional media publishers can learn much from tech companies, such as how they can embrace the interactive and the horizontal nature of social media. Some publishers still talk of having 'readers' and 'audiences' rather than appealing to communities of online users.

Jeff Jarvis (2014) states:

> Relationships – knowing people as individuals and communities so we can better serve them with more relevance, building greater value as a result – will be necessary for media business models.

He says media publishers will always sell journalism content, but content is not the end product. It is a means of learning more about the user.

The key questions Jarvis suggests you need to ask the user:

- What is she interested in?
- What does she know?
- Where does she live?
- What does she do?

Answers to these questions can be used to develop genuinely useful interactive and personalised services on the web, social media and apps. Building closer relationships is a matter of life or death for the big media players, warns Jarvis. They must change or face going out of business.

## What is social media?

So what is social media? The words most associated with social media include:

1) **Participation** – users often produce their own content, as well as viewing and engaging with content produced by others. Eyewitness user generated content (UGC) can be useful to journalists and is often shared on Twitter and YouTube.
2) **Community** – people gather in communities based on shared interests. This can often lead to participants to collaborate on projects together. You may have taken part in a Facebook Group – where online users meet to work on a specific project.
3) **Friendship** – social media traverse our private selves and public selves.

Christian Fuchs (2017) takes a broad definition of social media:

> All computing systems, and therefore all web applications, as well as all forms of media can be considered social because they store and transmit human knowledge that originates in social relations in society. They are objectifications of society and human social relations

**Mark Zuckerberg – the 'accidental billionaire'.**

*Figure 1.1* CEO Mark Zuckerberg speaking at the Facebook Innovation
Hub in Berlin, Germany, 25 February 2016

(dpa picture alliance/Alamy Live News)

Born in 1984, Mark Elliot Zuckerberg is the co-founder and chief executive officer (CEO) of Facebook. David Kirkpatrick (2011) portrays him as being a quiet and modest individual. Changes to the platform are viewed through a prism of the user experience – whether it will improve how its millions of members connect with each other and share content. At the time of writing Zuck, as he is known, is the fifth richest person in the world.

## Status in the community

As in offline communities, status is an important component for users. Whether you are on Facebook, Instagram or Twitter – it is always desirable to have a large number of friends, likes or followers of your content. In fact we often dismiss social media accounts with few followers.

Users report feeling a degree of excitement when they reach follower 'milestones', e.g. 1,000 Twitter followers or perhaps a few million, if you are a famous celebrity!

When a user shares a news article it is a vote of confidence in the content as they find it educational, informative, funny or otherwise significant. They share content because they think their friends or followers will also like it.

In this respect, we can view content as a form of 'social capital' in an online community. A large number of shares can amplify the power of the story. If this happens many times over, the content is said to have gone 'viral'. It may result in the journalist who originated the content gaining extra followers or likes.

When status is such a key element of online social communities it is unsurprising that there has been a rise in associated businesses. Klout (klout.com) will rate your online reputation not just on how many people follow your social media accounts, but also how influential it believes your friends and followers are.

Barack Obama has a near perfect Klout score of 99 out of 100. Sadly, Steve's score needs some improvement – he is rated a rather average 43! Journalists who are seeking experts to interview may study Klout scores. A hotel even offered better service to its high Klout scores guests to encourage them to post positive reviews online (Stevenson 2012).

### Isn't all news social?

The BBC *News at 10* is the most watched news bulletin in the UK, attracting an average of 4.5 million viewers (Foster 2016). To put this in context, the X *Factor*, one of the most popular TV shows in the UK, may get around 7 million viewers per episode.

At first glance, BBC *News at 10* appears to contradict everything we know about digital media. It is linear TV – the news is selected and presented in an order and at a time determined by the media producer (the editor). Using their editorial judgements, BBC journalists must determine what is important news and what isn't. Trust and authority are the bywords, which the BBC reinforces through its dramatic opening titles and sombre presentational style.

As a viewer, you may agree or disagree with the BBC's news judgement. But the reality is that as a viewer you can't engage with the programme or change its running order. Perhaps you would prefer them to cover the stories that interest you in more detail.

The way social news is shared on the web seems is very different to broadcast news. It comes more from a collective ethos of internet technology and the wisdom of the crowd. Social news is more like a 'conversation' that is shared person-to-person via mobile technology.

Steve Hill and Paul Lashmar (2014) state:

> A positive view of social journalism is that it can help on delivering one of
> the most important roles of giving a voice to people who traditionally lacked

access to the media. A critical view is that often it merely provides pseudo-empowerment to audiences.

Social journalism fills an important need in society. Frode Eilertsen (Tinius 2016a) states that, in a modern world, our basic human needs generally fall in three categories: the human, the citizen and the everyday being:

- The **Human** need is the manifestation of the fact that humans, at our core, are social beings. We seek and need contact with other human beings, and we cherish extensive and rich communication and interaction with others.
- The **Citizen** need is a reflection of those things that make us more than a mere beast. Our thirst for enlightenment in the form of knowledge and insight, as well as the practical need for being informed of the world around us that affects our lives.
- The **Everyday Person** represents our daily need to accomplish routine household tasks in our lives – small jobs, repairs, the purchase of products and services – and to be entertained. A large part of the internet economy is all about addressing our everyday needs in more convenient, faster or cheaper ways.

Eilertsen (Tinius 2016a) says 'news publishing represents one of the most essential pillars of human need and engagement' and is 'one of the most important engagement platforms in the digital era'.

## Smartphone addiction

We now turn to that little device in your pocket. You may call it a smartphone, but these are more like powerful computers. In the 1990s mobiles phones were dumb. People were happy being able to talk into them and perhaps send a text message or two. Smartphones became, well, smart, when networked to the internet via WiFi or mobile broadband. They also included other functionality, like global positioning system functionality or GPS, which told the world where you are.

It is easy to forget that the Apple iPhone is a little over ten years old, but in that short time smartphones have become essential to users' daily lives. There are 44.9 million smartphone users in the UK, the number doubling since 2011 (Statista 2017).

A study by Tecmark (2014) of 2,000 smartphone owners found users spend three hours and sixteen minutes every day using their device and rely on it to carry out on average 221 tasks a day.

We may feel a sense of loss when we are apart from our phone. The financial cost of replacing the device is often the smallest thing we worry about. It is the loss of access to data – the contacts, irreplaceable personal photos and videos. How will our friends contact us? The nightmare scenario is that we are forced to go 'off-grid' for a few days.

We use our devices to record and log important events. A forest of smartphones held aloft in the air greets bands when they appear on stage at concerts. Fans video every second of the concert for upload to YouTube at some future date. As humans we can feel a strong compulsion to document events, but we must balance this with living in the moment and enjoying the music.

Studies have examined what heavy use of mobile technology is doing to our brains. Smartphones appear to have improved our ability to multitask. A study commissioned by Microsoft (Watson 2016) states:

> While digital lifestyles decrease sustained attention overall, it's only true in the long-term. Early adopters and heavy social media users front load their attention and have more intermittent bursts of high attention. They're better at identifying what they want/don't want to engage with and need less to process and commit things to memory.

Young people consume more news content using their smartphones than older age groups. The *Digital News Report* found smartphones was the main platform for consuming news for under 25 year olds, beating all media platforms including TV news. Among older groups TV news was the most popular way of getting news (Reuters Institute 2016).

A key function of mobile devices is one of boredom killer. We access our smartphones during those 'micro-moments' when waiting for the bus or train and feel bored. In the past we would have read magazines or a newspaper.

James K. Williamson (Columbia Journalism Review 2016) states:

> Clearly, the appeal of mobile is about, well, mobility. It's convenient. It may also be about the physical touch, the handheld size, and the quiet intimacy that a phone brings. All that pulls people toward phones and away from their desktops.

## Mobile and social media – two sides of the same coin

Social media and mobile technology grew up together in the early 2000s. The technologies are so intertwined that it is hard to imagine how Instagram or Snapchat, for example, would work on a desktop or laptop computers. When Twitter launched in 2006, a year before the launch of the iPhone, smartphones were not at all commonplace. You could send Tweets from the twitter website, but it was far more common for people text their tweets to the platform using SMS. In the early days, Tweets were limited to 140 characters, a little less than a single SMS text message which was 160 characters (it reserved some characters for the username).

The technology analyst Benedict Evans (2015a) writes:

> the smartphone itself is a social platform – every app can see your friend list, access your camera, send you notifications and sit on the home screen two taps away from any other screen on your phone, so the friction of adopting them and of using more than one at once falls away.

Evans has an unassuming appearance – the rounded spectacles and jumper gives him a young and geeky appearance. But when it comes to mobile technology, he isn't averse to making big statements. He proclaimed 'mobile is eating the world' (Evans 2016) as he described how mobile usage is rising even in some of the poorest countries of the world. This provides journalists with opportunities to expand in emerging markets.

Smartphone and tablet apps provide unique functionality.

- **They can work out where they are** – location-based services, such as Google Now, knows where you live (spooky!). They know your daily commute and the types of news content you read.
- **They can see who your friends are** – by requesting access to your contacts.
- **Dating apps** – allow you to chat and date with people in your area.
- **They can access your photos.**
- **Money can be stored in an online wallet** – such as Apple Pay.

Mobile devices are also a form of converged technology – they can be used for the consumption *and* creation of multimedia content. This could be text, audio, video and digital still images. The rise of smartphone cameras has disrupted compact digital camera sales. Canon and Nikon, who dominate the market in cameras, now include phone-like facilities like WiFi and cloud storage for photos in their latest models. This is to appeal to social media users who wish to share their images online at a touch of a button.

Evans highlights more benefits of smartphone overs PCs:

> There's an old computer science saying that a computer should never ask you a question that it should be able to work out the answer to; a smartphone can work out much more. It can see who your friends are, where you spend your time, what photos you've taken, whether you're walking or running and what your credit card is.
>
> (Evans 2015a)

Smartphones apps use a combination of sensors, e.g. the phone's GPS (to see where you are) and accelerometer (your direction and speed) and APIs (application programming interface). An API is a method of communication between various software components. Facebook releases a number of APIs and its Graph API for example allows an application to access a user's Facebook data (photos, pages, people, etc), assuming the user has given the app permission. We discuss the inclusion of APIs

Evans (2015a) states:

> The sensors, APIs and data that are available (with permission – mostly) to a service you want to use on a smartphone are vastly greater than for a website isolated within a web browser on a PC. Each of those sensors and APIs creates a new business, or many new businesses, that could not exist on a PC.

Augmented reality (AR) and virtual reality (VR) provide new and exciting story-telling possibilities.

## Personalised, portable, social and always on

There are so many unique features that make mobile devices better for news consumption than laptops or desktop PC computers.

### Personalised

There was a time when the home PC – personal computer – was the height of technological development. But despite the name, PCs were not personal at all.

Smartphones, watches, tablets and other devices are individualised. Google Home, a voice controlled speaker, even recognises the sound of different people living in the same household.

We express our identity through or phones. Steve's 'wallpaper' image is that of a picture of his wife. In fact, it's pretty common for people to personalise their devices with images of their partner or children, much like they have personal photos on their desks at work. We express our identity through not just pictures, but also our ringtone, the apps we install and the colour of the device case.

Finally, smartphones are a tactile experience. We tap, swipe and touch the screens of our smart devices – this is a far more intimate experience than we have using a mouse with a desktop computer. It is no wonder we often feel very attached to these devices.

### Portable, but often used in the home

Mobile is a problematic term we use them at home, as well as on the go. They also act as second screens – we multitask using them while, for example, watching TV on the sofa.

Ben Evans (2015b) states:

> Most use of 'mobile' devices on the Internet is actually over WiFi. Most people use a smartphone when there's a laptop in arms' reach. And relatively little use of 'mobile' devices is when you're walking down the street or waiting for a coffee.

Mobile operating systems from Apple and Google are increasingly becoming the core to new internet of things devices – such as TVs, fridges and washing machines.

### Social and always on

We have said that mobile is a key driver of social media usage and vice versa. It began with SMS text messaging. The first SMS message was sent in December

1992 – it read simply 'Merry Christmas'. But this has largely been replaced by private messaging apps such as WhatsApp and Facebook Messenger, which each build upon the social nature of mobile technology.

---

### Whatever happened to the 'Facebook phone'?

Heard about the Facebook phone? We thought not. The HTC First phone launched in 2013 and was dubbed the Facebook phone as it ran an altered version of Android OS, known as Facebook Home. The company has a long history in creating hit software, but this phone was a rare failure. The company remains vulnerable in the mobile space because unlike Apple, Amazon or Google it neither manufactures devices nor has its own operating system. 'Apple and Google are the landlords, and Facebook is just a tenant', when it comes to being on mobile phones wrote Alex Heath (2017). Facebook won't have given up on the dream and it's likely it will launch smart devices in the future.

---

## Mapping the mobile and social media landscape

In this book the tech giants we will be mostly focusing are:

- **Apple** – the makers of the iPhone (smartphone) and iPad (tablet computer). It also runs the iOS operating system.
- **Google** – started life as a website search engine. However, it is its mobile operating system, Android, which interests us most.
- **Facebook** – by far the most important social media site for journalists. It also owns photo and video site Instagram and the messaging apps WhatsApp and Facebook Messenger.
- **Amazon** – is not really a player in smartphones, but has had success with Kindle Fire tablets and the Amazon Echo, featuring the voice command system, Alexa.

These tech giants dominate the lives of users. It is therefore highly likely that you will create multimedia interactive journalism content for display on many of these devices and platforms.

The power of these tech companies is massive. An article in *The Economist* (2016b) states:

> The most successful tech companies have achieved massive scale in just a couple of decades. Google processes 4 billion searches a day. The number of people who go on Facebook every month is much larger than the population of China. These companies have translated vast scale into market dominance and soaring revenues.

While old industrial giants used technology to reduce costs, we can see that the social media giants use technology to expand their user base.

### Social media user numbers

Social media sites ranked by number of active users worldwide (in millions) January 2017 (Smart Insights, 2017):

1. **Facebook – 1,871 (1.8 bn)**
2. **WhatsApp – 1,000**
3. **Facebook Messenger 1,000**
4. **QQ – 877**
5. **WeChat – 846**
6. **Qzone – 632**
7. **Instagram – 600**
8. **Tumblr – 550**
9. **Twitter – 317**
10. **Baidu Tieba – 300**

With over 1.8 bn active users or over 25 per cent of the Earth's population, Facebook dominates the social media landscape by some margin. Its global power is extended through the success of its products WhatsApp, Messenger and Instagram.

Emily Bell (Tinius 2016b) states:

> The responsibility they [Facebook] now have to distribute information fairly and transparently across countries and borders is a role Facebook did not necessarily seek. The civic and legal issues of this kind of power over information have not been close to properly explored …

You may well ask where is Snapchat in the top ten list? Positioned at 11, the social media site is expanding rapidly and is popular with under 25 year olds. However, it is not a rival to Facebook in news distribution, which is the most mainstream social media site being popular across a wide range of age groups, genders and countries.

### USA and China

'You get this feeling that you have to be out here' states Mark Zuckerberg (cited, Rao, 2011) on his decision to locate Facebook's HQ in Silicon Valley. Although in hindsight he said he would have preferred to stay where the company was founded in Boston.

Silicon Valley, a sprawling area south of San Francisco, houses giant headquarters of all the large American tech firms. There are streets with geeky names, such as Hacker Way where you will find Facebook and its 6,000 employees. Infinite

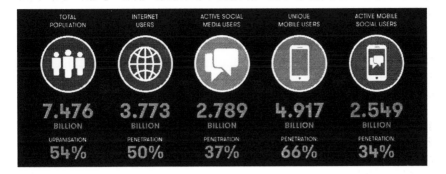

*Figure 1.2* Global Digital Snapshot – January 2017
By WeAreSocial/Hootsuite

Loop, a programming term, is the street where until 2017 you would have found Apple Campus, the tech giant's HQ. Not far away is GooglePlex where one can relax on Android Lawn. Here tourists take pictures surrounded by foam statues of the operating system's robot mascot.

The concentration of tech power in the USA, and Silicon Valley especially, is extraordinary. But there are more mobile phone users in India and China than in the USA. Tencent, the Chinese internet giant, who owns QQ (instant messaging), QZone (social media site) and WeChat (messaging) are serious rivals to Facebook. Baidu Tieba, an online forum system from search giant Baidu, is popular in Brazil, Vietnam, Japan, as well as in its native China. Huawei, Oppo and Xiaomi – all Chinese smartphone and tablet brands running Android – are becoming popular throughout the world.

## Mobile wars

We divide the mobile market into three key areas – devices, operating systems and networks.

### *Devices*

Apple is the largest tech firm in the world and creates popular mobile devices running iOS. It is hard to underestimate impact of the iPhone. It defined the market when it launched with its pleasant user experience and appealing looks. While not the first smartphone (Blackberry devices launched in 1999), it was the first to bring the concept of touchscreen when it launched in 2007.

Samsung is the second largest tech firm in the world and makes a wider range of consumer electronics than Apple, including televisions, compact cameras, washing machines and even virtual reality (VR) headsets. Its direct rival to the iPhone is the Galaxy S range of smartphones that run Android.

The *Digital News Report 2014* (Reuters Institute, 2014) found widely different usage patterns around the world:

> In general, richer Northern Europeans tend to favour Apple devices. The Spanish and Brazilians use predominantly other systems such as Android and Blackberry. Tablets see a more even split with Apple users driving almost half of all news usage.

There is no love lost between Apple and its archrival in the mobile arena, Samsung. In 2012 Apple sued its Korean rival for copying aspects of its iPhone and iPad features. *The Economist* (2012) reported at the time:

> The jury concluded that the company [Samsung] had violated a number of Apple's patents covering things such as a 'rubber-banding' feature in its firm's operating system, which makes lists jump back when pulled beyond their limit, and a 'pinch-and-zoom' feature which is now found in a wide range of mobile devices. It also upheld Apple's claim that Samsung had infringed on its design patents by copying aspects of the iPhone's design, such as the system used to display icons.

Journalists love to debate which company makes the best phones for recording audio and video. While most journalists seem to have a default preference for Apple products, it is worth remembering that cheaper Android phones are far more popular globally.

### Operating systems

The OS is the software that runs mobile devices. The battle is between two big US tech giants – Apple's iOS and Google's Android.

Steve Jobs, the late co-founder of Apple, said he would wage 'thermonuclear war' on Android to prevent it from beating iOS. He failed. Android powers around 80 per cent of all new smartphones including the entire Samsung range. It is also open-source software, meaning any phone company can adapt the program as needed and install it on its devices for nothing (*The Economist* 2016a).

## Technology and identity

Mobile and social are two sides of the same coin and technology and identity are also interlinked. We all have an online identity and offline identity. Sometimes these can be the same thing. However, some people also experiment with different identities online on social media message boards.

Real-world social relationships can be complex. Humans have become skilled at modifying what we say based on who we are talking to (the receiver), location and other contexts. You wouldn't necessarily share the same personal information with your parent as you do with, say, a close friend.

Human relationships also fluctuate in strength. Over time the close circle of friends we developed at school can break down as we develop new, deeper relationships, with others. The problem is that even the most sophisticated modern social media sites can struggle to keep up and fully represent these fluctuations.

---

### Why Google+ failed

Google+ (pronounced Google plus) launched in 2011 and aimed to take on Facebook in the social space. It attempted to represent the complexities of real human interactions, something that Facebook still struggles with, using a system called Circles. You may have a Circle of purely work colleagues – some of whom may or may not be close friends. You may have another Circle called 'dates' where, to save any uncomfortable situations, your dates won't be able to see each other! It was a great idea, but the complex nature of the platform meant is never took off in the UK. 'It looks like a cubicle farm and smells like a hospital. Posting anything on Google+ is like talking into a pillow', wrote John Herrman (2012). Ouch!

---

### Anonymous communication

Is it essential we know whom we are communicating with online? When Facebook launched it went out of its way to prevent it from being swamped with fake accounts. The company asks users provide all kinds of private information such as real name, mobile phone number, date of birth, location, schools attended and much more.

One of the best ways to verify people is by having them upload photos of themselves and to 'tag' friends in photos. This helps the Facebook algorithm to build up a picture of who the user is friends with in the offline world. The company has been successful in preventing the setting up of fake accounts. Users appreciate the fact that they can communicate with real people – that is to say, their online identity is the same as their offline identity. The platform also has been massively successful as an advertising platform, as companies can target particular demographics based on a user's age, location, gender, etc.

But Facebook's grab for private data is controversial. If you are seeking a social media site that is polar opposite to Facebook, you need look no further than the anonymous message board site 4Chan (4chan.org). Just about anything goes on 4Chan and users communicate with little censorship.

Christopher Poole, the creator of 4Chan, criticised Facebook:

> They set the bar in terms of what kind of control their users have over their identity online. They've been moving that bar slowly but surely in a direction

that they might call transparency, but what other people might call lack of choice.

(Krotoski 2012)

It raises privacy concerns as we must be aware of how much information we make available online which could be useful for corporations to advertise, the governments or hackers.

### *Is Big Brother watching?*

Security agencies, criminal hacker groups or large corporations may have an interest in viewing messages sent by journalists. Thanks to a series of documents leaked and published on WikiLeaks (wikileaks.org), we are aware that the CIA has the expertise to hack mobile smartphones.

Journalists who wish to communicate privately use apps such as Signal (signal. org), Telegram (telegram.org) and WhatsApp (whatsapp.com). These claim to provide 'end-to-end' encryption – the theory being only the communicating users can read the messages transmitted via the apps.

However, the British government claims these private apps are being used for terrorist and other criminal activities. The Home Secretary, Amber Rudd, stated after the Westminster terrorist attack in 2017:

> We need to make sure that organisations like WhatsApp, and there are plenty of others like that, don't provide a secret place for terrorists to communicate with each other.

(BBC 2017)

They have requested that private messaging systems companies provide them with a 'backdoor' to their system, essentially meaning that government spooks could view messages that the user is likely to believe are private. However, once a backdoor is created, hackers too could exploit the access.

Journalists and freedom of speech campaigners are concerned that their messages could be intercepted. So while these messaging apps provide a level of encrypted communication, they should not be relied upon.

## Conclusion

User behaviour on social media and mobile platforms is hard to analyse. Social media lacks the 'centrality' of traditional media. News no longer originates just from a few mainstream media brands such as the BBC, but comes from many small news sites and blogs. This makes for a noisy environment, where we are bombarded by information at all times.

Mobile and social media provide interactive experiences that are different to the way we watch the TV in the living room or a film in the cinema. For content to work on social media it really needs the user to engage with it – this could be a share, comment or like. Sadly, good engagement doesn't necessarily mean the content will generate big money from advertising.

## Further reading

Evans, B. (2015a) Mobile first. Available at: http://benevans.com/benedictevans/2015/5/14/mobile-first.

Technology analyst Benedict Evans writes extensively about mobile technology.

Kirkpatrick, D. (2011) *The Facebook Effect: The Real Inside Story of Mark Zuckerberg and the World's Fastest-Growing Company*. Virgin Books.

A comprehensive insight into the early days of the social media giant.

## References

BBC (2017) WhatsApp must not be 'place for terrorists to hide'. Available at: www.bbc.co.uk/news/uk-39396578.

Columbia Journalism Review (2016) In the race to win readers, which publisher will come out ahead? Available at: www.cjr.org/analysis/chaotic_world.php.

Evans, B. (2015a) Mobile first. Available at: http://ben evans.com/benedictevans/2015/5/14/mobile-first.

Evans, B. (2015b) Mobile, ecosystems and the death of PCs. Available at: http://ben-evans.com/benedictevans/2015/11/7/mobile-ecosystems-and-the-death-of-pcs.

Evans, B. (2016) Mobile is eating the world. Available at: www.ben-evans.com/benedictevans/2016/12/8/mobile-is-eating-the-world

Foster, P. (2016) BBC News at Ten extends ratings lead. Telegraph.co.uk. Available at: www.telegraph.co.uk/news/bbc/12126571/BBCs-News-at-Ten-extends-ratings-lead-over-ITV-after-launching-assault-on-its-rival.html

Fuchs, C. (2017) *Social Media: A Critical Introduction*. Sage.

Hill, S. and Lashmar, P. (2014) *Online Journalism: The Essential Guide*. Sage Publications.

Heath, A. (2017) Mark Zuckerberg wants to kill the smartphone so Facebook can control what comes next. Business Insider. Available at: http://uk.businessinsider.com/this-is-why-facebooks-mark-zuckerberg-wants-to-kill-the-smartphone-with-ar-2017-4?utm_source=feedly&utm_medium=webfeeds&r=US&IR=T.

Hermida, A. (2012) Tweets and truth. *Journalism Practice*, 6(5–6), 659–68, DOI: 10.1080/17512786.2012.667269

Herrman, J. (2012) Google doesn't understand its own social network. *BuzzFeed*. Available at: www.buzzfeed.com/jwherrman/google-doesnt-understand-its-own-social-network?utm_term=.vv7ROEjN2#.kb0dRa23j.

Jarvis, J. (2014) *Geeks Bearing Gifts: Imagining New Futures for News*. Cuny Journalism Press.

Jenkins, H. (2008) *Convergence Culture*. New York University Press.

Kirkpatrick, D. (2011) *The Facebook Effect: The Real Inside Story of Mark Zuckerberg and the World's Fastest-Growing Company*. Virgin Books.

Krotoski, A. (2012) Online identity: is authenticity or anonymity more important? *Guardian*. Available at: www.theguardian.com/technology/2012/apr/19/online-identity-authenticity-anonymity.

Rao, L. (2011) *Facebook's Zuckerberg: If I Were Starting A Company Now, I Would Have Stayed In Boston*, Techcrunch. Available at: https://techcrunch.com/2011/10/30/facebooks-zuckerberg-if-i-were-starting-a-company-now-i-would-have-stayed-in-boston/

Reuters Institute for the Study of Journalism (2014) *Digital News Report 2014*. Available at: https://reutersinstitute.politics.ox.ac.uk/our-research/digital-news-report-2014.

Reuters Institute for the Study of Journalism (2016) *Digital News Report 2016*. Available at: https://reutersinstitute.politics.ox.ac.uk/our-research/digital-news-report-2016.

Ronson, J. (2015) How one stupid tweet blew up Justine Sacco's life. *New York Times*. Available at: www.nytimes.com/2015/02/15/magazine/how-one-stupid-tweet-ruined-justine-saccos-life.html?_r=0.

Rosen, J. (2006) PressThink: The people formerly known as the audience. Available at: http://archive.pressthink.org/2006/06/27/ppl_frmr.html.

Shirky, C. (2008) *Here Comes Everybody: How Digital Networks Transform our Ability to Gather and Cooperate*. Penguin Press.

Smart Insights (2017) Top social network sites by number of active users 2017. Available at: www.smartinsights.com/social-media-marketing/social-media-strategy/new-global-social-media-research/attachment/top-social-network-sites-by-number-of-active-users-2017.

Statista (2017). Apple iOS: market share in the United Kingdom 2011–2017. UK Statistics. Available at: www.statista.com/statistics/271195/apple-ios-market-share-in-the-united-kingdom-uk [Accessed 11 February 2018].

Stevenson, S. (2012) What your Klout score really means. Wired. Conde Nast. Available at: www.wired.com/2012/04/ff_klout/.

Tecmark (2014) Smartphone usage statistics 2014 – Uk survey of smartphone users. Available at: www.tecmark.co.uk/smartphone-usage-data-uk-2014.

*The Economist* (2012) Copy that. Available at: www.economist.com/blogs/schumpeter/2012/08/apple-versus-samsung.

*The Economist* (2013) Lost between tablet and cloud. Available at: www.economist.com/blogs/babbage/2013/10/difference-engine-1.

*The Economist* (2016a). Android attack. Available at www.economist.com/news/business/21697193-european-commission-going-after-google-againthis-time-better-chance.

*The Economist* (2016b) Why giants thrive. Available at: www.economist.com/news/special-report/21707049-power-technology-globalisation-and-regulation-why-giants-thrive.

Tinius (2016a) A platform future for publishing. Available at: https://tinius.com/2016/05/18/a-platform-future-for-publishing/.

Tinius (2016b) The relationship status of journalism and platforms: it's complicated. Available at: https://tinius.com/2016/05/18/the-relationship-status-of-journalism-and-platforms-its-complicated.

Watson, L. (2016) Humans have shorter attention span than goldfish, thanks to smartphones. *Telegraph*. Available at: www.telegraph.co.uk/science/2016/03/12/humans-have-shorter-attention-span-than-goldfish-thanks-to-smart.

We are Social (2017) *Digital in 2017: Global Overview*. Available at: https://wearesocial.com/special-reports/digital-in-2017-global-overview.

# 2 The MoJo skillset

**This chapter will cover:**

- Taking a mobile first approach
- So what is mobile journalism (MoJo)?
- The role of the mobile editor
- The role of the social media editor
- Approaches to publishing on mobile
- Journalism and social media – best of frenemies?
- Predicting the future

## Introduction

In the past ten years humans have become glued to their smart devices. Whether it is on the bus, train or at home we love to tap on touchscreens. Smartwatches and voice-controlled devices deliver us news on-demand. We need to consider how journalists respond to the new opportunities and challenges the new technology provides. We will look at questions such as:

1) What exactly is mobile journalism or MoJo?
2) What are the key skills to be a mobile and social media editor?
3) What are the best ways to publish our content on social media?
4) What does the future hold in this fast developing area?

This chapter should come with a government-issued health warning – linear TV news still gets high ratings. BBC *News at Ten* presents the news at a time and in an order selected by journalists and remains popular despite an onslaught of new technology.

So just to be clear, we are not suggesting that a 'displacement effect' is necessarily occurring, i.e. usage of one medium (e.g. newspapers) decreases as another medium (e.g. online) grows in popularity (Hill and Lashmar 2014). People often multitask and consume news on mobile at the same time as watching the TV.

Clifford Nass (2010) writes:

> When people multitask with media they are consuming two or more streams of unrelated media content. It doesn't matter exactly what information they are taking in or what devices they are using.

The act of using two or more media streams simultaneously or multitasking can take many forms:

- watching *The Voice* on TV while tweeting pithy remarks about the contestants;
- tuning into YouTube while sending WhatsApp messages to a friend.

Younger people are particularly adept at multitasking, while older people can struggle to cope with too many channels of information.

While TV broadcast news remains popular, other consumption methods are struggling. The *Digital News Report* from the Reuters Institute shows an average of 62 per cent of users get their news via smartphones. In the UK they have taken over from desktop computers as a tool for news and entertainment (Reuters Institute 2018). If you thought people in the USA and UK were the heaviest users of social media for news, the reality is very different. The Reuters Institute found that urban Brazil leads the way, with 66 per cent of users getting their news from social media. Facebook, WhatsApp and YouTube are among the most popular social media outlets. Around 72 per cent of Brazilians surveyed access news via their smartphones.

## Taking a mobile first approach

It was possible to access the internet on non-smart mobile phones, but it was slow and inconvenient. The launch of the iPhone smartphone from Apple computers in 2007 revolutionised how content is consumed. Luke Wroblewski wrote in his 2011 book *Mobile First* that designers should create websites and apps that worked on small-screen devices first. Only later should they consider design for desktop or laptop computers.

Launched a year before the iPhone, BuzzFeed (buzzfeed.com) is a news brand for the mobile and social media age. It creates specially tailored content (known as native content) for individual social media platforms.

BuzzFeed UK editor, Luke Lewis, said it has drawn the majority of its traffic from mobile devices since 2013. He states:

> People are reading BuzzFeed posts at home in front of the TV and on their way home … When we have a huge break-out viral hit post 90 per cent plus come from mobile. You can't have a huge hit post on BuzzFeed without mobile devices.

(Cited, Ponsford 2014)

This book is about mobile and social media journalism. But for our audience (the users) these platforms are becoming so ubiquitous it is viewed as just another channel of content. Users move frictionlessly between different platforms for news at different times of the day. They are unlikely to reflect, as we do in this book, upon the different editorial, narrative and design skills required to output on so many platforms and devices.

Some media companies are taking a mobile and social media only strategy. Al Jazeera USA closed its cable news channel, stating that users preferred accessing its content on mobile and on-demand.

### Technological determinism

It is easy to become too focused on the latest technology and gizmos, at the expense of taking a user-centred approach. A determinist view may prioritise technology, such as platforms and devices, over the user experience or the need to produce high-quality content that follows journalism traditions. The reality is we must consider how people consume, share and interact with media in their day-to-day lives.

Cornelia Wolf and Anna Schnauber (2015) state:

> Studies concerned with the adoption of a new medium frequently focus on this single platform. This neglects the fact that the recipient may take advantage of a whole range of media options which affords many selection processes between offline and online media platforms.

Daniel Chandler (1995) states:

> Technological determinism seeks to explain social and historical phenomena in terms of one principal or determining factor. It is a doctrine of historical or causal primacy ... Technological determinism focuses on causality – cause and effect relationships – a focus typically associated with 'scientific' explanation.

A determinist approach suggests that journalism output is impacted by the digital workflow and software available to journalists in newsrooms. For example, if a website content management system (CMS) software makes it difficult for a journalist to embed video into a narrative, the journalist may produce less video. In this respect, determinism has a common sense logic. Technology restrictions can alter the types of multimedia outputs we produce. Conversely, today it is easy to produce live-streamed video and we have seen a huge amount of this appear online.

The concept of technology determinism warns us not to be blinded by the latest and greatest software and gadgets. Expensive software and content management tools are sold to media companies because they will improve efficiency, improve the quality of journalism or 'reduce costs' – often a euphemism for sacking journalists. The reality is that media companies often live to regret massive investments in technology when its worth has yet to be proven.

On the positive side, smart devices provide functionality and uses beyond older technologies such as desktop computers. Apple, for example, single-handedly popularised touchscreen navigation.

Journalism on mobile and social isn't without its practical and economic challenges, but for professional journalists these devices give us two important things:

A) **Wider reach** – as cheaper devices and faster speeds spread across emerging markets (e.g. Africa and South America), media brands find they can reach a new global audience.
B) **Better engagement** – mobile devices offer new and exciting interactive possibilities. 'Half of social network site users have shared news stories, images or videos, and nearly as many (46 per cent) have discussed a news issue or event.' (Anderson and Caumont 2014)

## So what is mobile journalism (MoJo)?

Definitions of mobile journalism, sometimes shortened to MoJo, are varied.

### A) Mobile for journalism production

MoJo is perhaps most associated with journalism video production. The backpack journalist – a 'jack-of-all-trades' who is skilled in the once distinct techniques of filming, sound recording and lighting – has now become the norm. Traditional broadcast news outlets have found cost-savings by arming their reporters with cheap mobile kit, rather than giving them dedicated cameras.

But this textbook takes a wider definition of MoJo. We go beyond video and audio production skills, although these remain important.

### B) MoJo and user generated content (UGC)

Ivo Burum (2016) relates MoJo to citizen journalism:

> Convergence and the proliferation of mobile technologies are resulting in unprecedented opportunities for citizens at grassroots levels, in particular those living in marginalized communities, to create and publish their own voice on a global scale ...

Burum highlights how citizens can tell empowering digital stories using just a smartphone, whether that be 'citizen witness' material or 'citizen journalism'. At a basic level, users may record eyewitness footage on a phone from a news event and share it with their friends on social media. Mobile technology is so ubiquitous that such footage commonly appears in mainstream news packages. Journalists need to develop skills in locating newsworthy and reliable UGC on the various social media sites. Anderson and Caumont (2014) state:

> 14 per cent of social media users posted their own photos of news events to a social networking site, while 12 per cent had posted videos. This practice has played a role in a number of recent breaking news events, including the riots in Ferguson, Mo.

Mobile technology is used in collaborative projects. The Knowle West Media Centre (kwmc.org.uk), a charity based in one of the most deprived areas of Bristol, in the west of England, brings together local residents with media professionals to create documentary videos. The aim is to empower people from disadvantaged groups to tell their own stories.

### C) *Researching stories using mobile*

Oscar Westlund (2013) states that mobile devices have enhanced the possibilities for journalists to work from location. He states:

> Internet connectivity and advanced search functionality, along with a myriad of intelligent and easily accessible apps, have obviously provided journalists with new and powerful tools for reporting news. Google queries, facts from databases, as well as gateways to informants are typically only a couple of clicks away.

Mobile and social journalists use the wisdom of the crowd or crowdsourcing techniques. This is based on the idea that the user (the audience) often knows more about a topic than a reporter does. Journalists will benefit by engaging with the user at every stage of the news production cycle and harnessing the expertise of the audience. Mobile journalism is an ongoing conversation between journalist and user. In this respect mobile journalism is not just a technological phenomenon, but has wider social and cultural significance than media platforms such as print and radio.

*What mobile journalism isn't.*

- Just videoing using phones – although there are numerous textbooks written on this topic.
- Just promoting our stories once 'complete'. Academic and journalist Jeff Jarvis (2016b) states:

> Too much of audience development is about using so-called social media to market our content. This is the last gasp of the old, mass-media reach-based business model.

*Figure 2.1* Diagram showing mobile journalism content planning
By Jools Oughtibridge / joolsoughtibridge.co.uk

## D) Devices

Smartphones, e-readers and tablets have been around for ten years and are considered to be mature technologies.

These devices may be controlled via touchscreen, rather than a keyboard and mouse. This gives smart devices a tactile experience that is very different to how we interact with a laptop. However, smart devices are given human-like properties when controlled not by touch, but by voice. Systems such as Amazon's Alexa and Apple Siri adopt a female robotic voice. Theory suggests that humans prefer female-sounding robotic voices to males as they are felt to be more trustworthy and comforting. Hence why it is an Amazon 'Alexa' rather than an 'Andrew'.

The rise of AR (augmented reality) and VR (virtual reality) has led to a new breed of immersive storytelling techniques. Wearing a wraparound headset, a user is transported to the scene of a news story.

Journalism is consumed via mobile apps. Media publishers may create their own dedicated news apps, but the social media apps are also hugely popular ways of interacting with content.

## The role of the mobile editor

So what is the role of the mobile editor? David Ho (2014), VP and Executive Editor at Hearst Newspapers Digital, states:

> The job often involves making sure graphics and images are mobile-friendly. It could be about working with developers, designers and product folks on setting a direction and helping create new news experiences. It might involve troubleshooting tech problems or testing new mobile advances.

To be a great mobile editor you need to be using the latest tools, apps, wearables and websites yourself.

Even as a mobile editor you have to be familiar with the core traits of traditional journalism – so you need to be able to write with clarity and very quickly. You need to understand the news agenda.

A mobile editor will represent the mobile user within the media company you work for. You need to encourage fellow journalists within your newsroom to think in a mobile first way. Understanding the user experience is core. Later on in this book, we examine how content is designed for websites and apps. This involves designing for various screen sizes, the orientation of the phone and its operating system (OS). There are various versions of OS available in use in 'the wild'. Many Android users still use quite old versions of the software; iPhone users tend to update their software more frequently. You also need to understand connection speeds and how that can impact the user's experience.

A mobile editor will need to be an early adopter of new technology. You will test it thoroughly to see how it can be deployed in journalism. Early adopters may beta test new products and provide feedback to the manufacturers so improvements can be made.

### Taking a user-centred approach

It is worth reflecting upon how you, your friends and family use mobile and social media technology in their day-to-day lives. As journalists, we can obsess over technology change and sometimes lose track of what ordinary folk do with their mobile devices.

Can you spot differences between how your family and friends use their devices based on age, gender or location?

Here are some key trends that have been summarised from the *Digital News Report* (Reuters Institute 2016 and 2018).

- Young people = heavy smartphone use, lower traditional TV viewing and radio viewing. Higher use of YouTube and podcasts.
- Older people = higher TV and tablet use.
- Paid print media newspapers are in decline among most age groups.

- Women = more likely to use social media apps to get news.
- Men = more likely to visit individual news sites and dedicated mobile news apps.

Here are questions you could ask your family or friends.

*A) What do you use news for?*

Academics often view news as playing an important role in the public sphere, a term coined by the German philosopher Jürgen Habermas. He described the public sphere as:

> an area in social life where individuals can come together to freely discuss and identify societal problems, and through that discussion influence political action.
>
> (De Beer and Merrill 2008)

But not all journalism is focused on the public sphere. Celebrity gossip news websites exist merely to entertain their users. These sites may wish to generate revenue for their owner, rather than educate or debate important political issues of the day. While perhaps a less worthy aim than of the *New York Times*, *Guardian* or BBC, such celebrity news sites can be extremely popular.

BuzzFeed (buzzfeed.co.uk) straddles the divide of entertainment and more serious news stories. It seeks to provide a mix of 'light' and 'shade' stories, i.e. both funny and serious content. People don't wish to be constantly depressed by the news.

*B) What role does technology play in your personal and work life?*

You don't have to be a computer programmer to have a view on this. Apps may attempt to solve a problem in the user's life, e.g. staying in contact with friends on social media or perhaps finding the route home using a mapping app. Consider how well does the app meet its stated aims?

*C) When do you engage with news?*

To understand media we no longer think purely in terms of technology and devices.

> It's actually about the right type of moments: How people behave – their intent – is the new way of thinking about media in the digital world,
>
> (Thomas Baekdal, in Tinius 2017)

Publishers can target micro moments – the five minutes or so when people are bored and need a distraction. Nobody accesses BuzzFeed looking for something;

people stumble across its content on their social media feed during those moments of boredom, often when they are waiting for something else to happen – like their bus to arrive. They wish to be entertained and informed.

A user-centred approach takes into account when, where and how people access content. So if you're working on a website aimed at young women, you may well wish to target smartphones rather than iPads. Perhaps focus your output on Instagram, which is used by more women than men.

Taking a user-centred approach sounds obvious, right? In reality there are many practical and mundane concerns that can stand in the way.

For example, there are many considerations when deciding on formats and narrative structures for a story. These may include:

- Interviews – access to experts?
- Deadlines – how much time do you have to turn the story around?
- Technology limitations of the website/social media platforms
- The user and their preferences
- Advertising – how is the content likely to generate views and ad revenue?
- How many shares/likes the story would gather.

When a class of journalism students at Westminster University were asked what influenced them most during the newsgathering process, it was the need to get interviews.

The students prioritised:

1. Could they get interviews easily?
2. Would interviewees go 'on the record'?
3. Would interviewees be coherent on camera?

Even experienced journalists can be resistant to change. They may insist on creating content in formats they understand. Those with a background in print may think in terms of text and images. Some journalists still view mobile and social multimedia outputs as secondary to writing a traditional text-based story. In reality, a far more integrated approach that embeds the needs of the user throughout the production process is required

How does journalism content generate revenue? We must factor in how we generate revenue from each platform. Media publishers must be able to make money, but banner adverts often make for a poor user experience. This is where things get very tricky. What is most popular and useful to the user often isn't what generates the most money through online advertising. Live streaming videos, such as those on Facebook Live, can gain high ratings, but low revenue.

Technology can impact news values in both positive and negative ways. Cheap equipment allows just about anyone to broadcast live. So mobile and social media are changing the way we do journalism. But it is often said that just because something is 'of interest to the public' and gets lots of clicks doesn't make it 'public interest journalism'. Similarly the rise of social media has gone hand-in-hand with poor-quality clickbait and fake news.

There are all kinds of competing practical and economic demands placed on us as journalists that can stand in the way of serving our users. You may be able to think of other limitations we face as journalists.

## The role of the social media editor

New technology has led to the development of new newsroom roles such as 'social media editor', 'audience developer' and 'community manager'. 'Platform relationship managers' coordinate relationships with social media and video companies.

As a social media editor you will need to:

- **Understand the user** – who is accessing your content, when and how? It is essential to develop a deep empathy with and understanding of the user.
- **Create content** – consider what types of content work best on each of the big social media platforms.
- **Generate revenue** – work with the platforms to generate advertising revenue.
- **Sponsorship** – you may wish to create branded content and other forms of sponsorship for advertisers.
- **Advocate a user-centred approach** – promote social media within your company.

You may be surprised to find that the role of social media editor is partly commercial, not solely a journalistic role. Decisions regarding content need to be evidence–based. You must consider the ROI (return on investment) on various media formats and formulate KPI (key performance indicators) to measure success. You will use various data tools and software to analyse reach, engagement, dwell time and revenue. It helps to be good with figures and data visualisation software.

BuzzSumo (buzzsumo.com) is a popular tool among social media editors. It allows you to analyse what content is most popular on a range of social media sites and the influencers who are amplifying it.

### Understanding communities

Online communities are brought together by:

- **Geography** – e.g. one served by a local newspaper or a hyperlocal site. People often identify with the cities and towns where they live and work. In the UK we refer to Brummies (from Birmingham), Geordies (Newcastle) and Scousers (from Liverpool) as having different traits.
- **Hobby** – The UK has a well-developed hobbyist consumer magazine sector. For example, Bauer Media (bauermedia.co.uk) publishes titles such as *Angling Times* – the UK's largest fishing newspaper which launched in 1953, MCN (Motorcycle News) breaks its bike-loving community down into even

smaller communities, e.g. for owners of Honda or Ducati bikes etc. The big bike manufacturers are keen to advertise in such communities.

- **Age/ethnic groups** – teens, the elderly, generation X, and millennial, etc – although these can be quite 'loose' in nature. Avoid stereotyping what elderly people are interested in. Many older people, an underserved user group, are tech literate and have embraced the use of tablet computers.

The role of the social media editor goes beyond creating content that appeals to the users or encouraging 'likes' and 'shares', although this remains important. The aim is to create genuine connections – user-to-user, user-to-journalists and with advertisers.

Social editors may help formulate internal codes of conduct regarding how staff interact on social media. So it is essential the social media editor also demonstrates best practice – avoid posting embarrassing images online!

## Approaches to publishing on mobile

Users access journalism through a range of different platforms – some the publisher owns (platform) and some they don't (off-platform). Journalists may create content that is native, i.e. specially designed for these individual sites and apps.

### Destination sites

Media brands run destination websites – e.g. the *Guardian*'s one is at Guardian. co.uk where users go to directly access content. But increasingly users find it more convenient to access news off-platform such as via the Facebook app.

### Apps and digital editions

Digital editions of newspapers and magazines often replicate the look and feel of their print counterparts. It is common to charge for digital editions and the *Guardian* has a digital edition which looks a lot like the printed newspaper. The *Guardian* also has a free live news app.

*Table 2.1* Platform versus off-platform publishing (by Steve Hill)

| Platform | Off-platform |
| --- | --- |
| **Media publisher's own news website** e.g. guardian.co.uk. Known as 'destination' websites. | **Social media apps** e.g. Guardian stories are shared on Facebook, Twitter and other social platforms newsfeeds |
| **News apps and magazine digital editions.** Sold through Apple Store or Google Play etc | **Aggregators** – apps such as Apple News, Upday and Flipboard host journalism content |

*Aggregation services*

These aggregate or bring together headlines from many different news sites. The likes of Apple News and Flipboard are popular with dedicated news junkies. But far more people access news via Facebook.

*Key jargon*

> **Responsive web design** – where a media provider sets up a website in such a way that it responds to the platform it is being viewed on, e.g. a website will change its design according to the screen size of the device.
>
> **Distributive news strategies** – where a media provider distributes content using a full range of platforms, in addition to their own website or app.
>
> **Adaptive storytelling** – Adaptive storytelling takes a platform-by-platform approach for creating content. It takes into account how users interact with the platform.
>
> **Native formats** –Many publishers create exclusive content for particular platforms, e.g. Snapchat. Creating content for social media isn't without its challenges. 'Each platform they work with has its own technical requirements, processes, hurdles and pace of evolution', states Jack Marshall (2016).
>
> **Direct consumption** – Facebook wishes to becomes a platform for direct consumption of news. Users shouldn't have to leave its site (i.e. go to a news website) to actually read a full news story. This strategy is controversial as it reduces the amount of traffic going to publishers' news websites and advertising revenue.

## Top social networks for news

The *Digital News Report* (Reuters Institute 2018) in a survey of users in 12 countries lists the most popular social media sites for news consumption:

1. Facebook – 36 per cent
2. WhatsApp – 15 per cent
3. Twitter – 11 per cent
4. Facebook Messenger – 8 per cent
5. Instagram – 6 per cent

It is easy to see that Facebook dominates the market – with no rival social media site being as influential around the world. Not only is it the world's most popular social media site, it is number one for news.

**Where journalists should publish content**

- For global reach, across all age groups: Facebook
- For young professionals interested in news: Twitter
- For video: YouTube
- For audio: SoundCloud or Audioboom
- For personalisation: Messaging services such Snapchat Discover and WhatsApp
- For younger and female users: Instagram
- For older users and professionals: LinkedIn

Here we profile the key social media sites.

### A) *Facebook – the dominant name in social media*

Anderson and Caumont (2014) state:

> Unlike Twitter, where a core function is the distribution of information as news breaks, Facebook is not yet a place many turn to for learning about breaking news.

Where Twitter once dominated breaking news content, Facebook has become a serious player since 2014. Facebook's algorithm, the set of rules that the company uses to prioritise what users see on their newsfeed, has changed to prioritise breaking news.

It is impossible to exaggerate Facebook's influence on journalism. It is by far the most important network for finding, reading, watching, sharing and commenting on news in most Western countries. It's this dominance that concerns many media publishers.

The figures are staggering. Facebook is most popular in Malaysia and Mexico, where over 60 per cent of those surveyed use it on a weekly basis for news (Reuters Institute 2018). It is the most mainstream platform in the UK, being used equally by both genders. It also has broadest spectrum of age groups compared to other social platforms.

It is highly convenient for users. A publisher will create a public Facebook Page (note this is different to a private personal profile that most people are familiar with) and users can then 'like' or 'follow' the page. For example, over 44 million people like the Facebook Page of *National Geographic* magazine (December 2017). Users will then be notified of updates to the page through their personalised newsfeed. Facebook includes auto-play video content and live-streaming video – this has led to a renewed interest in online video. The company is hosting augmented (AR) and virtual reality (VR) content.

### B) YouTube – the TV stars of the future?

Google-owned YouTube is limited to video sharing – however it is massively popular for news and is a home for virtual reality (VR) news content. Video content from mainstream publishers mixes with a new breed of successful pro-am (professional amateur) vloggers or video bloggers. There are large vlogospheres in the genres of fashion, beauty, video games and technology journalism. Younger people are spending less time watching mainstream TV and more time with online video.

*The stars of YouTube*

The top five most influential YouTubers in the UK based on data from social media research firm Fizziology (Foster 2017):

1. **Zoella (beauty)**
2. **Ksi (music/comedian)**
3. **Joe Sugg (comedian)**
4. **Dan Middleton (video games)**
5. **Tanya Burr (beauty)**

Beauty vlogger, Zoella, whose real name is Zoe Sugg is a veteran YouTuber. She started out in 2009 by offering make-up tips from her bedroom to an audience of mostly teen girls, but today has over 12 million subscribers to her channel (December 2017). As with most professional vloggers, she has ditched her bedroom for a professional TV studio. She generates revenue from pre-roll adverts and sponsorship deals from a well-known British supermarket.

### C) Twitter – 'outsized influence'

Even when President Donald Trump makes policy announcements via the platform, Twitter's influence can be overstated. Its users are skewed more towards young professionals and the highly educated and so it's not nearly as mainstream as Facebook.

Nevertheless, Twitter is in second place as a news source at 12 per cent in both the UK and in the USA. The largest percentage of people using Twitter for news was in Turkey, where it acts as a massive online political public sphere (Reuters Institute 2018).

Journalists use the platform to gather user generated content (UGC). The Brussels attack in March 2016 demonstrated how breaking news spreads on the platform.

> More than 92,000 tweets with links to stories on the attacks were posted within the first 24 hours after they occurred, according to Parse.ly's data.

About a third of those tweets were sent within the first six hours after the attacks.

(Lichterman 2016)

But Twitter is also losing ground to private messaging services such as WhatsApp and photo sharing sites such as Instagram.

### D) *Snapchat and Instagram – image and video sharing sites*

Launched in 2011, the Snapchat app has an unusual and scrappy appearance. It seems to both please and frustrate its young users in equal measure. It is best known for photo and video sharing, but news consumption remains a minority activity compared with its rivals Twitter and Facebook. It was slow to launch a suite of analytics tools – these are tools that media publishers user to measure views and engagement with content. This made it hard for publishers to monetise (generate revenue from) their content.

The BBC and Sky News create content on Snapchat to bring younger users into the brands. A typical viewer of a 24-hour news TV channel is over 45 years old and male. Snapchat's demographics are skewed to younger and female users.

*The Economist* and *National Geographic* magazines are also using Snapchat to encourage young people to become subscribers to their print products. BBC Shorts, where 15-second self-contained videos are uploaded to an Instagram page, have proved popular.

Maria Grechaninova, senior broadcast journalist with the BBC's Global Content Hub, states:

> Sometimes we feel that some people in our audience don't necessarily follow our website and for them, [Instagram] is their way of being exposed to BBC material.

(Ciobanu 2015)

### E) *WhatsApp for messaging*

Facebook-owned WhatsApp has become the place to share news with friends. As *The Economist* (2015) states:

> The prospect may surprise those who thought messaging apps were just another way for teens to share this week's tragic news about One Direction (a pop group, apparently). But their continuing explosive growth suggests that they will be a lasting phenomenon.

Slack, Telegram and WhatsApp can be used by teams of journalists working on a story as a group communication tool. 'It's something we've been using for major deployments for some time now', says BBC Singapore bureau editor Liz Corbin. She adds: 'It is superb for information sharing and crucially for team morale. I am repeatedly struck by how vital it is in terms of getting a story right and quickly' (BBC College of Journalism 2016).

However, WhatsApp is private and is therefore weak as a source of UGC. Twitter, which is more open, is a much better source for eyewitness material.

### Journalism and social media – best of frenemies?

#### Frenemy = part friend, part enemy

We've already hinted at the risks of having so much content distribution power in the hands of a relatively small number of (mostly) American tech firms. This isn't just a theoretical discussion, publishers and journalists have to decide which of the social media providers they distribute their content across and how much money and time they invest in creating native content.

Generating revenue from online journalism (monetising content) is challenging. Advertising revenue is moving from news websites to social media platforms. This has led to a sometimes fraught relationship between content publishers and social networking platforms.

Tina Brown, editor of numerous magazines including *Vanity Fair* and the *Daily Beast*, states in a *Time* magazine interview (Moore 2017) that there has been a 'fantastic resurgence in journalism' in the last few years. But she states:

> I think it's high time that Facebook and Google created a vast philanthropy fund to fund journalism. They have stolen so much [revenue from journalism] that it's high time they gave some of it back.

Brown has a point. A few tech companies invest in journalism. Google News Initiative (newsinitiative.withgoogle.com/) was set up to encourage high-quality online journalism, but the money is a drop in the ocean compared to the amount of revenue lost by news publishers.

A report from global consulting firm OC&C Strategy Consultants (Mayhew 2016) stated that the UK news industry could lose up to £500m in revenue to online platforms such as Facebook, Twitter, Google News and Apple News in the next decade. The figure is equal to 10 to 15 per cent of the industry's revenues.

Toby Chapman, associate partner at OC&C Strategy Consultants, states:

> The reaction of incumbent brands will be critical to what happens next. There are strategies that can be taken – by news and other industries vulnerable to the threat of online platforms – to avoid a similar fate.

> (Cited Mayhew 2016)

When a user's attention moves away from news websites to social media platforms, the advertisers tend to follow. This has meant reduced spending on banner adverts on news websites. Chapman argued that a 'collaborative and industry wide response' is required.

However, taking a user-centred approach, it is easy to see that accessing news through an aggregate and personalised feed on Facebook, Twitter or another social media site is highly convenient. Frequently the social media apps offer a better experience than the dedicated news apps.

The traditional rule of publishing is that control of the platform and distribution is control of the audience relationship. The power of social media to promote or demote stories at will, a process usually determined by an automatic algorithm, worries publishers who rely on them to reach new users.

Emily Bell, the academic and journalist, says social media provide 'a new paradigm' which has been unseen before as news is now distributed by social media companies who are not rooted in traditional journalism principles or a public service remit. She states:

> On the one hand, journalists can reach far greater audiences immediately than was the case in the past. On the other hand, journalists and publishers have very little control now over how information reaches the world and there is limited transparency.
>
> (Reuters Institute 2010)

Should the social media platforms invest more in supporting journalism? On one hand, the social media platforms give news publishers unprecedented access to new users. So maybe new publishers should be paying even more to be on the platforms? But the social media sites also need journalism content to keep users on their sites. News publishers say they deserve to be paid more for the content they supply.

## Predicting the future

In 1957 former British Conservative Prime Minister Harold Macmillan famously noted that, thanks to a rising economy, Britons 'have never had it so good'. For many people, the same could be said for our media landscape. It feels like we have unlimited choice of journalism outlets and online entertainment. No longer restricted to a few TV channels and newspapers, content is all around us and much of it is free at the point of consumption.

Academic Ian Hargreaves (2014) describes a modern phenomenon he terms 'ambient news'. He states: 'News, which was once difficult and expensive to obtain, today surrounds us like the air we breathe.'

We consume content through streams of content on Twitter and Facebook and curated collections on Instagram and Snapchat. The stream never stops – 24 hours a day and seven days a week a conversation is taking place and some people even claim they suffer from FOMO anxiety – fear of missing out.

The features of the mobile ecosystem include the following.

*Table 2.2* Usage of media (by Steve Hill)

| Old media strategy – print/broadcast | A mobile first strategy |
| --- | --- |
| Scarcity of content | Abundance of content |
| Appointment to view – users waits for news to appear | On-demand/24 hours/seven days a week |
| Media companies run printing presses and TV stations | Tech giants control modes of distribution |
| Journalists as information gatekeepers | The social web/sharing culture |
| Revenue – paid for by user and/or advertisers | Revenue – hard to charge directly for online content. Use of ad blockers. |

### Abundance of content

In the past there was information scarcity. The rise of digital media led to an abundance of content that is distributed, copied and stored at minimal cost.

### On-demand

In the pre-web days we waited for the news to be delivered. We waited for the paperboy (or girl) to deliver our newspaper through our letterbox – a habit that has all but disappeared in many communities. We also waited for the *News at Ten* to appear on TV. Today news is available on-demand at a time, on a platform and device of the user's choosing.

### Tech giants control the means of distribution

Dead tree distribution (i.e in paper) is a very expensive business. It involves running a large printing press and a network of trucks to distribute your magazines. But this had one key advantage – only the rich could do it. Now the social media companies have taken control of online distribution networks for news.

### Gatekeeping

In the pre-Web era journalists acted as the content gatekeepers and were often key opinion formers in the sectors they operated in. They acted as controllers of information appearing in the public domain. Today anyone can publish on social media with little editing or quality control.

### Where now?

Mobile and social media has had a transformative impact on journalism.
    The *Stanford Social Innovation Review* (2017) describes five key trends:

1) A radically diminished funding base for print media;
2) Increasingly fragmented audiences;
3) An accelerating pattern of random and instantaneous digital dissemination of information;
4) Video's increasing displacement of the written and spoken word;
5) Diminishing amounts and lower quality of civic education, and related declines in knowledge of public affairs.

It warns: 'Individually, these trends are problematic; together they pose a severe threat to democracy.'

*The Times* newspaper in London that was launched in 1785 – an incredible 206 years before the World Wide Web was made available to the public in 1991.

In the last 20 years *The Times*, along with all national newspapers in the UK, has faced the twin threat of a decline in circulation and advertising revenue.

Imagine being the editor of *The Times* and having to cope with so much technological change. In the 1990s the paper set up a website (thetimes.co.uk) for electronic distribution on desktop machines. But then smartphones came along – so you need to distribute content via apps, alongside your website. Then tablets became popular and then you need to factor in the ever growing importance of social media sites.

As an editor you may be begging for the pace of change to stop, but you have to take into account the rise of new devices based around:

- Virtual reality (VR)
- Augmented reality (AR)
- Voice control – such as Amazon Alexa and Google Home.
- Artificial intelligence (AI) devices

Investment in these technologies all requires money, purchase of new content management systems and the employment of staff with expertise. Yet declining sales of print has meant far less revenue from advertising, subscriber and newsstand sales.

There is also far more competition in news than ever before. Traditional names such as *The Times* have been joined by digital-only news sites such as Vice, BuzzFeed and the Huffington Post. The *Independent* newspaper closed its print title in 2016 and went digital-only. Well, if you can't beat 'em, join 'em!

In fact *The Times* newspaper hasn't suffered badly compared to its Fleet Street newspaper rivals, who are losing around 10 per cent of print readers each year. Just over 400,000 people buy *The Times* today. While its circulation is half of what it was in 1997, a solid digital policy is helping it hold its own online (Ponsford 2017).

And who knows what changes are in store in the next ten years? Editors, faced with limited budgets, have to determine which technologies they will invest in.

## Conclusion

It is clear there is a fundamental reshaping of media occurring, much of it brought about by mobile technology, some of it is very positive. *The Economist* (2011) states:

> The industry is being reshaped by technology – but by undermining the mass media's business models, that technology is in many ways returning the industry to the more vibrant, freewheeling and discursive ways of the pre-industrial era.

Academic and writer Jeff Jarvis (2016a) advises a more radical reimaging of mainstream media where 'conversation is the kingdom'. This is different to old media models where content or distribution was king.

He adds:

> What has died thanks to the abundance and choice the internet enables is not print or newsstands, longform or broadcast. What has died is the mass-media business model – injuring, perhaps mortally, a host of institutions it symbiotically supported: publishing, broadcasting, mass marketing, mass production, political parties, possibly even our notion of a nation.

So what does this all mean? As journalists we need to develop relationships with the tech giants while remaining focused on what we do best – producing independent journalism.

The job of social media and mobile editor is one of techno-optimist and advocate for experimentation of new technology. But we must remain grounded in the traditions of journalism as we will see in the next chapter.

Ken Lerer, a co-founder of the Huffington Post, described the challenge editors faced from changes in technology:

> 'You have to fix the plane while you're flying it.' He said some media company 'planes' are going to land safely, 'but most of them are going to crash and burn.'

(Desjardins 2016)

**Expert interview – Dina Rickman**

**Former head of social, the *Independent* (independent.co.uk)**

*Figure 2.2* Dina Rickman

The key skills I look for in a new recruit working in social media tend to be more about their personality. By that I mean their ability to show resilience.

I also look for intelligence which could be anything from a really top degree in journalism or an example where they've done something different and adapted really quickly. The actual skills that you need to use the platforms can be picked up relatively quickly by intelligent and resilient people.

My career highlight is the 2017 general election. Statistics from NewsWhip [a social media monitoring company] show the *Independent* was the most successful social publisher during the election with almost three times as much engagement as our nearest rival.

The social media platform we use most for promotion and engagement is Facebook. For some publications Twitter will be top. It is important to learn how to use Google Analytics [analytics.google.com] and CrowdTangle [crowdtangle.com – a free tool that allows publishers to discover how news spreads on the web]. They should also look at a public social analytics tools such as SimilarWeb [similarweb.com] and BuzzSumo [buzzsumo.com].

## Further reading

Reuters Institute for the Study of Journalism (2016) *Digital News Report 2016*. Available at: https://reutersinstitute.politics.ox.ac.uk/our-research/digital-news-report-2016.
The annual survey of news usage around the world. It is well worth downloading the latest edition.

## References

Anderson, M., and Caumont, A. (2014) How social media is reshaping news. Pew Research Center. Available at: www.pewresearch.org/fact-tank/2014/09/24/how-social-media-is-reshaping-news.

BBC College of Journalism (2016) – For breaking news, WhatsApp can be a strong team. BBC Blogs. Available at: www.bbc.co.uk/blogs/collegeofjournalism/entries/00a10ab9-0923-4a4d-817c-0a9d9715ba8c.

Burum, I. (2016) *Democratizing Journalism through Mobile Media the Mojo Revolution*. Routledge.

Chandler, D. (1995) Technological or media determinism. Available at: http://eldar.cz/mishutka/mn/%C2%9Akola/technologie/Technological%20or%20Media%20Determinism.doc

Ciobanu, M. (2015) Why publishers are using Instagram to connect with their communities. Journalism.co.uk. Available at: www.journalism.co.uk/news/why-publishers-are-using-instagram-to-connect-with-their-communities/s2/a578551.

De Beer, A. S., and Merrill, J. C. (2008) *Global Journalism: Topical Issues and Media Systems*. Pearson.

Desjardins, J. (2016) The slow death of legacy media. Business Insider. Available at: www.businessinsider.com/the-slow-death-of-legacy-media-2016-10?IR=T.

Foster, A. (2017) Zoella has been crowned the most powerful YouTube star in Britain. *Evening Standard*. Available at: www.standard.co.uk/lifestyle/london-life/zoella-has-been-crowned-the-most-powerful-youtube-star-in-britain-a3494211.html.

Gates, B. (1999) *Business at the Speed of Thought*. Warner Books.

Hargreaves, I. (2014) *Journalism: A Very Short Introduction*. Oxford University Press.

Hill, S., and Lashmar, P. (2014) *Online Journalism: The Essential Guide*. SAGE Publications Ltd.

Ho, D. (2014) News in motion: six ways to be a good mobile editor. Poynter. Available at: www.poynter.org/2014/news-in-motion-six-ways-to-be-a-good-mobile-editor/244675/?utm_content=buffer45ea1&utm_medium=social&utm_source=twitter.com&utm_campaign=buffer#.UzHiInDdyE0.twitter.

Jarvis, J. (2016a) Death to the mass? Available at: https://medium.com/whither-news/death-to-the-mass-eb33c08dc3b6.

Jarvis, J. (2016b) Meeting and exceeding the news business' hiring needs. Available at: https://medium.com/whither-news/meeting-and-exceeding-the-news-business-hiring-needs-bbca85aec93a.

Lichterman, J. (2016) Twitter has outsized influence, but it doesn't drive much traffic for most news orgs. Nieman Lab. Available at: www.niemanlab.org/2016/04/twitter-has-outsized-influence-but-it-doesnt-drive-much-traffic-for-most-news-orgs-a-new-report-says.

Marshall, J. (2016) The rise of the publishing platform specialist. *Wall Street Journal*. Available at: www.wsj.com/articles/the-rise-of-the-publishing-platform-specialist-1458896683.

Mayhew, F. (2016) UK news industry could lose £500m in revenue to online platforms over next decade. *Press Gazette*. Available at: www.pressgazette.co.uk/uk-news-industry-could-lose-500m-in-revenue-to-online-platforms-in-next-decade-report-warns/.

Moore, M. (2017) Editor accuses web giants Facebook and Google of 'theft' from journalists. *The Times*. Available at: www.thetimes.co.uk/article/editor-accuses-web-giants-facebook-and-google-of-theft-from-journalists-0xcfdsh6h.

Nass, C. (2010) Thinking about multitasking: it's what journalists need to do. Nieman Reports. Available at: http://niemanreports.org/articles/thinking-about-multitasking-its-what-journalists-need-to-do/.

Ponsford, D. (2014) News on the move: how BBC is going mobile-first. *Press Gazette*. Available at: www.pressgazette.co.uk/news-move-how-bbc-going-mobile-firstmetros-online-success-storywhy-times-reader-first-not-digital.

Ponsford, D. (2017) Print ABCs: seven UK national newspapers losing print sales at more than 10 per cent year on year. *Press Gazette*. Available at: www.pressgazette.co.uk/print-abcs-seven-uk-national-newspapers-losing-print-sales-at-more-than-10-per-cent-year-on-year.

Reuters Institute for the Study of Journalism (2010) Journalism in the age of social media. Available at: https://reutersinstitute.politics.ox.ac.uk/our-research/journalism-age-social-media.

Reuters Institute for the Study of Journalism (2015) Executive summary and key findings of the 2015 report. *Digital News Report*. Available at: www.digitalnewsreport.org/survey/2015/executive-summary-and-key-findings-2015.

Reuters Institute for the Study of Journalism (2018) *Digital News Report 2018*. Available at:. www.digitalnewsreport.org/

Stanford Social Innovation Review (2017) The civic media crisis and what philanthropy can do. Available at: https://ssir.org/articles/entry/the_civic_media_crisis_and_what_philanthropy_can_do.

*The Economist* (2011) Coming full circle. Available at: www.economist.com/node/18904158.

*The Economist* (2015) The message is the medium. Available at: www.economist.com/news/business/21647317-messaging-services-are-rapidly-growing-beyond-online-chat-message-medium.

Tinius (2017) The new reality of media. Available at: https://tinius.com/blog/the-new-reality-of-media.

Westlund, O. (2013) Mobile news. *Digital Journalism*, 1(1), 6–26. DOI: 10.1080/21670811.2012.740273

Wolf, Cornelia, and Anna Schnauber, Anna (2015) *News consumption in the mobile era*. *Digital Journalism*, 3(5), 759–776. DOI: 10.1080/21670811.2014.942497

Wroblewski, L. and Zeldman, J. (2011) *Mobile First*. A Book Apart.

# 3  Fake news and trolling

**This chapter will cover:**

- What is fake news?
- Hyperpartisan news
- Causes of fake news
- Filter bubbles
- Information segregation
- Trust in journalism
- Freedom of expression
- False balance
- Independence
- Taking on the trolls
- Solutions

## Introduction

The Karri Twist, an Indian restaurant in South London, became infamous for the most bizarre reason. An article claimed the restaurant was using human meat as an ingredient and bodies were stored in a freezer on the premises.

If it all sounds like a joke, the owners of the Karri Twist weren't laughing. 'When people started calling asking me if we were selling human meat, I couldn't believe it', recalled employee Shinra Begum (BBC News 2017). 'I was completely shocked when I eventually found the article online and being shared all over Facebook', stated Begum. 'We even had a member of the public come in and say it was lucky we had shutters over our windows because he would have bricked them in' (BBC News 2017).

The story was a hoax. Yet the anonymity of internet communication and the speed with which rumours can spread makes social media a fertile ground for gossip, rumour and speculation. This chapter looks at both fake news and the trolling of journalists – two online threats that are not as unconnected as they first appear. Both distort the public debate and can even threaten democracy. The victims of fake news and trolling can feel powerless to prevent it.

Many early users regarded the internet, or cyberspace as it was known, as a type of utopia. They celebrated unrestricted freedom of speech that was very different to that offered in mainstream media. Cyberspace is a 'a world of complete freedom and anonymity, and where users say and do what they like, uncensored, unregulated, and outside of society's norms' (Bartlett 2016).

Internet freedom of expression, where anyone can publish content without censorship, has plenty of supporters. The sending of repeated abusive messages, often known as 'flaming' was a feature of early Usenet newsgroups – these text-based community message boards predate the launch of the World Wide Web. 4Chan (4chan.org) is regarded as the modern web equivalent to Usenet. Pretty much anything goes on its anonymous message boards and users meet to plan hacking and doxing attacks, although unlike Usenet 4Chan has some limits.

There is a clear clash of cultures between internet freedom of speech and the restricted communication of mainstream mass media. What we produce as professional journalists is regulated by both laws, e.g. libel, and voluntary ethical codes of conduct, such as those from the Independent Press Standards Organisation (IPSO). It is this unresolved conflict that is at the heart of the debate over fake news, trolling and the role of social media in democratic society.

## What is fake news?

John H. Johnson (cited Attkisson 2018) has a broad definition of fake news that includes:

1. News that is entirely false
2. News that is slanted and biased
3. Pure propaganda
4. Stories that misinterpret and misuse data
5. Imprecise and sloppy reporting

This broad definition reflects the fact fake news comes in many different flavours. At one extreme, President Donald Trump has accused respected news organisations such as the *New York Times*, BuzzFeed and, most frequently, CNN, of producing fake news. Yet what he is saying is that these organisations produce news reports that scrutinise his administration. This is precisely what good journalism should be doing as part of its role in the fourth estate.

At the other extreme, there are fake news stories that are generated solely to mislead the consumer. These stories can be extremely convincing and journalists can be caught out.

'Fake media tried to stop us from going to the White House. But I'm president, and they're not', said Donald Trump at a rally in July 2017 (Grynbaum 2017). Trump constantly referred to CNN as being garbage journalism.

Veteran media commentator Ray Snoddy (cited Harrison 2017) states:

> '… mainstream media' has changed from a general description into a term of abuse. We've seen trust in media ebb and flow over many years but there's been nothing like this before. There is now a completely different way of self-manufacturing and distributing news outside of the mainstream.

This attack on the mainstream media from politicians, and it's not just Trump, is strategic and is viewed as a way to win votes. Yet it poses a threat to journalism. The politicians' aim is to convince supporters that only they can be believed and that mainstream media should never be trusted.

Here are three fake news headlines:

- Nine Italian nuns pregnant after offering shelter to North African immigrants.
- Scientists in Saudi Arabia say women should be categorised as mammals, not humans.
- KFC accused of kicking out girl, 3, scarred in pit bull attack.

What makes for the best fake news articles? 'When it comes to the fake stuff, you really want it to be red meat', states the founder of National Report, a fake news outlet, who goes by the pseudonym Allen Montgomery (Murtha 2016). He highlights the importance of reflecting a 'hot button issue' – something that is politicised or will anger people. He states:

> It doesn't have to be offensive. It doesn't have to be outrageous. It doesn't have to be anything other than just giving them what they already wanted to hear.
>
> (Murtha 2016)

Plenty of theory suggests we are most susceptible to fake news when it is supporting our own political bias or prejudice. No professional journalist should be involved in producing fake news. Verification is at the heart of journalism and professional codes of conduct. Where journalists make mistakes they correct errors as soon as possible and in a transparent way. We will take a look at some journalist errors later on in this chapter.

### US presidential elections 2016

Fake news has been manufactured on a giant scale. Facebook admitted in November 2017 that 150 million Americans may have seen content created by Russian operatives, much of it supporting Donald Trump. Senator Dianne Feinstein stated: 'What we're talking about is the beginning of cyber warfare' (White 2017).

A study by BuzzFeed (Silverman 2016) found the most shared fake story was:

**Pope Francis shocks world, endorses Donald Trump for president**

The story had picked up 960,000 Facebook engagements by November 2016 – this is the number of likes, shares and comments. What we don't know is exactly how many of these comments were saying that the headline was garbage, but fake news is certainly influential.

The BuzzFeed report states:

> In the final three months of the US presidential campaign [of 2016], the top-performing fake election news stories on Facebook generated more engagement than the top stories from major news outlets such as the New York Times, Washington Post, Huffington Post, NBC News, and others.
>
> (Silverman 2016)

Fake news seeks to:

- Make money (through online advertising or other commercial messages);

and/or

- Influence politics, e.g. propaganda that influences how people vote in elections.

Once released, fake news is amplified and shared virally via social media and will spread rapidly around the world. Sometimes even mainstream media news websites accidently report fake news as fact.

The speed with which false information can spread via social media is immense. Kevin Rawlinson (2016) states:

> Within minutes or hours, a claim can morph from a lone tweet or badly sourced report to a story repeated by dozens of news websites, generating tens of thousands of shares. Once a certain critical mass is reached, repetition has a powerful effect on belief.

Rawlinson says that rumour can appear true to readers 'simply by virtue of its ubiquity'.

## Hyperpartisan news

Hyperpartisan political blogs and independent news outlets have risen in prominence. These news sites often mimic the appearance of mainstream media brands and will promote their political stories on Twitter and especially on political forums on Facebook.

*Figure 3.1* Alex Jones of Infowars protesting in Dallas
By Sean P. Anderson

Facebook's algorithm during the 2016 US election prioritised news based on the most shares or comments, rather than reliability. Hyperpartisan sites created stories with outrageous or controversial headlines in a bid to get more shares and appear high up the newsfeed. Facebook has now changed its algorithm and hyperpartisan sites have had their stories demoted.

Two of the most influential hyperpartisan political sites in the USA are the right-leaning Breitbart (breitbart.com) and Alex Jones' Infowars (infowars.com). Both have attacked mainstream media for alleged bias against Donald Trump. Infowars ran a bizarre campaign in 2017 to 'expose' CNN as 'terrorist media' and to 'fight MSM' (mainstream media) (Infowars 2017).

Academic Yochai Benkler states that a right-wing network of hyperpartisan sites anchored around Breitbart:

> developed as a distinct and insulated media system, using social media as a backbone to transmit a hyperpartisan perspective to the world. This pro-Trump media sphere appears to have not only successfully set the agenda for the conservative media sphere, but also strongly influenced the broader media agenda, in particular coverage of Hillary Clinton.
>
> (Benkler et al. 2017)

In this respect, hyperpartisan sites can influence mainstream reporting. Benkler noted that Breitbart's influence extends way beyond its own users and successfully influenced mainstream media to frame the debate around immigration in terms of terror, crime and Islam. This worked to benefit Donald Trump.

If there was a British equivalent of Breitbart it would be The Canary (thecanary.co). The left-leaning news site was a cheerleader for Labour leader Jeremy Corbyn.

BuzzFeed News found during the first two weeks of the 2017 UK general election campaign, left-leaning sites 'are consistently and repeatedly going more viral than mainstream UK political journalism' (Waterson 2017).

It is a simplification to say hyperpartisan news is automatically fake news. What unites these sites is a commitment to report stories that they believe that mainstream media ignores. In this respect, they see a role of expanding media plurality and provide a platform for alternative voices. Kerry-Anne Mendoza, Canary editor, states the site's aims:

> Today, a handful of powerful moguls control our mainstream media. As such, its coverage is largely conservative. But we have created a truly independent and viable alternative. One that isn't afraid to challenge the status quo, to ask the hard questions, and to have an opinion.
>
> (Canary n.d.)

Their skilled use of social media optimisation when promoting stories on social media has meant their stories are often widely shared.

In some respects they share the traditions of journalism, e.g. they usually seek to break exclusive stories and expand the public debate. But with a strong commitment to a particular political cause their reporting is by definition one-sided. Indeed, this may be the primary reason for their popularity.

## Causes of fake news

There are two key concepts that run through online communication:

A) Freedom of expression.
B) Anyone can publish – i.e. they can set up a website, blog or social media account and publish content to the Web.

When the Web launched in the early 1990s many celebrated the democratisation of media. You no longer needed an expensive printing press or to own a TV station to publish content. This enhanced the range of voices and opinions that could be heard.

Around the year 2000 we saw the launch of free and simple to use blogging platforms, most notably Blogger.com in 1999 and Wordpress.com in 2005. This led to an explosion in personal blogs and the launch of independent news sites, most notably the Huffington Post in 2005 and BuzzFeed a year later.

Easy to use blog technology allows anyone to publish online content. Therefore, the Web is far more democratised than traditional media. A new wave of democratisation occurred as technology, such as mobile camera equipment, became cheaper than before. The third wave of democratisation came with the launch of live video streaming services such Periscope in 2015 and Facebook Live in 2016. It is now possible for anyone with a smartphone to set up his or her own TV station or do a live broadcast from the street.

Quality control is clearly a factor when anyone can publish. Andrew Keen in his classic text *The Cult of the Amateur*, published in 2007, with great foresight predicted:

> … all this is that democratized media will eventually force all of us to become amateur critics and editors ourselves. With more and more information online unedited, unverified and unsubstantiated, we will have no choice by to read everything with a sceptical eye.
>
> (Keen 2007)

Keen was writing before recent concerns about fake news. He continues: 'Most of us assume that the information we take in can be trusted … But when the information is created by amateurs it rarely can be.'

He took a polarised position, crudely summarised as – professional journalism is good, amateur journalism is bad. This is clearly a simplification. Professional journalists embed UGC from social media where it is newsworthy. The 'us' (mainstream media) and 'them' (amateur) rivalry has evaporated, more so than he could imagine.

But Keen was offering an important warning for the future. Social media platforms are confusing environments where breaking news from mainstream media sources appear side-by-side with news from bloggers, hyperpartisan sites and gossip shared by friends. Users don't know what news to trust as at first glance fake sites look identical to those from mainstream providers. Perhaps we don't care where news comes from these days?

## Filter bubbles and virtue signalling

Social media algorithms aim to provide personalised newsfeeds – that is to say, based on our past reading, they attempt to predict what news we will find most relevant. News shared by our friends tends to appear more prominently in our feed. Algorithms also take into account the type of content we have liked, commented on or shared in the past. Perhaps most importantly, paid-for posts get the most prominence.

Paid-for adverts and posts are the new battleground in politics. Facebook has always taken commercial advertising. Companies take out adverts targeting users based on their gender, age, location, who the user is a friend with, relationship status and political affiliation and hobbies. This allows for much more tailored targeting of consumers than provided by other advertising methods – such as display adverts in a newspapers or TV adverts.

Political parties have now got in on the act, except they are trying to sell policies and influence elections, rather than selling cans of beans. Tim Ross and Tom McTague say that British political parties can target tiny batches of voters – as low as 1,000 in marginal constituencies in the UK. In 2015 the Conservatives spent £1.2 million on Facebook advertising alone. They were running 350 adverts promoting then Prime Minister David Cameron, each with slightly different messages and all carefully targeted at specific age groups, gender and locations (Ross and McTague 2017). Of course, users won't necessarily know they are being selectively targeted to see specific adverts or paid-for social media posts.

There are some positives. In an era of information overload where content is everywhere, these algorithms attempt to automatically extract the most useful content. However, unlike reading a newspaper or watching TV news, this is content based on our existing political bias and personal tastes – it's perhaps best described as news-u-like. This can lead to filter bubbles where people only read news or opinions that reinforce their own pre-existing beliefs.

We are often friends with people with similar outlooks on life. Perhaps you supported the UK's membership of the European Union? A YouGov poll in 2016 (Goulard 2016) showed that 75 per cent of those aged 18–24 voted to remain in the EU during the June 2016 referendum. Many people were shocked to discover that outside their social media filter bubble not everyone in the UK agreed. Laura Marcus (2012) states:

> The net actually makes it easier to avoid people you don't agree with or who may challenge your view … However, all social networks tend to be homogenous. Why should the net be any different?

While some Twitter users like to have 'adversarial friendships', it's more common to engage with 'like-minded individuals', states Marcus.

Matthew d'Ancona (2017) writes that technology is 'herding us into like-minded political tribes'. He states that they 'congregate with the like-minded and to ignore information or analysis that conflicts with our presumptions'. He adds: 'It is a bleak irony: the greatest source of information constructed in human history is being used to tamp down what we know and think already.'

But not everyone agrees. Yochai Benkler believes the concept of the filter bubble is an oversimplification. He suggests there are differences between how supporters on the right and left of politics consume and share news, even when they used the same technology platforms – a term he calls 'asymmetric polarisation'.

Benkler (2017) states:

> Our analysis challenges a simple narrative that the internet *as a technology* is what fragments public discourse and polarizes opinions, by allowing us to inhabit filter bubbles or just read 'the daily me.'

The concept of virtue signalling is often seen on Facebook and Twitter during political discussions. Essentially, this is all about showing off to others about how virtuous you are, i.e. what a good and considerate person you are. James Bartholomew (2015) states:

> Sometimes it is quite subtle. By saying that they hate the Daily Mail or UKIP [The UK Independence Party], they are really telling you that they are admirably non-racist, left-wing or open-minded

He says that the great thing about virtue signalling is that it does not require actually doing anything virtuous: 'It does not involve delivering lunches to elderly neighbours or staying together with a spouse for the sake of the children. It takes no effort or sacrifice at all.'

The creation of filter bubbles and the rise of people virtue signalling reminds us that the online and offline communication can be very different. It pays to be sceptical when handling social media content.

## Information segregation

Does online communication act to expand or limit the range of opinions and diversity of news? If you think social media can limit our news diet, you may believe in a concept known as information segregation.

In the past our news diet was limited by geographic access (e.g. the newspapers that were sold in our area) or cost (payment for newspapers and media channels). Today we enjoy access a vast range of international media sources offering a wide range of news and opinions.

Mainstream media provide us with what we call 'broad brushstroke' coverage, e.g. a newspaper will serve up a broad range of news topics, such as home news, international, business and sport. The weekend newspapers often have an additional culture section.

The web is not limited by space and is great for deep and narrow news. So we can explore our topics of interest – known as 'vertical' channels. So fans of niche sports, such as table tennis or perhaps handball that may rarely get coverage in newspapers, can find dedicated news websites. So, on the face of it, we have much wider choice in our news diet than before.

*The Economist* (2011) states:

> there is much to celebrate in the noisy, diverse, vociferous, argumentative and stridently alive environment of the news business in the age of the Internet.

Flaxman et al. (2016) state that the use of internet tools – social media and web searches – can lead to more choice:

increased choice and social networks lead to greater exposure to diverse ideas, breaking individuals free from insular consumption patterns ... substantial fraction of ties in online social networks are between individuals on opposite sides of the political spectrum, opening up the possibility for diverse content discovery.

Flaxman states that, taken together, 'web search and social networks reduce ideological segregation'.

But while it possible to read widely, many of us have restricted news diets. Many people only consume news from social media. Why is this the case? In an age of information overload, users perhaps naturally become more selective about the news sources they consume. Ellie Rennie (2018) states:

> As moral psychologist Jonathan Haidt has shown, polarisation is a mix of our evolutionary groupishness – our desire to build self-narratives that correspond with grand political narratives in order to bind ourselves to others.

Humans seek out information that makes them feel sure of themselves. Rennie adds: 'News delivery via social media works on a business model that exploits the same need for self-validation that Haidt has identified.'

Users should seek out alternative perspectives to avoid information segregation that could ultimately weaken decision-making and the democratic process.

## Trust in journalism

We've identified what fake news is, why it is a threat and how it can spread rapidly via social media algorithms that have no concept of what is true or false. Journalists now, more so than ever, need to prove to the public they can be trusted.

*The Elements Of Journalism*, the classic text on media ethics by Bill Kovach and Tom Rosenstiel (2014), lists ten key principles that are worth remembering as we contend with the rise of fake news:

1. Journalism's first obligation is to the truth.
2. Its first loyalty is to citizens.
3. Its essence is a discipline of verification (fact checking and accuracy).
4. Its practitioners must maintain an independence from those they cover.
5. It must serve an independent monitor of power
6. It must provide a forum for public criticism and compromise.
7. It must strive to make the significant interesting and relevant.
8. It must present the news in a way that is comprehensive and proportional.
9. Its practitioners have an obligation to exercise their personal conscience.
10. Citizens have rights and responsibilities when it comes to the news as well – even more so as they become producers and editors themselves.

The Missouri School of Journalism describes what it calls the tenets of good reporting (Timokhina 2012):

- Be accurate.
- Avoid biases.
- Present multiple viewpoints or perspectives.
- Pursue the truth.
- Use factual data, yet develop people skills.
- Maintain community ties and 'connect the dots'.
- Be open and transparent.
- Evoke emotion.
- Think visually; have vision.
- Integrate new developments and technology.

The key elements of truthfulness, accuracy, multiple perspectives and independence from those whom you write about are essential traits of good journalism.

Journalists must be open and transparent about where and how they obtain their information. It is good practice in online stories to link through to your source material, if it is available online. If you make a mistake, admit to it and print a clear correction.

## Freedom of expression

The debates regarding fake news and trolling highlight a clash of cultures. Social media companies are relatively unregulated, in comparison to content providers. The latter work under legal and ethical codes about what they can publish.

The right to freedom of expression is sacrosanct for those who believe in the 'anything goes' ethos of cyberspace where users publish what they want with no limits. This contrasts with mainstream media where freedom of expression has limits. Editors act as gatekeepers – they control the release of news into the public domain and also act as quality controllers.

Aiden White (n.d.) states that journalism is 'about constrained expression, not free expression'. As private citizens on social media we 'are not obliged to be truthful, honest, transparent, or decent and public-spirited'. He states that this right to "self-regarding" free expression underpins much of the communication on social media. This is very different to serious journalism that is "other regarding" i.e. promotes truth-telling, accuracy and a responsibility to others.

Critics of mainstream media may regard the newspaper role of editors as gatekeepers negatively. Gatekeepers are said to have acted to limit the range of voices that are heard and in some cases have prevented important information appearing in the public domain. Some celebrate the more open and free nature of social media discourse where news is created and shared among users often with no fact checking or quality control at all.

## False balance

Most journalists are taught the need to be fair and balanced in news reporting – this normally involves including at least two sides of any debate. This is generally very sound advice, but what do you do when your own research tells you that one side is simply wrong. Do you allow their factually wrong version of events airtime? Or are you acting as censor of content?

CNN's Christiane Amanpour (2016) said that journalism needs to be 'truthful, not neutral'. She states:

> There is a difference here. Truthful is bringing the truth. Neutral can be creating a false equivalence between this side and that. I really want you to know that I go out of my way to bring you the truth.

She says that facts exist and being neutral, in some cases, can create a false moral equivalence to two sides. Here are two exampes of this.

*Figure 3.2* Christiane Amanpour of CNN – AIB Television Personality of the Year 2015
By Association for International Broadcasting

### Climate change

A classic example of times where there may be false balance is during debate over climate change. The vast majority of respected scientific sources believe the climate system is warming, even if they debate the extent to which it is occurring, cause and impact. However climate change deniers often present 'alternative facts' to say it doesn't exist.

### Brexit

Broadcast news has a duty to be impartial, unlike newspapers in the UK. This meant covering the EU Referendum of 2016 was a nightmare, with BBC News being criticised for giving false equivalence to both sides of the debate. James Harding, its director of news and current affairs, said some were concerned it was giving the 'same treatment to respected experts as to know-nothings and lightweights'. But he concluded: 'The fundamental charge – that BBC reporting resulted in a false balance in which fanciful claims got the same billing as serious insights – is not true' (Harding 2016).

## Independence

In 2015, the *Daily Telegraph*'s chief political correspondent, Peter Oborne, resigned over the newspaper's lack of coverage of a tax story relating to the banking giant HSBC. Oborne claimed journalists were self-censoring to avoid upsetting the bank, which at the time was a prominent advertiser in the newspaper. He described it as a 'form of fraud on its readers' (cited Plunkett and Quinn 2015). He claimed the traditional distinction that exists in newspapers between the advertising and editorial departments had collapsed. The paper denied the claims.

Oborne (cited Plunkett and Quinn 2015) states:

> It has been placing what it perceives to be the interests of a major international bank above its duty to bring the news to Telegraph readers. There is only one word to describe this situation: terrible.

Aside from advertisers, government bodies and the PR industry also seek to influence the news agenda.

## Advocacy journalism

Journalists need to be independent, this is core to Bill Kovach and Tom Rosenstiel's ten principles. However advocacy journalism or campaigning journalism, as it is sometimes known, subverts this core principle. The popular news site Vice (vice.com) regularly includes such journalism. It may be the case that the journalists themselves are participants within the story, e.g. volunteering as political activists etc.

Supporters of this type of journalism say it often covers issues that are publicly important, is often investigative and often seeks to give a voice to the voiceless. The aim is often to hold power to account and bring about change.

But poor advocacy journalism ignores inconvenient truths or distorts the facts to promote a particular agenda. At its worst it can replicate a hyperpartisan blog and fake news.

Mathew Charles (2013) states that advocacy journalism focuses on a 'shift away from objectivity towards the arguably more ethical practice of attachment'. He adds that, with advocacy journalism: 'The neutral and detached reporter, who remains outside of events and reports only facts, becomes a campaigner immersed in a story to call for and foster real social change.'

Tadhg Kelly (2014) warns that this style of reporting appeals to audiences who prefer the subjective to the objective. He states:

> Successful journalism is often about the advocacy of narratives because the audience has long flocked to the subjective over the objective, to emotion and identity and expression of belief over information.

He adds that readers may say that they want objective news, 'but when they vote with their clicks they tend to do so with their hearts'.

Advocacy journalism certainly has a role in the modern media landscape. It often appeals to journalists who have strong political beliefs, although they need to be wary of allowing their passion and personal bias to rule over factual reporting.

## Taking on the trolls

The rise of trolling – the posting of abusive messages – presents similar philosophical, regulatory and technical challenges as dealing with fake news. For some, the right to troll is a celebrated part of freedom of expression online, much like the spreading of fake news. The argument goes that, if you don't like it, you only need to close your social media accounts and uninstall your apps.

But there is an irony with trolling. While the trolls justify their actions under principles of freedom of speech, they seek to silence the voices of their victims – whether they are journalists or social media users. A Pew Research Center survey (Duggan 2014) found 40 per cent of people have been bullied on the Web, and the majority of those people (66 per cent) say it most recently happened on a social network; 73 per cent of people reported seeing someone else being harassed online.

- **Doxing** – This is where the victim is harassed by having private information – such as their home address, phone number, private photos, etc – published on message boards.
- **Bots** – Trolling can occur using fake social media accounts that are controlled by bots – short for robots, this is software that runs automated tasks.

- **Diversity** – Female journalists and those from ethnic minorities are more likely to be subjected to online bullying.

Dick Costolo, CEO of Twitter, admitted in a leaked memo in 2015 that the company 'sucks at dealing with trolls and abuse' (Metz 2015). Twitter highlights the 'challenge of stamping out unacceptable behaviour without eroding the character of an inherently unruly and combative community' (Metz 2015).

### Journalists subjected to abuse

The *Guardian* conducted a wide-ranging study on online abuse in its own comment sections and found 'articles written by women attract more abuse and dismissive trolling than those written by men, regardless of what the article is about' (Gardiner et al. 2016). While the majority of opinion writers at the *Guardian* are 'white men', it was ethnic minority journalists and women who received the bulk of abuse. The Gamergate controversy of 2014 highlighted how female journalists writing in male-dominated sections of the media (in this case, games journalism) can be vulnerable to attack. Gamergate sought to highlight unethical practice in games journalism, but it took on misogynistic overtones as female games journalists received the most abuse.

It can be difficult to understand why people troll, yet it is remarkably common. The anonymity of online communication, whether real or imagined, emboldens the perpetrators. Jamie Bartlett, author of *The Dark Net*, (2016) cites John Suler who studied the behaviour of participants in early internet chatrooms:

> He [Suler] found that participants tended to be more aggressive and angry online than offline. He suggested this was because, when protected by a screen, people feel that real-world social restrictions, responsibilities and norms don't apply.

Bartlett highlights how anonymous online communication can allow people to explore and experiment with their own identities. Yet it also allows them to 'act without fear of being held accountable'.

It is very rare for trolls to be prosecuted in the UK for their actions. The Malicious Communications Act 1988 covers the sending or delivery of letters or other articles for the purpose of causing distress or anxiety. However, many believe the law is inadequate for the modern era.

### Dealing with trolls as a journalist

TrollBusters (troll-busters.com) was set up by journalist Michelle Ferrier. In the mid-2000s, she was driven to quit her job for the *Daytona Beach News-Journal* after receiving barrages of racist hate mail. Fearing for her life, she moved to another state and even bought a gun for protection.

TrollBusters employs vetted volunteers who respond to incidents as they happen. The aim is to overwhelm the feed by posting supportive comments on social media. This tactic is used to prevent 'pile-on' behaviour where trolls join each other during attacks. This highlights that trolls often launch coordinated attacks, even though they are generally viewed as being loners.

Amy Gahran (2015) says of the trolls:

> Their demeaning, dismissive, insulting and even threatening comments can completely derail a conversation, chilling the expression of a diversity of voices.

Journalists who are on the receiving end of abuse are advised to differentiate between criticism about ideas (i.e. what they write or produce) and between all-out harassment. Criticism of ideas may well be offensive, but legal. These types of users can be ignored or blocked if there is a problem.

The latter, harassment, can have racist or sexist overtones. Where there are threats of physical harm it should be reported to the police.

## Solutions

A range of solutions are proposed to limit the impact of fake news and trolling on the online public debate.

### *Fact checking*

Dedicated fact-checking sites will verify suspect content – whether this is speeches from politicians, mainstream media reports or conspiracy theories:

- **FactCheck** – factcheck.org
- **Full Fact** – fullfact.org
- **Politifacts** – politifact.com
- **Snopes** – snopes.com

Snopes is perhaps the most well-known fact-checking site. It began by interrogating urban myths – such as the recurring claim that the moon landings were staged. Its 50 Hottest Urban Legends (snopes.com/50-hottest-urban-legends) is a frequently updated list of questionable stories currently doing the social media rounds.

### *Regulating the social media providers?*

The social media sites, after years of denial, are aware they have a problem. The European Commission has called for much tighter controls on the tech giants to combat fake news and online harassment. Specifically they have argued that

Facebook should be classified as a media publisher rather than a technology platform.

Why does this matter? By classifying it as a media company it can then be regulated in line with traditional TV, radio and newspapers – so they would need to obey established media laws about what they can and cannot publish. This poses practical and ethical challenges to the companies.

### The case for regulation

Currently, moderators at the social media companies are to a limited extent filtering content. They remove videos of beheadings by terrorist groups and will close their accounts. Facebook in 2016 reversed its decision to remove an iconic Vietnam War photo known as 'napalm girl', which features nudity. It stated: 'While we recognize that this photo is iconic, it's difficult to create a distinction between allowing a photograph of a nude child in one instance and not others' (Levin et al. 2016).

So there is an argument that social media companies are making editorial decisions by determining what will appear. They are also similar to media companies as they sell advertising.

Josh Constine (2016) states that Facebook writes community standards and act as editors by pulling content (such as nude photos) that break its rules. He adds:

> Facebook writes the code that applies these algorithms and policies like a technology company, but it also makes editorial decisions about what to prioritize and permit, like the editor of a media company.

Facebook has sought to reduce fake news. It experimented with warning a user if the truthfulness of content they are planning to share has been disputed. It also educates the public on how to spot fake news. However, others say the companies will only take their role in the public debate seriously if they are regulated.

As Margaret Sullivan (2016) writes:

> Yes, social media platforms are businesses. They have no obligation to call their offerings 'news' or to depict their judgments as editorial decisions … Given their extraordinary influence, they do have an obligation to grapple, as transparently as possible, with extraordinary responsibility.

### The case against increased regulation

Freedom of speech campaigners argue the online world is distinct from mainstream media and shouldn't be regulated. From a practical perspective, it is hard to see how a social media company could view or edit every post before submission.

Mark Zuckerberg in August 2016 claimed he runs a tech company, not a media company. He used the distinction that it does not produce content, but it simply delivers it. Perhaps more than anything, the company doesn't want to get into the time-consuming and ethically problematic business of attempting to determine what is or isn't fake news. He states (2016):

> We need to be careful not to discourage sharing of opinions or to mistakenly restrict accurate content. We do not want to be arbiters of truth ourselves, but instead rely on our community and trusted third parties.

Patrick Walker, Facebook's head of media partnerships, said in December 2016: 'We believe it's essential that Facebook stay out of the business of deciding what issues the world should read about. That's what editors do.' (Heath 2016).

From a state of near denial, the social media companies are taking their responsibilities more seriously. They know that if they don't do something they may well face being regulated out of business.

## Conclusion

The twin concepts of freedom of expression and the fact that anyone can publish run deeply through internet communication. Limiting either of these freedoms, poses significant challenges.

The debate around fake news has become highly politicised. Politicians and their supporters accuse respected traditional media outlets of producing fake news, when they are just doing their jobs – namely holding the powerful to account.

### Expert interview – Aidan White

*Founder and President, Ethical Journalism Network*

*Figure 3.3* Aidan White

Fake news is the deliberate fabrication of information with the intention to deceive. When journalists make mistakes, and of course they do occasionally, they are under an obligation to correct them. Professional journalists don't seek to mislead or produce articles that are intentionally false.

Fake news is also not satire like you see in *Private Eye* magazine. The aim of satire is not to deceive people, it exists to entertain. Fake news is potentially much more sinister than this. In many cases it is political, it intends to change how people vote or otherwise act. It can also be used to encourage people to buy products or take certain positions. It disturbs the idea of democratic pluralism. Fake news creates uncertainty in people's lives.

Social media sites are unwilling to take responsibility for the content that appears on their platforms. Facebook, Google and Twitter have got immensely rich off a business model that makes no distinction between journalism as a stream of information which is in the public interest and other material – commercial messages, abusive messages or pornography.

Their only interest is whether the content generates clicks and advertising. So they will resist anything that stops them doing this. I don't like laws generally. When it comes to communications I prefer voluntary self-regulation. But if the social media companies don't accept self-regulation they are inviting governments to do something. Within ten years it is highly likely antitrust laws will break them up, much like the oil companies were in the early 20th century because they had too much power.

## Further reading

Bartlett, J. (2016) *The Dark Net: Inside the Digital Underworld.* Melville House.
Traces the early concepts of cyberspace, online freedom of speech and the rise in trolling and online abuse.
Kovach, B., and Rosenstiel, T. (2014) *The Elements of Journalism: What Newspeople Should Know and the Public Should Expect.* Three Rivers Press, CA.
The classic text on ethical journalism is even more relevant in an era of fake news.

## References

Attkisson, S. (2018) *Smear: How Shady Political Operatives and Fake News Control What You See, What You Think, and How You Vote.* Harper Collins.
Amanpour, C. (2016) Interview on the *Daily Show.* Comedy Central, 20 July.
Bartholomew, J. (2015) I invented 'virtue signalling'. Now it's taking over the world. *Spectator.* Available at: www.spectator.co.uk/2015/10/i-invented-virtue-signalling-now-its-taking-over-the-world/.
Bartlett, J. (2016) *The Dark Net: Inside the Digital Underworld.* Melville House.
BBC News (2017) Restaurant hit by 'human meat' fake news claims. BBC Newsbeat. Available at: www.bbc.co.uk/newsbeat/article/39966215/restaurant-hit-by-human-meat-fake-news-claims.

Benkler, Y., et al. (2017) Study: Breitbart-led right-wing media ecosystem altered broader media agenda. *Columbia Journalism Review*. Available at: www.cjr.org/analysis/breitbart-media-trump-harvard-study.php.

Canary (n.d.) Values. Available at: www.thecanary.co/values/.

Charles, M. (2013). News, documentary and advocacy journalism. In: K. Fowler-Watt and S. Allan (eds), *Journalism: New Challenges*. Poole: CJCR, Centre for Journalism and Communication Research, Bournemouth University, pp. 384–392,

Constine, J. (2016) Zuckerberg implies Facebook is a media company, just 'not a traditional media company'. TechCrunch. Available at: https://techcrunch.com/2016/12/21/fbonc/.

d'Ancona, M. (2017) Technology is herding us into like-minded political tribes. British GQ. Available at: www.gq-magazine.co.uk/article/technology-effect-on-politics.

Duggan, M. (2014) Online harassment. Pew Research Center: Internet, Science & Tech. Available at:www.pewinternet.org/2014/10/22/online-harassment.

Eddy, M. (2016) Obama, with Angela Merkel in Berlin, assails spread of fake news. *New York Times*. Available at: www.nytimes.com/2016/11/18/world/europe/obama-angela-merkel-donald-trump.html.

Flaxman, S., Goel, S., and Rao, J. M. (2016) Filter bubbles, echo chambers, and online news consumption, *Public Opinion Quarterly*, 80(S1), 298–320. doi: 10.1093/poq/nfw006.

Gahran, A. (2015) TrollBusters: strategies to preserve constructive online discourse. Available at: www.knightdigitalmediacenter.org/blogs/agahran/2015/03/trollbusters-strategies-preserve-constructive-online-discourse.html.

Gardiner, B., Mansfield, M., Anderson, I., Holder, J., Louter, D., and Ulmanu, M. (2016) The dark side of Guardian comments. *Guardian*. Available at: www.theguardian.com/technology/2016/apr/12/the-dark-side-of-guardian-comments.

Goulard, H. (2016) Britain's youth voted Remain. Politico. Available at: www.politico.eu/article/britains-youth-voted-remain-leave-eu-brexit-referendum-stats.

Grynbaum, M (2017) Trump tweets a video of him wrestling 'CNN' to the ground. *New York Times*. Available at: www.nytimes.com/2017/07/02/business/media/trump-wrestling-video-cnn-twitter.html.

Harding, J. (2016) A truly balanced view from the BBC: don't blame us for Brexit. BBC Blogs. Available at: www.bbc.co.uk/blogs/aboutthebbc/entries/e5f8951f-cec7-4d8a-8504-15016235617f.

Harrison, A. (2017) Can you trust the mainstream media? *Observer*. Available at: www.theguardian.com/media/2017/aug/06/can-you-trust-mainstream-media.

Heath, A. (2016) Facebook is going to use Snopes and other fact-checkers to combat and bury 'fake news'. Business Insider. Available at: http://uk.businessinsider.com/facebook-will-fact-check-label-fake-news-in-news-feed-2016-12?r=US&IR=T.

InfoWars (2017) 200K cash prizes! Infowars launches operation: expose terrorist media/Kathy Griffin. Infowars. Available at: www.infowars.com/200k-cash-prizes-infowars-launches-operation-expose-terrorist-mediakathy-griffin/.

Keen, A. (2007) *The Cult of the Amateur: How Blogs, MySpace, YouTube, and the Rest of Today's User-Generated Media are Destroying our Economy, our Culture, and our Values*. Doubleday.

Kelly, T. (2014) What is journalism anymore? TechCrunch. Available at: https://techcrunch.com/2014/11/09/what-is-journalism-anymore/?ncid=rss.

Kovach, B,. and Rosenstiel, T. (2014) *The Elements of Journalism: What Newspeople Should Know and the Public Should Expect*. Three Rivers Press (CA).

Levin, S., Wong, J. C., and Harding, L. (2016) Facebook backs down from 'napalm girl' censorship and reinstates photo. *Guardian*. Available at: www.theguardian.com/technology/2016/sep/09/facebook-reinstates-napalm-girl-photo.

Marcus, L. (2012) Is Twitter anything more than an online echo chamber? *Guardian*. Available at: www.theguardian.com/technology/2012/aug/22/twitter-online-echo-chanber-leftwing.

Metz, R. (2015) How technology might help Twitter curtail harassment. MIT Technology Review. Available at: www.technologyreview.com/s/535031/can-twitter-fix-its-harassment-problem-without-losing-its-soul.

Murtha, J. (2016) How fake news sites frequently trick big-time journalists. *Columbia Journalism Review*. Available at www.cjr.org/analysis/how_fake_news_sites_frequently_trick_big-time_journalists.php

Rawlinson, K. (2016) How newsroom pressure is letting fake stories on to the web. *Guardian*. Available at: www.theguardian.com/media/2016/apr/17/fake-news-stories-clicks-fact-checking.

Rennie, E. (2018) The robots are polarising how we consume news – and that's how we like it. The Conversation. Available at: http://theconversation.com/the-robots-are-polarising-how-we-consume-news-and-thats-how-we-like-it-64730.

Ross, T., and McTague, T. (2017) *Betting the House: The Inside Story of the 2017 Election*. Biteback Publishing.

Silverman, C. (2016) This analysis shows how viral fake election news stories outperformed real news on Facebook. BuzzFeed. Available at: www.buzzfeed.com/craigsilverman/viral-fake-election-news-outperformed-real-news-on-facebook?utm_term=.kymyQVd65A#.jcbRZQY5xb.

Sullivan, M. (2016) Face it, Facebook: you're in the news business. *Washington Post*. Available at: www.washingtonpost.com/lifestyle/style/face-it-facebook-youre-in-the-news-business/2016/07/10/cc53cd70-451a-11e6-bc99-7d269f8719b1_story.html?utm_term=.83d2062ca349.

*The Economist* (2011) Back to the coffee house. Available at: www.economist.com/node/18928416#prin.

Timokhina, E. (2012) Revisiting the basics of journalism. Missouri School of Journalism. Available at: https://journalism.missouri.edu/jan-2012/journalism-basics.html.

Waterson, J. (2017) How a small group of pro-Corbyn websites built enormous audiences on Facebook. BuzzFeed. Available at: www.buzzfeed.com/jimwaterson/the-rise-of-the-alt-left?utm_term=.saN8mxZ6N#.bgzyQWG3Z.

White, A. (n.d.) Journalism is other regarding: it is not the same as free expression. Ethical Journalism Network. Available at: http://ethicaljournalismnetwork.org/resources/publications/ethical-journalism/other-regarding.

White, J. (2017) Facebook under fire as it reveals 150m Americans saw Russian election propaganda. *Independent*. Available at: www.independent.co.uk/news/world/americas/us-politics/facebook-russia-ads-trump-election-2016-how-many-americans-saw-a8031881.html.

Zuckerberg, M. (2016) A lot of you have asked what we're doing … Available at: www.facebook.com/zuck/posts/10103269806149061.

# 4 Finding the story

## Verifying the news

**This chapter will cover:**

- Journalism as verification
- Scepticism and cynicism
- Verification in practice
- Verifying human sources of information
- Verifying websites and search results
- The dark web
- Verification of social media
- Verifying images and video
- Verifying places
- Verification for reporters at the scene
- Shades of grey – verification case studies
- Coping with trauma
- Live blogs

## Introduction

In September 2003, 17-year-old Shafilea Ahmed disappeared from her family home in Cheshire in north-west England. The case was notable for its numerous twists and the fact it took seven years to bring the culprits to justice.

Shafilea was missing for five months and during this time her father and mother – Mr Iftikhar and Mrs Farzana Ahmed – invited journalists into their home to make appeals for help. Often appearing distraught, as you might expect, they portrayed themselves as loving middle-class parents.

The case became a murder hunt when the teenager's body was found. But it took police years to get a breakthrough when, in a bizarre twist, Alesha Ahmed, Shafilea's sister, ordered an armed gang to rob the family home in 2010.

Alesha, who was now a university student, confessed to the crime and then told her lawyer something extraordinary. She said aged 15 she had seen her parents suffocate her sister with a plastic bag and dispose of her body. Based on this evidence, both parents were arrested and later sentenced to life imprisonment in what was described as a 'honour killing' of their daughter, who was due to take part in an arranged marriage (BBC 2012).

Mr and Mrs Ahmed lied repeatedly on camera regarding their involvement and in the process had both police and sceptical crime reporters fooled. While an extreme case, it also highlights how sources can embellish, distort or be economical with the truth when they speak to journalists.

Therefore systematic verification of information is at the heart of professional journalism and can be time-consuming and complex. It raises practical and ethical concerns as we walk a fine line in being sceptical, but not cynical in our approach. This practical chapter outlines some key tools to use when verifying material.

## Journalism as verification

The main role of the reporter in a breaking news situations is to establish the truth. Breaking news events can attract hoaxers, trolls and those who wish to exploit circumstances for political or financial reasons. It is essential to be transparent about uncertainty and credit or link to the sources you are drawing on, so the reader can determine where you got your information.

Attribution ensures that the source is accountable for the information they are giving you, and helps the user to make a judgement about how reliable that information might be, and any vested interests that might have motivated the statement.

If you are relying on information circulating online, familiarise yourself with basic techniques such as checking for 'red flags' that can indicate hoax social media accounts. Recently created accounts or those with few followers should be treated with particular wariness; you should also see what other information you can find about the person (including other social media profiles and contact details), and what connections they have. We list some software and websites that can help verify people beneath.

---

### Ethical codes

The importance of accuracy is highlighted in the two main ethical codes of conduct for journalists in the UK.

### The National Union of Journalists – NUJ – Code of Conduct (nuj.org. uk/about/nuj-code)

A journalist: Strives to ensure that information disseminated is honestly conveyed, accurate and fair. Does her/his utmost to correct harmful inaccuracies. (NUJ 2011)

**Independent Press Standards Organisation – IPSO – Code of Practice (ipso.co.uk/editors-code-of-practice)**

i) The Press must take care not to publish inaccurate, misleading or distorted information or images, including headlines not supported by the text.

ii) A significant inaccuracy, misleading statement or distortion must be corrected, promptly and with due prominence, and – where appropriate – an apology published. In cases involving IPSO, due prominence should be as required by the regulator. (IPSO 2016)

## Scepticism and cynicism

Professor Stephen Greenspan (2008) believes we should 'cultivate scepticism, but not cynicism'. Being sceptical means we query and test the reliability of sources – whether this is in text, photographic, video or audio format. Our aim is to seek some independent proof, often through triangulation with other sources.

You may find yourself hearing two conflicting versions of the same event. We warned in a previous chapter about giving false balance in your attempts to reflect all sides of the story. Reporting 'he said–she said' situations is increasingly frowned upon, so you should attempt to fact-check what your sources are telling you. If the source is unable to provide evidence to back up a claim, it is important that this too is reported. This is part of acting in a transparent and open way.

During verification, we need to be wary of our own personal or political bias. Professor Greenspan warns we are vulnerable to being hoaxed when source material aligns with our pre-existing worldview. In this way, we are more likely to give a 'free pass' to politicians or celebrities whom we like or agree with.

This tendency has its own name: confirmation bias – and it has been widely researched. One study of news consumption, for example, noted different effects on 'proattitudinal news exposure' (seeking news that confirms our own biases) and 'counterattitudinal news exposure' (avoiding news that challenges them) (Song 2016).

The research confirmed that news consumers make different decisions on what stories to read based on levels of fear and anger – highlighting not only our role as journalists in exposing readers to stories that may challenge what they believe, but also our own vulnerability to the same behaviour. For example, you may think you have a story and seek out information that backs that up, while ignoring signs that the story might be different, or false.

As journalists it is important to recognise that we are all subject to confirmation bias – the evidence suggests it happens at an unconscious level (Mooney 2011). The solution, then, is not to seek to 'avoid' confirmation bias happening at all but rather to assume that it is happening all the time and incorporate that knowledge into your processes.

This means taking steps to research contradictory sources, and consider alternative story angles. That story about a shocking weather image, for example? Perhaps it might instead be a story about 'Shocking weather image turns out to be fake' or '15 fake images from today's storms' or 'The person behind the weather image that fooled Twitter' or 'How a joke image led to 55 police calls'.

Confirmation bias is a powerful thing. Research suggests that, even when we read reports from different points of view, we are more likely to *recall* information from those reports that confirm our own biases. In fact there are so many dimensions of confirmation bias that one person has created a helpful 'cheat sheet' listing them (betterhumans.coach.me/cognitive-bias-cheat-sheet-55a472476b18) – it may be worth pinning this up on your wall to remind yourself of all the ways your brain can trick you!

Returning to the classic journalist's motto, 'If your mother tells you she loves you, check it out': it presents an interesting exercise: consider how you would find the evidence to prove and then disprove it. Do you have family photos, video material or quotes from relatives that could help?

Cynicism is different to scepticism because it is a belief that people are motivated purely by self-interest. This can be dangerous – it may lead us into following internet conspiracy theories and refusing to trust anything we read, regardless of its source. In this respect, a peer-reviewed journal article is dismissed as easily as a social media share from a friend. But the two are not the same.

As we attempt to combat fake news, it is important to remember that real provable facts do exist! The earth is not flat and, yes, the vast majority of climate scientists say the earth is warming.

It is common to hear people complain that politicians are liars and they all are as equally corrupt as each other. The author of this chapter has interviewed many politicians and has found that when you meet them face-to-face they come across as hard-working individuals who are committed to public service. They often get into politics precisely because they want to make the world a better place.

Rather than taking a cynical view of politics, a more nuanced view is that there are numerous economic and political forces at play that prevent politicians from carrying out their manifesto promises. But it is rare to read about the complexities of policy making in the newspapers and large numbers of people continue to regard politicians to be untrustworthy.

## Verification in practice

So far we have highlighted that verification is at the heart of journalism. Newsrooms should have robust verification processes in place. When planning coverage of diary news events (such as public events or company announcements) it is possible to anticipate how information will be sourced on social media and the verification process that will be implemented. For example, you can seek out lists of reliable sources of information on social media in advance and set up 'follows' for the accounts of people you know will be at the scene.

*Create a decision tree*

This is a type of verification workflow – essentially a checklist of 'tests' or yes/no questions that information must 'pass' before it is published. A well-structured and logical decision tree workflow can go a long way to reduce the chance of errors. You can create it using simple software such as FreeMind (freemind. sourceforge.net).

We've researched a large number of verification software tools for this chapter and we've tried to recommend only the best which we think will stick around. Unfortunately, tools come and go frequently. Topsy is a case in point. This was an excellent analytics tool that allowed journalists to manage social media accounts, measure engagements and keep an eye on rival news organisations. However, Apple bought it in 2013 only to kill it off two years later.

---

### Staying up to date

Verification tools come and go and it pays to stay up to date. Journalism. co.uk (journalism.co.uk) reviews new tools as they emerge. However, don't become too reliant on any single tool – who knows if it will disappear?

---

## Verifying human sources of information

Julie Posetti (2014) writes:

> There are two key elements: the source of a piece of content, and the content itself. These two components must be independently verified, and compared against each other to see if they tell a consistent story.

She says that it can be the case that the content is genuine, but the person sharing it isn't the original creator. It is also possible that your 'reliable source' has fallen for a hoax and is unintentionally sharing fake news.

We love social media, but some journalists are guilty of attributing too much credibility to material found through social media. Actually calling people on a mobile phone is one of the best ways to verify who they are. It is easy to lie via social media messages or email. Aim to speak to a source face-to-face if you can.

Unfortunately, journalists can be prevented from carrying out full verification. Some modern newsrooms may represent something more akin to 'news factories' where journalists scour the web for stories and spend their days rewriting press releases rather than making phone calls and meeting contacts in person. These types of websites are very vulnerable to being duped and reporting fake news.

Social media can help us in verification and improve the range and depth of journalism we produce (Duffy and Si 2017). It is easier than ever to track people down and do interviews, but research into the use of social media by journalists suggests a need for a new set of skills around verification (Lecheler and Kruikelmeier 2016).

The best journalists build up large contact databases of reliable sources so they know who to call in any breaking news situation. When you are starting out you may have few contacts, but you will soon build them up. Try to get all the key contact information – email addresses, social media accounts and mobile phone numbers – for your contacts database.

As a tool to prevent being hoaxed, many journalists will prioritise content from known reliable sources whom they have met in person in the past. These are people who are usually experts in some way. This doesn't mean that unknown sources at a scene of a new story are automatically untrustworthy, but the journalist will flag them for full verification before publication. Even if you know a source, and/or believe them to be reputable, you should still be sceptical.

A verification process for human contacts may go something like this:

1) Who is the contributor? Do they have expert knowledge or first-hand experience. How reliable are they likely to be?
2) Can their content be verified?
3) How is the information passed to you and presented?
4) Do they have a vested interest in you reporting what they have said?

### Software to help with contacts

Most journalists are familiar with the power of TweetDeck (tweetdeck.twitter.com) and Hootsuite (hootsuite.com) in organising social media contacts. Both tools launched in 2008 and are used in newsrooms.

Kred (kred.com) produces a 'score' indicating how influential a user is deemed to be – taking into account the scores of who follows them. Be suspicious of users with very new Twitter accounts – they may be fake.

Pipl (pipl.com) is useful for finding contact information for sources. It searches multiple social media sites and contacts databases. Unless your subject lives their life entirely off-grid, Pipl is likely to help locate them.

SocialMention (socialmention.com) allows you to track what people are saying about any topic in real-time. It monitors 100+ social media properties including more obscure ones like Digg. It also has sentiment analysis and a full range of ways to filter results.

## Verifying websites and search results

Most journalists know to treat information on amateur blogs and social media sites with great care, but may have no qualms in republishing stories stolen from other news sites. Ripping off stories from other news sites without attributing it is common, but also very poor practice. Never, ever, reproduce court cases stories without checking the details carefully. It is very lazy and there could be costly legal problems if there are mistakes in the original story.

Journalists will benefit from expanding the range of tools they deploy to verify stories. A survey of American journalism students during a news day exercise by Julia Tylor (2014) found a heavy reliance on search engines to verify news. It found that students searched using Google, followed by Bing and LexisNexis. The report warned that students trusted the credibility of search engine results despite them being 'based on highly selective ranking algorithms that rely more on keywords than credibility' (Tylor 2014).

It is unsurprising that Google is popular with journalists, as it has by far the most users of any search engine. Globally around 80 per cent of searches are on the site. The next biggest search engines – Bing and Baudu – have a market share only in the region of 8 per cent (NetMarketShare 2017).

Google searches around 130 trillion pages which sounds impressive until you realise this is tiny fraction of the web. Marc Goodman (2015) states:

> According to a study published in Nature, Google indexes no more than 16 per cent of the surface Web and misses all of the Deep Web. Any given search turns up just 0.03 per cent of the information that exists online (one in 3,000 pages).

So we are just scratching the surface of the Web if we only use Google. As Goodman warns: 'It's like fishing in the top two feet of the ocean – you miss the virtual Mariana Trench below.' We also don't know how Google compiles its search results, which sites it includes and those it may leave out. The company claims such information is commercially sensitive.

---

### The right to be forgotten

A European Court of Justice [ECJ] ruling from 2014 requires that search engines and social media sites remove links to pages that 'appear to be inadequate, irrelevant or no longer relevant or excessive … in the light of the time that had elapsed' (Court of Justice 2014).

The idea behind the ruling is sound – i.e. that individuals shouldn't be stigmatised for mistakes they have made in the past. This replicated the offline world where the concept of 'spent convictions' exists for former prisoners. Similarly, former criminals may wish to have old stories in a newspaper written about their crimes de-linked by the search engines. The phrase 'de-linked' is important – the content isn't actually removed from the search engine, it's just made much harder to find. But some argue that this is censorship and have demanded the 'right to remember' rather than forget. Google's Transparency Report (transparencyreport.google.com) lists examples of the material it has been compelled to de-link and it makes for fascinating reading.

### Search tools for journalists

It is tempting to follow the crowd and just use Google for searching the Web, but there are some decent alternatives.

Microsoft's Bing has a solid video search tool. The Chrome browser extension – Storyful Multisearch – allows you to search numerous social sites in one go including Tumblr, YouTube and Storyful itself. Extensions (chrome.google.com/webstore/category/extensions), as the name suggests, are small programs that extend the functionality of Chrome. There are plenty of time-saving extensions, which can help with newsgathering.

Google Trends (trends.google.co.uk) is a zeitgeist site and provides visualisations of the most popular stories that people are searching for in real time. For example, during the London mayoral elections in 2016 a funny Google search was 'How tall is Sadiq Khan?' The then Labour candidate, now mayor, is five foot six inches in stature. It's not being rude to say that the London Mayor is on the short side for a man. Conservative rival Zac Goldsmith, who ran against Khan, towered over him at six foot two inches tall during election debates. One of the most common questions people were typing into Google search in the run-up to the European referendum vote was 'What is Brexit?' The fact that this suggests people didn't know what they were voting for was rather worrying.

Google Trends is great for generating ideas for explainer style articles. It also gives insight into the weird issues that the public care about. Most of the social media sites have Top Ten 'trending' lists that can provoke ideas.

Another Google service, Alerts (google.co.uk/alerts), is a great research tool that allows you to monitor new stories about your patch. Try setting up an alert for a favourite sports team or your hometown. Google will then email you links to news mentioning the keyword.

## The dark web

The dark web is mostly associated with criminal activity when it is discussed in the media. An infamous example of a dark web site was Silk Road – an online marketplace for illegal drugs. There are many legitimate uses for the dark web, but those who visit have to be mindful of the fact shady activities are going on in its darker corners. Avoid downloading files you don't recognise which may contain viruses or worse.

So what is it? *Tech Advisor* magazine defines it as a:

> collection of websites that exist on an encrypted network and cannot be found by using traditional search engines or visited by using traditional browsers

(Egan 2018)

You need browser software to view it. Tor (torproject.org) – short for The Onion Router – is one of the most popular. It uses secret pages with .onion suffixes – rather than .com – that are only accessible with a Tor browser. Tor is very secure and it doesn't reveal your IP address, which is rather handy for those who wish to communicate privately.

As with the open web, you need a search engine to locate things on the dark web. DuckDuckGo (duckduckgo.com) is anonymous. You may wish to access the dark web using a secure virtual private network (VPN) and there are many companies that offer such technology.

## Verification of social media

Steve Schifferes et al. (2014) found journalists use social media in verification for:

1. Predicting or alerting breaking news
2. Verifying social media content – quickly identifying who has posted a tweet or video and establishing 'truth or lie'
3. Listening – following high-quality people/networks to find out about interesting/relevant stories
4. Tracking trends and sentiment to inform programmes and news agenda
5. Easily distribute content, find a new audience and get feedback on what people thought of it
6. Getting quick access to eyewitnesses or other trustworthy informants
7. Crowdsourcing questions about a story in development – asking a network for advice

But Schifferes said journalists are frustrated with verification tools and sought more tools to automate what was often laborious work, such as for searching for stories across multiple social networks. As well as finding text-based material, journalists needed better tools to find multimedia material such as images and video. Journalists also wanted help with verification, such as how to determine who is a reliable source. They also wanted improved tools to filter fake video and images and to cross-check images with geo-location data. There is certainly more room for automation in verification and improved software.

### Tools for handling social media

Twitter has long been viewed as the best social media site for breaking news. It frequently beats the news wires such as those from Reuters, Press Association (PA) and Associated Press (AP). However, Facebook and other social media sites are making inroads and stories are being streamed on Facebook Live in particular.

It is worth breaking down social media into a three-stage process:

- **Discovery and verification** – the main aspect we are interested in here;
- **Curation** – bringing social media together to form a narrative;
- **Publication** – getting it out there on a news website or app.

A few tools help with all three stages, while others specialise in just one area.

*Facebook for Media (facebook.com/facebookmedia)*

The Facebook Signal dashboard has had a peculiar history. It launched in 2015 although it has had a long test phase. A dedicated dashboard for journalists opens on three main columns: 'Trending now/Emerging' topics (which can be further filtered by category), 'Trending Posts' (by users) and 'Live'. Other parts of the service provide quick access to 'Public figures' (with a heavy US bias) and a powerful search tool for both Facebook and Instagram. The service is designed to encourage the embedding of Facebook updates in news stories and not just tweets. It also has the facility to curate Facebook content into publishable 'collections'. It is free, but you need to apply for access.

*Banjo Discovery (discovery.banjoapp.com)*

This dashboard provides interesting ways of discovering and organising social media content (e.g. by time and location) to publish breaking news as it happens. It aims to allow for the curation of content from a range of social media sources including China's Weibo. It is free, but you need to apply for access.

*Cronycle (cronycle.com)*

A solid research tool which will appeal to all researchers – whether they are journalists, students or academic. It allows you to curate and publish social media content.

Twitter is so important for breaking news and there many tools that can help journalists during news discovery phase.

*Dataminr (dataminr.com)*

A powerful Twitter monitoring and analysis tool. It is outside the budget of individual journalists, but many news organisations have institutional subscriptions. Its main use is for real-time alerting of potentially newsworthy tweets based on a combination of authority (official accounts, for example, tweeting announcements) and keyword analysis (such as references to explosions, crashes and evacuations), but it can also be used to find tweets in real time as events develop, or perform historical analysis to analyse trends.

## Verifying images and video

Images and video verification techniques are also important. People can try to pass off images from previous news events as being from a current event, so use the reverse image search facility provided by Google Images to see if an image is older than it seems. Hoax images can be very hard to spot when they have been manipulated in editing tools such as Photoshop.

An image's EXIF data provides information on when the image was taken, on which camera, and with what settings – look for 'EXIF checking' tools online which allow you to check this. Verification expert Eliot Higgins offers helpful case studies on how these techniques, and others, have been used on his website bellingcat.com.

UGC expert Claire Wardle (Silverman 2014) states that there are four main elements in verifying social media content:

- Provenance (is this the original piece of content?)
- Source (who uploaded the content?)
- Date (when was the content created?)
- Location (where was the content created?)

Journalists need to verify many different types of multimedia material that come their way, including images and video content.

Photos often contain hidden information within them. The IPTC (n.d.) website states:

> Metadata is a set of data that describes and gives information about other data. Photo metadata allows information to be transported with an image file, in a way that can be understood by other software, hardware, and end users, regardless of the format.

It states that there are three main categories of metadata:

- **Administrative** – identification of the creator, creation date and location, contact information for licensors of the image, and other technical details.
- **Descriptive** – information about the visual content. This may include headline, title, captions and keywords.
- **Rights** – copyright information and underlying rights in the visual content including model and property rights, and rights usage terms.

We are mostly interested in the administrative detail, such as the location where the image was shot. You can upload an image to websites such as Jeffrey's Image Metadata Viewer (exif.regex.info/exif.cgi) to see what EXIF has been embedded in the image. There may be GPS coordinates embedded in images taken with smartphones. This allows us to map quite precisely where in the world the image was taken.

This can then be verified by calling the person who took the photo. Ask them to explain where they were and what type of camera they used and check for inconsistencies with the EXIF data.

You can also take an image through a process known as error-level analysis (ELA) which attempts to show the differing levels of compression throughout an image, which can be a giveaway that the image has been manipulated, perhaps in Photoshop. Fotoforensics (fotoforensics.com) offers ELA and metadata analysis for free and is a great free tool for verification.

### Tools for image and video verification

*Photodesk (photodesk-app.com)*

Instagram is important to most journalists, but especially those working in fashion and lifestyle where it is hugely influential. Photodesk for Mac is a cheap desktop app that allows you to search for images using keywords, tags and usernames and locations. You can also make lists of content creators to keep track of reliable sources, package and publish the material. Pictodash (www.picodash.com) is another cheap rival that works for both PC and Mac.

*Google Images (images.google.com) – reverse image search*

Google Images compares your image of uncertain provenance with billions of other web images to locate similarities. Click on the camera icon next to the search bar to upload an image or paste a URL. It is pretty common for journalists to do reverse image searches, so you may wish to install the Chrome browser extension RevEye (chrome.google.com/webstore/detail/reveye-reverse-image-sear/keaaclcjhehbbapnphnmpiklalfhelgf?hl=en) which allows access to a vast range of databases in one hit.

*YouTube Dataviewer (citizenevidence.amnestyusa.org)*

Created by Amnesty International, it aims to extract metadata from videos hosted on YouTube. The tool attempts to identify the first upload of the video (i.e. the original) from any copies and re-posts. Controversial videos can disappear quickly off the web, so use a Tube Catcher (atube.me) to save offline.

## Verifying places

If you are sent an image of plane that has crash-landed into a side of a mountain, it pays to be sceptical. You may have local contacts on the ground, who can get to the scene of the accident. But this is another case where technology can help.
Google's three main mapping tools are essential:

- **Maps** – google.co.uk/maps
- **Street View** – the fastest access is via a third-party site Instant Street View (instantstreetview.com)
- **Google Earth Pro** – google.com/earth

The free Earth Pro software includes the ability to measure radiuses on the ground, go back in time (very useful during natural disaster stories) and publish high-resolution satellite images. Using Google Maps, Street View and Earth is usually free to journalists, although images generated need crediting.

### Software that can help with place verification

*Wolfram Alpha (wolframalpha.com)*

Not a search engine, it describes itself as a 'computational knowledge engine' – whatever that is. It gives access to useful databases – it keeps a searchable record of historical weather conditions which is useful when verifying images and video.

*Wikimapia (wikimapia.org)*

Wikimapia, an open source project, which is trying to map the whole world and get as much detailed information about buildings as possible.

## Verification for reporters at the scene

Ushahidi (ushahidi.com), which translates as 'testimony' in Swahili, was developed to map UGC reports of violence in Kenya after the post-election violence in 2008 and is a well-known tool for collating UGC during natural disasters.

Security is a big issue for reporters on the ground in dangerous parts of the world. They can become targets for security forces, but these mobile phone apps can help reduce the dangers on the ground.

*Figure 4.1* Google Earth Pro software
By Google, 2018

### Umbrella app (Android only)

From sending emails, travelling in hostile environments to attending protests, journalists need to work securely. This free and open source app provides a lot of useful tips. Needless to say, information on the app is encrypted and in one swipe you can hide the app.

### Reporta app

The International Women's Media Foundation (IWMF) designed the app to help journalists working in hostile environments. It provides a useful check-in system to alert your newsroom of your whereabouts and an SOS button to call in help.

## Shades of grey – verification case studies

In this part of the chapter we have included examples of verification dilemmas. Some things may be impossible to prove. Wardle says: 'The best advice is to be transparent and honest if you have doubts' (Silverman 2014).

To publish or not? Peter Verweij (2012) states:

> At the end of the day there will also be a decision to make: publish or not? There are two things to consider here. First, how urgent is it? And second, what is the damage in case of falsehood? … Falsehood damages your credibility, but if true, you win the race with a scoop.

### Case 1: Hurricane shark

During Hurricane Sandy, which hit the state of New Jersey in 2012, a huge amount of UGC material appeared on social media. At its peak, users of Instagram were posting ten photographs of the devastation every second, with around half a million photos being posted overall (Laird 2012).

One such image on Facebook appeared to show a big shark swimming down a flooded street in New Jersey. So, what do you think? Do you publish it? Journalist Tom Phillips (Silverman 2014) had to make the call. He writes: 'One aspect of the images, is that they were strange enough to make you suspicious, yet they weren't implausible enough to dismiss out of hand.'

Key questions to ask:

#### A) Similar sightings?

Who else has seen the shark? Phillips found no other evidence. But unlike a plane crash, it is plausible that it could be a one-off sighting.

## B) Image source?

The image appeared on a Facebook profile. It was clear the user lived in New Jersey and had other genuine pictures of flooded streets on his profile.

## C) Reverse image search?

An extensive reverse image search was done on the shark fin. An original image showing a fin emerging from water was discovered. This had been inserted into a legitimate picture of flooding in New Jersey. It appeared this was a harmless social media prank that got out of hand.

Animal stories are popular, but journalists must take care. In September 2010, ITV's West Country regional TV news bulletin reported as fact that a polar bear was washed up on a Cornish beach. It was eventually identified as a dead cow.

## Case 2: Court case picture mix up

Thankfully animals can't sue journalists for libel. However, a simple image mix up caused trouble for a celebrity website.

In 2013 Ian Watkins of the rock band Lostprophets went on trial for a series of horrific sex offences, some involving children. E! Online, a celebrity website, mixed the defendant's picture in a report on the case with that of Ian 'H' Watkins, formerly of Steps, a British ABBA-inspired pop group.

This simple mistake had the potential for devastating consequences. 'H' Watkins, who had built a career based on a cheeky and clean-cut personality, started to receive abusive messages. Yet he had nothing to do with the sexual assault allegations.

E! Online did just about everything possible to reduce the damage:

1. Quickly replaced the photograph with the correct one.
2. An editor's note was added to the story stating clearly: 'This story was originally published with an image of Ian "H" Watkins of the band Steps rather than Ian Watkins of the Lostprophets. E! Online deeply regrets this matter'
3. E! Online emailed and rang 'H' Watkins' manager to apologise.

Journalists need to balance the need for speed against accuracy. 'Being first is rewarded by increased web traffic, which tends to encourage snap (shallow?) judgements and a failure to adequately check the veracity of sources', writes Anthony Zurcher (2014). E! Online behaved transparently by not just replacing the image very swiftly, but also highlighting an error had been made. This helped limit the damage.

## Case 3: Proof of 'obscene act'

Should you report accusations which you can't prove? In September 2015 the *Daily Mail* broke the story alleging that the then British prime minister, David Cameron, had committed an 'obscene act with a dead pig's head' (Ashcroft and Oakeshott 2015) as part of what it calls an 'outrageous initiation ceremony' when Cameron was a student at Oxford University. The exclusive story was political dynamite and the *Daily Mail* legitimately claimed it was in the public interest.

The article listed the source of the contentious allegation as a 'Distinguished Oxford contemporary, now an MP' (Ashcroft and Oakeshott 2015) – which left everyone guessing who it was. It is not unusual for journalists to include off-the-record comments. But the journalist would be expected to verify such a shocking allegation. It was clear that there was no video or photo evidence. Doubts were raised whether the story was true or merely gossip. Isabel Oakeshott who wrote the story was asked if she had any proof. She states:

> We couldn't get to the bottom of that source's allegations … So we merely reported the account that the source gave us … We don't say whether we believe it to be true.
>
> (Channel 4 News 2015)

Katharine Viner, Editor, *Guardian* newspaper, described Oakeshott's comments as 'an unusually brazen defence' and commented:

> It seemed that journalists were no longer required to believe their own stories to be true, nor, apparently, did they need to provide evidence.
>
> (Viner 2016)

## Case 4: Death knock by social media

The death knock has an important significance in journalism. It symbolises, perhaps more than any other story type, the importance of doing face-to-face interviews. A reporter is dispatched to knock on the door of a relative of someone who has died in tragic circumstance to get quotes and a picture of the deceased. The death is rarely of natural causes; it is most likely to be murder, suicide or a freak accident.

In Liverpool, the saying goes when someone dies you expect a visit from 'the police, the priest and the Liverpool Echo' – the latter being one of the great northern city newspapers (liverpoolecho.co.uk). The order is important – it should *always* be the police who break the news of a death to the relatives.

A more recent phenomena is for relatives to set up Facebook tribute pages to loved ones. This has allowed for a new style of reporting – the virtual death knock. For the reporter it saves time and means they won't have to bother the relatives. But a study by academics Jackie Newton and Dr Sallyanne Duncan found that relatives preferred that journalists do the death knock and interview them in person rather than obtaining images from social media.

Newton and Duncan (cited Pugh 2012) stated that a number of families in this study had been 'prepared by the police for intense media interest in the death of their loved one'. However, 'When it did not arrive, or when their loved one's death was ignored or covered briefly without contact with the family, they felt let down'. They added: 'One mother of a murder victim said this perceived lack of interest added a further layer of hurt to her bereavement.'

The death knock is viewed as the bread and butter of local news reporting and it's often the first test for any rookie reporter. Never assume that relatives of the deceased won't want to be interviewed. A face-to-face interview is always the best way of getting to the truth and is preferable to telephone or, worse, interviews via email. It may save time and the potential for uncomfortable situations, but avoid pinching quotes or images off social media. It is lazy, can cause upset to the relatives and possibly lead to legal issues.

## Coping with trauma

Doing the death knock can be very difficult, but vicarious trauma is the emotional damage that journalists can experience as a result of overexposure to disturbing images.

Margaret Sullivan (2016) of the *Washington Post* states:

> When Diamond Reynolds logged on to Facebook after her boyfriend, Philando Castile, was shot by a police officer Wednesday in Falcon Heights, Minn., her first words as she started recording were 'Stay with me.' Millions did.

The 2016 shooting of Castile by a cop through the window of a car was streamed on Facebook Live in all its horrific detail by Diamond Reynolds. It provoked a debate about the responsibilities social media platforms have in censoring content.

The stream will haunt anyone who has viewed it, but it was important story. At a time of rising police brutality against black Americans, Minnesota's governor was forced to bring in the Justice Department to investigate what might have otherwise been ignored.

Trauma is recognised as an issue facing not just journalists on the front line, but anyone dealing with user generated content (UGC) which may include traumatic material. The BBC provides guidelines for its journalists and First Draft's guide Journalism and Vicarious Trauma (firstdraftnews.com/journalist-guides) has plenty of tips on how to cope with trauma.

There has been a run of distressing stories in recent times – the Syrian Civil War, terrorist attacks and the beheading of hostages. These stories have produced often gruesome UGC images and video that require verification. Terrorist organisations run surprisingly professional media operations that create broadcast-quality propaganda videos for distribution to 24-hour news channels.

The coverage of terrorist attacks by the media must be proportional. That is to say we must balance the public's right to know, while ensuring we don't give terrorists what has been referred to as the 'oxygen of publicity' for their cause. While gruesome videos are often shared widely online, as journalists we have to be careful about what we choose to show.

P. Kim Bui (2016), who reports on human rights for Reported.ly, states:

> We pass over a lot of footage at Reported.ly: often when it's too brutal, it's unnecessary to the story, it furthers terrorist agendas. It is good practice to be transparent in this area and state in the story if a video for example is too brutal to show.'

As well as protecting ourselves, it is also important that we don't accidently put our users in harm's way. For example, in extreme weather conditions it can be dangerous to invite users to contribute UGC material or to live video streams. During storms in 2014 the Coastguard SOS campaign tweeted to the Sky News account warning them to:

> STOP asking people to send in photos of coastal storms and instead warn people to KEEP AWAY FROM COASTS.

> (CoastGuardSOS 2014)

## Live blogs

Live blogs provide commentary on an event while it takes place, usually through frequent and short updates. It is essentially a raw feed that allows the journalists to curate a range of multimedia material from original sources and third parties and provide comment. During a live blog the editors often have to make verification decisions at great speed.

Live blogs are structured in a very different way to a traditional inverted summary style news story. It is the rawness of the live blog format that has led some to challenge their accuracy.

So are live blogs a legitimate form of journalism? There is no doubt live blogs can be extremely popular. A BBC News website source told the author that it is common for more people read its live blogs than listen to its radio coverage during breaking news events.

But Thurman and Walters (2013) found that some journalists complained that live blogging was done away from than the scene of a story. Paul Lewis, who was at the *Guardian* at the time of interview, states that journalists need to go to the story and shouldn't over-rely on second-hand sources. Reporting a story on the ground is always the best approach. Lewis states:

> They [live blogs] can be really useful ... but your vantage point is a computer screen in an office block in London, and as a journalist you always find out more when you're there. Always.
>
> (Quoted in Thurman and Walters 2013)

It is good practice to signpost the source material used in a live blog clearly and transparently, allowing the users to make up their own minds. And in an environment where news events are reported live by participants, live blogs offer an important service in filtering, contextuality and checking information and media that would otherwise be subject to none of those procedures.

Journalists should highlight the information that they have verified and seek help from the audience with verifying the stuff you can't. It is also good practice to highlight information that you are currently missing.

## Conclusion

Most journalism courses instil a habit of checking and rechecking questionable information and consider how to establish 'reliable sources' of information. It is essential to verify information, often through a process of triangulation with other independent sources. However, it is common for journalists to complain they either don't have the time or the technical resources to do it for every story.

Nick Davies (2009) states: 'For journalists, the defining value is honesty – the attempt to tell the truth. That is our primary purpose. All that we do ... must flow from the single source of truth-telling.'

**Expert interview – Matt Cooke**

**Head of Partnerships & Training, Google News Lab, Google News Lab**

*Figure 4.2* Matt Cooke

We launched the Google News Lab (g.co/newslab) back in 2015, the core objective was to collaborate with journalists to experiment and think of new ways technology could be used to enhance storytelling. We've worked with newsrooms to consider how they can innovate with new virtual reality technology such as our partnership with The Guardian for their first foray into VR [6x9 – A Virtual Experience of Solitary Confinement – theguardian.com/world/ng-interactive/2016/apr/27/6x9-a-virtual-experience-of-solitary-confinement]

Personally, when I speak to journalists in Europe they don't say they often make errors in verification, but they do say it takes a lot of time. Whilst no digital tool will replace the individual judgement of a journalist – there is no silver bullet – there are tools and techniques that can help you come to a decision or give you more information to help.

A simple example – you find or receive an image of an event, use Google reverse image search to find out if the image has surfaced elsewhere or is related to other connected photographs. We've worked with First Draft to strengthen the training of journalists and the awareness of the verification process – it's an industry wide challenge.

But, what about video? Frame By Frame For YouTube (a Chrome extension) can help you interrogate a video. Google Maps and Google Earth are also used for verification. I recommend Eliot Higgins [Founder of online investigation website Bellingcat and a visiting research associate at King's College London] who has case studies of how various tools are used in practice (firstdraftnews.com/author/eliot-higgins).

## Further reading

Silverman, C. (ed.) (2014) *Verification Handbook* (verificationhandbook.com).
A definitive e-book guide to verifying digital content for emergency coverage.
First Draft (firstdraftnews.com).
This coalition of news providers and fact checkers was founded in June 2015 'to raise awareness and address challenges relating to trust and truth in the digital age'.
Google News Initiative – (newsinitiative.withgoogle.com).
Plenty of free training courses in verification.

## References

Ashcroft, M., and Oakeshott, I. (2015) British Prime Minister and an obscene act with a dead pig's head: how David Cameron took part in sordid initiation ceremony after joining Oxford University dining society as a student. *Daily Mail*. Available at: www.dailymail.co.uk/news/article-3242550/Cameron-pig-bemused-look-face-future-PM-took-outrageous-initiation-ceremony-joining-Oxford-dining-society.html#ixzz57Bzquxvi.

BBC News (2012) Shafilea Ahmed's sister talks of 'relief'. Available at: www.bbc.co.uk/news/uk-england-18194131.

Bui, P. K. (2016) There are real world consequences to sharing social footage. Medium. Available at: https://medium.com/1st-draft/there-are-real-world-consequences-to-sharing-social-footage-no-matter-who-you-are-880e31a6d10b.

Channel 4 News (2015) David Cameron allegations: Toby Young vs Isabel Oakeshott. Channel 4 News. 21 Sept. Available at: www.youtube.com/watch?v=rm_Bli5h0Ns.

CoastguardSOS (2014) Stop asking people to send in photos. Twitter. Available at: https://twitter.com/Coastguard_SOS/status/419380592317591552.

Conn, D. (2016) How the *Sun*'s 'truth' about Hillsborough unraveled. *Guardian*. Available at: www.theguardian.com/football/2016/apr/26/how-the-suns-truth-about-hillsborough-unravelled.

Court of Justice (2014) An internet search engine operator is responsible for the processing that it carries out of personal data which appear on web pages published by third parties. Court of Justice of the European Union. Available at: https://curia.europa.eu/jcms/upload/docs/application/pdf/2014-05/cp140070en.pdf.

Davies, N. (2009). *Flat Earth News: An Award-Winning Reporter Exposes Falsehood, Distortion and Propaganda in the Global Media*. Chatto & Windus.

Duffy, A., and Si, J. T. R. (2017) Naming the dog on the internet. *Digital Journalism*, 1–18. doi: 10.1080/21670811.2017.1377092.

Egan, M. (2018) Thinking of venturing on to the Dark Web? You might want to change your mind. Tech Advisor. Available at: www.techadvisor.co.uk/how-to/internet/dark-web-3593569/.

Goodman, M. (2015) Most of the web is invisible to Google: here's what it contains. Popular Science. Available at: www.popsci.com/dark-web-revealed.

Greenspan, S. (2008) *The Annals of Gullibility: Why we Get Duped and How to Avoid it.* Praeger.

IPSO (2016) Editors' code of practice. IPSO. Available at: http://ipso.co.uk/editors-code-of-practice/.

IPTC (n.d.) What is photo metadata. Available at: https://iptc.org/standards/photo-metadata/photo-metadata/.

Laird, S. (2012) Instagram users share 10 Hurricane Sandy photos per second. Mashable. Available at: http://mashable.com/2012/10/29/instagram-hurricane-sandy/#KyWvQFH0Raq.

Lecheler, S., and Kruikemeier, S. (2015) Re-evaluating journalistic routines in a digital age: a review of research on the use of online sources. *New Media and Society*, 18(1), 156–171. doi: 10.1177/1461444815600412.

Mooney, C. (2017) *The Science of Why we Don't Believe Science.* Mother Jones. Available at: www.motherjones.com/politics/2011/04/denial-science-chris-mooney/.

NetMarketShare (2017) Market share for mobile, browsers, operating systems and search engines. Available at: https://netmarketshare.com/.

NUJ (2011) Code of conduct. National Union of Journalists. Available at: http://nuj.org.uk/about/nuj-code/.

Posetti, J. (2014). Trends in newsrooms: back to basics with social media verification. http://blog.wan-ifra.org/2014/07/09/trends-in-newsrooms-3-back-to-basics-with-social-media-verification.

Pugh, A. (2012) Bereaved say 'death knocks' better than social media. *Press Gazette.* Available at: www.pressgazette.co.uk/bereaved-say-death-knocks-better-than-social-media/.

Schifferes, S., Newman, N., Thurman, N., et al. (2014): Identifying and verifying news through social media. *Digital Journalism*. DOI: 10.1080/21670811.2014.892747]

Selby, J. (2013) Steps star Ian 'H' Watkins gets court apology for Lostprophets paedophile mix-up. Independent. Available at: www.independent.co.uk/news/people/news/steps-star-ian-h-watkins-gets-court-apology-for-lostprophets-paedophile-mix-up-9015816.html.

Silverman, C. (ed.) (2014) *Verification Handbook: A Definitive Guide to Verifying Digital Content for Emergency Coverage.* European Journalism Centre, Maastricht.

Song, H. (2016) Why do people (sometimes) become selective about news? The role of emotions and partisan differences in selective approach and avoidance, *Mass Communication and Society*, 20(1), 47–67. doi: 10.1080/15205436.2016.1187755.

Sullivan, M. (2016) Face it, Facebook: you're in the news business. *Washington Post.* Available at: www.washingtonpost.com/lifestyle/style/face-it-facebook-youre-in-the-news-business/2016/07/10/cc53cd70-451a-11e6-bc99-7d269f8719b1_story.html?utm_term=.92c4ff740e3e.

Thurman, N., and Walters, A. (2013) Live blogging – digital journalism's pivotal platform? *Digital Journalism*, 1(1), 82–101. DOI: 10.1080/21670811.2012.714935

Tylor, J. (2014) An examination of how student journalists seek information and evaluate online sources during the newsgathering process, *New Media and Society*, 17(8), 1277–1298. doi: 10.1177/1461444814523079.

Verweij, P. (2012) Seven top tips for verifying tweets, Memeburn. Available at: https:// memeburn.com/2012/01/seven-top-tips-for-verifying-tweets/.

Viner, K. (2016) How technology disrupted the truth. *Guardian*. Available at: www. theguardian.com/media/2016/jul/12/how-technology-disrupted-the-truth.

Zurcher, A. (2014) Journalistic ethics at internet speed. BBC News. Available at: www. bbc.co.uk/news/blogs-echochambers-27553248

# 5   The art of storytelling

**This chapter will cover:**

- Choosing the most appropriate ways to tell the story on new platforms
- Writing for mobile
- Raw versus packaged news
- Breaking news: liveblogging and live tweeting
- Curation and aggregation
- Explainer journalism
- Long form and immersive features
- Telling stories with data
- Horizontal storytelling and the 'Stories' format

## Introduction

Journalism skills fall broadly into two categories: the techniques used to find stories, and the skills to tell those stories effectively. A good journalist needs to develop both those sides of their skillset: after all, a story is only as good as the raw material you have to work with, and there's no point getting a great scoop if no one wants to read it. One of Kovach and Rosenstiel's ten principles of journalism, for example, is that: 'It must strive to keep the significant interesting and relevant' (Kovach and Rosenstiel 2007).

The internet has seen a massive expansion of both sets of skills, with many new ways to tell and find stories. As a result, journalists have revisited many of the basic principles of storytelling: the importance of character, setting and movement, for example; and techniques of sequence, editing and composition.

In this chapter we outline some of the techniques that are being used to tell stories effectively across different platforms, and the concepts informing the decisions behind those.

## Choosing the most appropriate ways to tell the story

In April 2016 Scott Rensberger told the mobile journalism conference MojoCon: 'Storytelling is the most powerful thing in the world – it connects the dots of our communities.' Regardless of the technology, he argued, storytelling was 'still everything', with the power to affect your mind, heart or wallet – and great stories could do this without needing expensive production, technology, filters or transitions (Scott 2016).

For professional storytellers this is a hugely exciting period to be part of: with dozens of new platforms, and few barriers to creating content on those, there are huge opportunities for creating new ways of telling stories, and discovering new rules for what works best.

But this dizzying array of possibilities also represents a massive challenge: instead of focusing on just one approach, most journalists need to be able to get to grips with multiple platforms, with multiple media options. It is a lot easier to make those choices – and make the right ones – with some understanding of core story-telling concepts and techniques.

### Genre and format

Broadly speaking, journalism belongs to the 'factual' genre. Within that, however, broadcast and print journalism has developed various genre formats, from the NIB (News In Brief) and the inverted pyramid to the interview feature and broadcast package. Some of these formats have been carried over into online publishing in what are described as 'extant subgenres', but the internet – and particular mobile media – has also seen an expansion of new, 'spontaneous genres': those which 'never existed in other media; a novel genre that arises with no clear antecedent genres in non-electronic form' (Shepherd and Watters 1998).

Formats and genres help journalists to report quickly and efficiently when stories break – and time is a key factor in deciding which format is chosen. More rigid formats are used when time is of the essence, whereas formats which require more time (such as features and documentaries) offer more scope for creativity. Subject matter is also be a factor. If colourful characters or locations are involved and are accessible, for example, editors might choose to commission an interview or package. These factors still come into play now we have access to a much wider range of formats – but a wider understanding of those formats is also needed.

- Are things changing so fast that a traditional 'story' format is going to be inadequate? Then live updates via Twitter, Facebook, a liveblog or a combination of those may work better.
- Is there a wealth of material out there being produced by witnesses? Some sort of curation-based format might work well.
- Have you secured an interview with a key expert? A Facebook Live chat, or Twitter Q&A, may work well.
- Is there a set of locations or items that tell their own story? Visual formats on Instagram, Snapchat, Pinterest or similar platforms might work well.
- Are you on the scene and raw video of the event is going to have the most impact? Streaming live video could work well.

- Does the event take place over a geographical area, so users will want to see the movement or focus on a particular location? Then a map might be most appropriate.

Many publishers have begun to establish their own formats for different social platforms, which have then been adopted by other publishers too. See for example the way that captions have become conventional on social video, how GIFs are used in Twitter updates or emojis in mobile notifications. It is important to read, watch and listen to a variety of formats on social and messaging platforms, and look for styles which recur – as well as techniques which break those conventions effectively.

And some formats have been invented by social platforms themselves: perhaps the best example of this is Snapchat's 'stories' format, a sequence of vertical images or short videos that can be tapped through. Since its introduction in 2013 the format has been imitated by Instagram, Facebook, Twitter, Medium and a number of media organisations' mobile apps.

### Medium and media

The medium of a story is sometimes closely related to the genre format: the gallery genre format relies on still images, for example; livestreaming tends to be video; and a live blog format may be primarily text-based. However, you can also choose to mix still and short moving images in your gallery, or include visual, audio and video updates in your live blog. And livestreaming can be audio-only too.

Interviews can be realised in any single medium – from a purely text-based piece, to an audio interview or one which is recorded on video – or any combination: text-based pieces may embed video and/or audio clips and still images; an audio interview can use a strong illustrative image, or be turned into an audio slideshow by using a sequence of several images.

The choice of medium will be shaped by the nature of the story itself – how important or meaningful are the sights and sounds involved? But also by the time available – and the platforms being used by the audience …

### Device

In 2013, when most of the industry was only just beginning to shift to a 'mobile-first' approach to publishing, senior *Washington Post* staff were looking further ahead, to what they were calling 'adaptive storytelling', around devices and timing.

A key figure in this development was Cory Haik, the *Post*'s then-executive producer and senior editor for digital news. In a post on her blog she used the example of a live blog of the Presidential inauguration to illustrate the concept: viewers watching the event on TV while following the live blog on their phone, she suggested, should be given 'headlines and some version of a curated social conversation that's happening', while those following the live blog on desktop (and therefore unlikely to have a TV on) should get live video too (Haik 2013). Time of day, platform and location could also be used to determine what content to serve up – as well as the environment in which they were using the platform, and the functionality of the device being used (e.g. its ability to geolocate the user) (Edge 2014).

The chief revenue officer of the *Washington Post*, Kevin Gentzel, summed up the concept succinctly: 'Reader experiences must be designed not from a mobile-first perspective,' he argued, 'but from a device-first sensibility' (Gentzel 2013).

---

### Writing for mobile – the basics

Graeme Parton (2015) has the following tips when writing for mobile: (econsultancy.com/blog/66669-five-tips-on-writing-content-for-a-mobile-audience):

**Get to the point, fast** – 'Nine times out of ten you're killing time between other activities,' he says when we read on the go. 'You also have a million other things to do on your device, messaging, calling, gaming, so distractions are plentiful.' He says 'there's no time for long paragraphs full of unnecessary words. Write with a sense of immediacy and get to the point quickly.'

**Design matters** – Break up body copy text into small blocks. 'I'm talking about short, subtitled sections populated by bulleted lists, succinct bites of information and relevant quotes.'

**Write hard-hitting headlines** – 'Keep it short and sweet. It's worth aiming for around 8–12 words. Anything more and you risk losing the reader's interest before they've even clicked through.'

**Optimise everything** – Your website must be optimised for mobile display, that is obvious. Parton goes further: 'Got links in your article? That's great, you should have, but think about where they lead to before hitting "publish". There's little point including anything clickable if the destination pages aren't as mobile-friendly as your own.'

**Analyse and capitalise** – 'Use your analytics reports to measure and research your mobile audience until you can measure and research no more. The better you understand their needs and expectations, the better positioned you'll be to meet them.' We recommend free tools such as Google Analytics and Google Webmaster Tools.

Peter Marsh (2014) (inma.org/blogs/ahead-of-the-curve/post.cfm/5-tips-for-news-writing-with-mobile-eyes-in-mind) says that mobile-only audiences tend to fall into two camps:

- Busy on-the-go news readers who want something to look at while standing in line or sitting at a coffee shop.

- In-depth news readers who check their smartphones several times a day looking for new or engaging content to delve into.

Marsh states: 'Good writing is good writing. Period. As an old software guy, I like to say that writing for mobile is akin to programming in the days of severely limited memory and available disk space. The focus must be on tight editing and efficiency. There's no space to waste.'

1.  **Provide maximum information with minimum words** – 'Make every word count. Cut out the fluff and get to the point. Use short, tight sentences, and remove every superfluous word.'
2.  **Create attention-grabbing headlines** – 'Keep your titles brief, relevant, and descriptive. Avoid jargon.'
3.  **Focus on strong introductions and compelling summaries** – 'Mobile audiences have no time for introductions that dance around a topic', says Marsh. We too would discourage long 'delayed' or 'drop' style introductions which are so common in feature article writing.
4.  **Use the medium to benefit your message** – Images and video can look stunning on high definition mobile screens.
5.  **Lists and links are the lifelines of an effective mobile story** – Marsh writes: 'Ordered or unordered lists; it doesn't matter. Lists are succinct and easy to read. They clearly show the reader where one point ends and another begins.'

### Scheduling: 'dayparting' for the web

Cory Haik framed the concept of adaptive publishing as being a 'content-parting' strategy equivalent to 'dayparting', a term from broadcasting which refers to the idea of scheduling different types of content at different times of the day (for example, children's programming is typically scheduled in the times before they go to school, and when they return home). And dayparting has spread into online and mobile publishing too, with publishers typically focusing on different platforms and formats at different times of the day, and different days of the week.

At the most basic level, we might assume that our audience is on their mobiles first thing in the morning, on desktop computers during the day and tablets in the evening. But data on user behaviour can provide more detailed insights, such as when your particular target audience is likely to be commuting (and on mobile), when they are on their lunch break and when they relax at home in the evening.

Specific platforms can provide further granularity: one study of social media usage found that on weekends 'Twitter activity falls to almost half of its weekday amplitude … whereas Facebook activity seems to be less affected … It is interesting to note that Facebook is most consistently used throughout the day on Sundays' (Spasojevic et al. 2015).

## Platforms: strengths and weaknesses for storytelling

Different platforms provide different opportunities for storytelling – but also bring different expectations and behaviours on the part of the audience. Users of Instagram expect storytelling to be primarily visual and most Facebook video is watched without sound (Patel 2016). Twitter and mobile notifications bring the promise of breaking news. Messaging platforms and email should be used sparingly, or users will treat updates as spam.

Stories can also be told across more than one platform – an approach which Henry Jenkins calls 'transmedia' storytelling (Jenkins 2006). Modern liveblogging tools, for example, allow you to automatically pull in your own updates from Twitter, Facebook and elsewhere – and to automatically push them out from the live blog to your social media accounts. And it is relatively easy to embed social media updates – including Facebook Live streams – in a website article.

There are some exceptions to this: at the time of writing, for example, Instagram stories cannot be seen outside of the mobile app, while Snapchat and messaging apps have no web URLs for updates, and cannot be embedded either. For that reason, if you are choosing to publish to one of these 'closed' platforms it is important to consider how that material might be made available to audiences on other platforms, and in the future.

Messaging apps' strength is also their biggest weakness: their ephemerality lends a certain urgency to updates that leads users to want to click through while they still can. This is an extreme example of what is often called the 'Fear Of Missing Out' (FoMO for short), a concept that initially referred to the appeal of social media and defined by one study as: 'a pervasive apprehension that others might be having rewarding experiences from which one is absent … the desire to stay continually connected to what others are doing' (Przybylski et al. 2013).

Mobile apps push notifications can also play into similar desires: in 2015 USA Today's new sports app was described as employing 'FOMO-as-editorial-strategy, designed specifically to prey on the worries of the sports-obsessed' (Ellis 2015). However, as users only tend to regularly use a handful of apps, it is extremely hard to get users to build a regular habit with a specific news app, leading many publishers to shift their attention to 'chatbots', which operate within already popular mobile apps such as Facebook Messenger, Slack, Kik and Viber.

Chatbots – sometimes simply called 'bots' – are automated scripts that provide users with a way to interact with content in the same way as they might interact with a person, or robot. The most basic chatbots, for example, greet the user every morning with an introduction to the day's biggest story, asking if they want to know more, or presents them with a choice of top stories. If the user answers 'yes', or chooses a particular topic, then a summary of the story is pulled into their chat, typically with a link to the full story online. Another bot format presents information in the form of a multiple choice quiz, where users can guess the answers and compare them against the answers.

More advanced chatbots can handle more complex responses, and/or display more personality in the process. Some can also function as a way to gather users' input: the *Washington Post*'s Feels bot, for example, offered to 'track how your feelings change in this last stretch of the election and even compare them to others–putting focus on the emotional, not political, spectrum' (*Washington Post* 2016).

### Understanding social algorithms

When you decide to tell stories on social platforms you are also agreeing – in most cases – to those platforms deciding whether your followers, and their friends, get shown it. These decisions are automated, using algorithms (essentially recipes for handling information) which those platforms keep closely guarded.

Facebook is perhaps best known for its use of algorithms. For the first few years of its existence the service had displayed friends' updates in reverse-chronological order, but in 2009 it introduced a major change, ordering updates based on their popularity (measured by the amount of engagement it had experienced). In what was to become a familiar pattern, many users objected to the change – but it stuck anyway.

In 2016 Instagram also switched from showing images based on recency to ordering them based on an algorithmic judgement that a user might want to see it more (because, for example, they had interacted with images from that person much more than others), and the same year Twitter turned on its 'best tweets first' ordering by default.

The reasoning behind this algorithmic sorting is clear: the average user of Facebook has the potential to see around 2,000 updates when they check into the app – are they really only interested in the most recent ones? Algorithms take recency as just one of a number of factors to weigh up in ordering those updates, but also look at others, such as whether the user seems to be more interested in the person behind it, and whether the content itself has particular qualities (text, video or image for example) and generated a lot of interest – or none at all.

But it is the potential for social platforms to skew these algorithms to favour their own objectives over those of users' which has been of particular interest to news organisations. This has been particularly evident in Facebook's decision to push its own video services: studies suggested that the platform was more likely to show users video uploaded directly to the site than when users shared YouTube videos instead (Csutoras 2015; Corcoran 2015).

Rather than challenge such editorial meddling, news organisations have adapted their own strategies to accommodate them, uploading 'native' video rather than linking to video on other platforms. But this also leaves journalists and publishers subject to changes in algorithms, which can often come without warning: when Facebook tweaked its algorithm in 2016 to favour 'friends and family' updates, it was blamed – along with the decision to prioritise Instant Articles – for a noticeable drop in traffic to publishers' websites (Moses 2016). A year later publishers were once again expressing concerns about unusual drops in Facebook traffic (Moses 2017).

## Raw versus packaged news

Although this chapter is all about storytelling, it is important to note that alongside more 'packaged' formats in news reporting there has also been a significant increase in what might be termed 'raw' formats that have not been through a production or editing process.

This increase might be partly attributed to a compression and blurring of the stages of news production facilitated by digitisation: where previously different employees in a news organisation might be involved, respectively, in newsgathering (reporters), production (sub editors, typesetters or designers, printers) and distribution (delivery staff), now it is possible for reporters to gather, produce, publish and distribute their stories all at the same time. In addition, mobile technologies have made it increasingly easy to record and publish 'raw' material before it enters the production process.

Initially these raw storytelling forms were pioneered by non-journalists as part of what was branded 'citizen journalism' or user generated content (UGC). But increasingly journalists began producing their own unedited material too, from jerky footage of news events and shaky images, to sketchy live updates as news unfolded across their network.

The shift raises a number of legal, ethical and quality considerations for journalists in reporting across multiple platforms. Ultimately journalists will always be involved in a trade-off between speed and quality: should you seek to be the first to a story – or take longer to produce something which may have more depth? How much of a 'draft' should the 'first draft of history' be?

Certainly one thing that publishers and broadcasters discovered quickly during the first wave of UGC was that audiences didn't particularly care about technical quality when something was newsworthy: the iconic images of the 7 July bombings or Hudson River landing were not of particularly high quality – but they conveyed the moment effectively, and provided something that no image captured later by a professional photographer or videographer would.

Put another way, there is a difference between an image or video being technically 'good', and *telling a story*. Sometimes the rushed nature of footage is part of its narrative value – although this does not mean a journalist should not know how to compose a good shot or keep it steady. Equally, journalists should record raw footage with an eye for character, setting and movement: what to film, and when to start recording, and stop, are decisions that are informed by this.

Indeed, although 'raw' news might not have been through a formal production process, it is likely that some sort of implicit editing process has been employed, in the reporter's mind. Experienced journalists will do much of their editing before they even begin recording, making editorial decisions about where to position themselves, what to record, what to ask, when to start recording and when to stop. These decisions – shaping subject, composition, beginning, middle and ending – still impose a narrative structure on the 'raw' footage. In a protest march, for example, a reporter might anticipate the climactic moment of a speech and begin filming as that approaches. They might look for sites of conflict (movement), or interesting characters or settings.

Almost all journalists are expected to take images and video when arriving upon the scene. But this does not mean that reporters should always publish their raw material. Judgements of news value apply as always: does this have value or merit? And the role of the material in the overarching narrative should be considered as well: the most commonly used narrative format for raw material is the 'running commentary' on events that the reporter is covering (the reporter narrates the video that he or she is filming, or posts a series of text updates on events they are observing) – but raw footage can also be incorporated into a more packaged format later on, as a form of illustration or even in formats such as galleries or curation (see below).

Ultimately the reporter has to bear both forms in mind: capturing the information needed for the packaged report while catering to those following her activities live. And if there's a choice to be made between the two, it often comes down to just how time sensitive the information is.

## Breaking news: liveblogging and live tweeting

Breaking news represents a particular form of news reporting that combines a packaged format with raw material. Online, the typical breaking news format is the liveblog, a reverse-chronological (most recent top) ordering of updates relating to a particular news event. Alternatively, or in addition, live updates might be 'live tweeted' direct to Twitter, or pushed to other platforms (Facebook, Instagram and Snapchat have all been used to provide similar live coverage of breaking news situations).

Third-party liveblogging tools include Coveritlive, Liveblog Pro, 24liveblog and Scribble Live, but many publishers also have their own internal liveblogging tools. These typically combine a space to type updates alongside a dashboard to monitor and pull in updates from elsewhere.

The *Guardian*'s Readers Editor Chris Elliott describes liveblogging as 'the trunk of the tree from which individual stories branch off. Live blogs need to be written with care and restraint, or they can appear too breathless' (Elliott 2016). Although breaking news coverage might be seen as formless, there are in fact a number of conventions that news organisations have adopted in reporting stories using the liveblog format. These include an introduction which establishes the background, updates which aim for variety in source and medium, an ending which rounds up the key points and where readers can find more, and above it all throughout an evolving bullet-point list of key events or stories from the coverage, including links to any stores which have 'branched off' from it (Bradshaw 2017).

If you are publishing live updates from a breaking news event to Twitter or another platform, those updates may be pulled in to a liveblog too, and the same principles apply: begin by establishing the background and what is known before digging deeper. Aim for a variety of media if possible – video, images, audio and text – and a range of sources and types of information: experts, authorities and

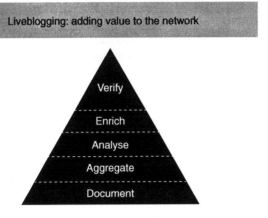

*Figure 5.1* Liveblogging pyramid. When liveblogging, ask yourself how you can add value to what people are already doing in covering the event

By Paul Bradshaw, 2011

eyewitnesses; quotes, data and documents. Play to the strengths of your position in the story, whether that is being on the ground and able to check or chase things in person, or able to access multiple sources from the newsroom.

## Curation and aggregation

Liveblogging, which typically combines original reports with updates from others across the Web, is just one form of curation – the process of collecting and combining elements to create something new. Curation is often confused with aggregation, but typically aggregation refers to an automatic gathering of similar content (for example, pulling in feeds from multiple sources on a topic), whereas curation normally involves some sort of editorial judgement.

Curation can occur at the platform level (you might argue that Facebook's algorithms codify a series of editorial judgements to 'curate' what they judge to be the updates you'll be most interested in), the publication level (selecting and combining articles) or the article level.

One of the best established curation tools, for example, is Flipboard, which allows you to create your own personalised magazines by selecting a collection of articles (for example, around a particular theme). Media organisations from the *Guardian* and the *Telegraph* to CNN and StyleList have created editions customised for the app. The blogging platform Medium also offers a 'publications' feature which allows users to combine content from the site into a branded magazine-like experience (users can also 'submit' articles to publications).

In email newsletters curation is particularly common: many newsletters offer to round up or highlight the 'best' or 'must-see' links from that week, day or month.

Services such as MailChimp (mailchimp.com) allow you to create these emails from templates, monitor metrics of performance, and manage subscribers. Some, such as Nuzzel (nuzzel.com) also offer to create automated email newsletters based on the most shared links from people on a particular Twitter list.

When curating in this way it is helpful to have clear criteria to inform your judgements on what to include. In their blog post 'How We Curate: Guidelines and Principles', for example, Medium list six types of content that they are 'particularly' focused on curating, including those that are timely, 'authentic', 'groundbreaking', 'diverse and undiscovered', interesting but not doing well, and 'innovative or experimental' (Medium 2016).

### Listicles, timelines, maps and galleries

At the article level, curation is particularly used in the 'listicle' format: articles with titles like '21 Brilliant British People Problems' (BuzzFeed) are often based on highlights from an online discussion (in this case, the Reddit thread British Problems), but they can be used to bring serious stories to life as well: 'Baroness Warsi's Nine Most Controversial Moments' (Huffington Post UK), for example, is a breezy way of reporting 'politician makes controversial move' alongside some context.

Well-written listicles don't just curate the best of something – they think about how to create a narrative arc in the *ordering* of those elements, choosing a strong beginning and ending, and a journey in between.

Other curation-based formats include galleries, timelines, maps and playlists. In most cases third-party tools have been created to serve the need for these: the social site Playbuzz, for example, offers many of these in its 'Create' section (playbuzz.com/create), while Timeline JS and Storymap JS are just two of many map-creation tools used in news, and playlists can be created on YouTube or Vimeo (where they're called 'albums').

### Curating reactions: events and obituaries

Curation is also often used to report on responses to events. When former chancellor George Osborne announced he was to stand down as an MP, social media manager Jono Read used Twitter's 'Moments' feature to curate 'George Osborne's political career in GIFs' (Read 2017), while Vogue curated reaction to Instagram's change of logo in the story 'The Best Meme of the Week Goes to Instagram's New Logo'. GIFs, memes and jokes are a regular feature of curation pieces.

Obituaries now regularly use curation in a range of ways: when David Bowie died in January 2016 news outlets used a liveblog (*Telegraph*), gallery (*Mirror*), video playlist (*Telegraph*) and listicles ranging from the 'best of' his output, to 'quotes' and 'facts and myths' (*NME*, *International Business Times* and BBC) (Bradshaw 2016). Perhaps the most creative and labour-intensive response was from the Press Association: 'Every word of Space Oddity made up of single lyrics David Bowie fans have tweeted out'.

Curation, however, raises particular ethical and legal issues around privacy and consent: is it ethical to draw on content that users have posted to social media and discussion threads? Legally users retain copyright over all content that they have posted online, so journalists should seek permission before reproducing it – but don't always do so. Sometimes there is confusion over the concept of 'public domain': the term has two meanings – copyright-free, and 'in the public domain' – but they are not the same.

## Packaged journalism

While breaking news and curation often react to events, more carefully packaged formats such as explainers and longform features typically seek to dig deeper into an issue or story. With more words – and time – at their disposal, the journalist must think more carefully about how best to arrange the ingredients to maintain the reader's attention for a longer time period.

### Explainer journalism

Explainers seek to help the reader understand something complex. That might be a new scientific breakthrough or the causes of a disaster, a proposed new law or a long-running conflict. Or it might be a theme in the news, like immigration or recession.

It is a well-established format in journalism – but it has found particular popularity online, where website analytics showed they performed well (Garber 2011). That popularity hit a particular peak in 2014 with the launch of dedicated explainer sites Vox and FiveThirtyEight, while publications such as the *New York Times*, Bloomberg, Slate and *The Economist* launched dedicated sections. *The Economist's* top ten explainers of 2013, for example, included 'What is the difference between Sunni and Shia Muslims?', 'How does Bitcoin work?', 'Why are there so many tunnels under London?' and 'Why are your friends more popular than you?'

It is an example of what is sometimes called 'evergreen' content: articles whose value does not fade markedly with time. Part of this can be attributed to the role of search engine optimisation in users finding content: a large proportion of searches are information-seeking, often following a news story, so it makes sense to try to capture that traffic by writing stories explaining the background to the Israel–Palestine conflict, offshore tax or the housing crisis, especially when you anticipate there to be regular news events related to the topic in the coming years.

Initially typically long and text-driven, explainers now come in all shapes and sizes, particularly in social video where outlets have seen an opportunity for animated explainers: in 2017 the *Guardian* announced that their 'dabs' explainers project – a platform-specific video series focusing on complex subjects – had just reached 200 million views on Facebook. One interview with Paul Boyd, multimedia editor for innovation and audience at the *Guardian*, noted that 'The tone of the script, music, visuals and transitions were all carefully chosen to suit on-the-go, promiscuous audiences … watching on their mobile phones, predominantly with the sound off' (Scott 2017).

After The Flood, a creative agency who were commissioned to create explainer videos for the BBC, explain the narrative considerations behind the format on their website. They particularly emphasise the importance of 'a story "hook" that is fundamental, understandable and repeatable' (After The Flood 2014), and suggest considering the way that the voice-over and the visuals work together, and providing ways for viewers to move on to related content. Their 'BBC Explainers Guide' is worth reading in full at aftertheflood.co/projects/explainers-videos.

The *Wall Street Journal*'s audience development editor Sarah Marshall identifies at least six types of explainer that the publication uses (Marshall 2014), many of which can also be found on the BBC's Explainers page (bbc.co.uk/news/explainers), including:

- Listicle explainers such as '5 questions about the ECB's lending program';
- 'The Numbers'-based explainers (CBBC Newsround's 'Wimbledon 2017 in numbers');
- 'At a glance' explainers ('Takeaways from Jackson Hole');
- 'The short answer' explainer ('What is the West Lothian question?');
- Video-driven short answer explainers; and
- The 'unpacking' animation ('Scottish Referendum: What is the United Kingdom?')

In addition, there are also longer explainers which are designed to be added to and amended over time. Online magazine Mother Jones is a particularly big user of these longer formats, often adopting a Q&A format so that users can skip directly to the section that addresses their information needs, and typically linking to a number of ongoing updates. Updates are clearly labelled: 'The Trayvon Martin Killing, Explained', for example, includes 46 updates between 19 March and 21 June 2012, from 'UPDATE 1, 12 p.m. EDT, Monday, March 19: More details on Florida's self-defense laws' to 'UPDATE 46, 7:10 p.m. EDT, Thursday, June 21: New evidence released, including police reenactment video'. The article offers a link to skip to the latest update at the top (Weinstein et al. 2012).

But make sure that you kick off your explainer with a hook that makes it newsworthy. Heidi N. Moore, the *Guardian*'s US former finance and economics editor, recommends leading with 'the most important or surprising elements of a story and then work down to the details' (Thiruvengadam 2013)

### Infographics

The same principles apply to the infographic – another form of explainer which has experienced a boom in popularity online, fuelled in part by infographic creation tools such as Infogr.am, Piktochart and Easel.ly. Unlike standalone data visualisation (see below), infographics tend to combine charts, graphs or maps with standalone figures, quotes and even images. The *Mirror*'s 'History of Dr Who

Companions' infographic, for example, runs 'key facts' for each companion (with an image) down one side, alongside charts and tables on the other illustrating quantitative measures such as gender breakdown, appearances and popularity.

Like all good stories, an infographic should not merely be a list of facts, but instead have a beginning, middle and end. In his book *Cool Infographics*, Randy Krum describes this as the 'Introduction/Foundation' that establishes the thing we are looking at; the 'A-Ha!' section that tells us something new or surprising; and the 'Conclusion/Call-to-action' (Krug 2014).

In journalistic contexts, then, the top of an infographic might focus on the 'big picture' or 'shocking statistic', before drilling down into some interesting details behind that. For a strong ending, you might choose a piece of information which connects with the 'what happens next' question, or link to your ongoing reporting. The *Mirror*'s Doctor Who companion infographic, for example, ends on a fact box on 'The Doctor's next companion'.

### Longform and immersive multimedia features

Long-form journalism – typically referred to in its online format as a single word: longform – has seen a similar boom. The launch of the iPad in 2010, and Amazon's Kindle Singles in 2011, helped create a market for the format in what was branded the 'race for the tablet market' (Dowling and Vogan 2014), but it was a *New York Times* 2012 story about an avalanche – 'Snow Fall' (Branch 2012) – which perhaps did most to show what longform journalism was capable.

'Snow Fall' combined thousands of words of text with video, galleries, animation and JavaScript transitions that moved and faded elements as the reader scrolled through the story. It was not only beautifully realised (the story took six months and at least ten staff), but also boasted impressive user engagement statistics, with the story getting over 10,000 shares on Twitter and the average reader spending 12 minutes on the page (Dowling and Vogan 2014) – there were over 3.5 million readers of the story in its first week. Equally importantly, 'Snow Fall' diverged from the standard news website article design by being created outside the *New York Times* content management system (Koc 2015) to remove banner adverts and site navigation, resulting in an elegant approach to story design that was adopted elsewhere, including the launch of platforms dedicated to the form such as Byliner, Beacon, Longform.com and Medium.

There is no common agreement on how many words a piece of journalism needs to be to be considered 'longform' – it has been used to refer to any feature which is longer than a traditional news report – and so increasingly the term 'immersive' journalism has been used instead to refer to Snow Fall-like journalism that includes non-textual elements such as video and images and avoids distracting page clutter.

But an immersive appearance is only one dimension of longform journalism: more important is a consideration of the ingredients needed for a longform report, and the narrative devices which will help you keep a story going over thousands of words. In this regard longform journalism borrows heavily from traditional techniques used in feature writing for over a century: instead of using the 'inverted pyramid' structure of shorter news reports which begins with the newest information, for example, features might begin with a key scene or individual.

The longform investigation into Olympic torchbearers, '8000 Holes', for example, begins like this:

> Jack Binstead is one of the UK's most promising young athletes: a wheelchair racer in with a chance of competing in the next Paralympic Games. Born with brittle bone disease he has, says his mother Penny, broken 64 bones in his body over just 15 years.
>
> (Bradshaw and Miers 2012)

Starting like this does two things: first it introduces a human element, which we can easily connect with; but secondly, it represents a 'hook' – the reader is, hopefully, intrigued why the writer has chosen to focus on this individual and what is going to happen to him which justifies this focus.

That justification is crucial: the choice to begin with a particular individual represents an implicit promise on the part of the reporter: the promise that this person is indeed important, and the story big enough to justify patience on the part of the reader. If you cannot deliver on that promise, it may be that longform is not the appropriate format.

Another approach – typically used when the story centres on dramatic events – is to use a setting. The *Guardian*'s longform immersive 'Firestorm', for example, which tells the story of a violent Australian bushfire, begins like this:

> What everyone remembers about that morning; it was a beauty … A cloudless sky; no wind to speak of. Not too hot, yet. Something else they remember: there were no birds.
>
> (Henley 2014)

The 'no birds' is an example of using mystery as a hook, something that the BBC's 'Body on the moor' uses effectively with an intro of just 11 words: 'It was the position of the body which somehow seemed strange' (Manel 2016)

Structuring the middle of a longform piece often relies on splitting the story into chapters based on different themes or scenes: '8000 Holes' (leanpub.com/8000holes), for example, devotes one chapter to the big picture of how sponsors managed the public applications process, another chapter to the detail of the corporate executives who appeared carrying torches, and a third to the political reaction when it was revealed that promises had not been met. Firestorm's first chapter sets the scene of the place where the fire started; its second chapter moves to the fire service; and a third chapter takes a step back into the history of bush fires in Australia before subsequent chapters return to the scene of the fire. This switching between scenes or themes is what gives a narrative its movement, before endings typically return to the situation now and look ahead to what happens next – or is failing to happen.

To cover such a range of themes or scenes the writer must gather sufficient material: typically this might involve case studies of those affected by the story, experts, authorities, and/or those working in the field. Interviews – which may need to be professionally recorded so they can be added as multimedia elements – should aim to gather not just information about events and facts, but 'colour': details about settings, sounds, smells, tastes and feelings that you may need to bring scenes to life. You might also ask for images or video that interviewees have of events or key individuals.

Background research will provide a historical dimension to your story as well, which can be woven in to break up quotes, or add extra colour. You might look for documents or archive material to embed, too, and you can also create visual elements built on this research, such as timelines, flow charts, charts, video explainers and infographics (see above).

There are a number of tools which make it easy to create stories with immersive features. Medium, which has a mobile app and email updates, is perhaps the easiest to use, although its functionality is limited. More powerful tools include Atavist.com (atavist.com), FOLD, and Shorthand Social (social-landing.shorthand.com) which also optimises stories for mobile.

### How long should mobile articles be?

There is some dispute among journalists and academics around how long articles should be on mobile. The large screens on tablet devices such as the iPad make reading longer feature articles much easier than before. But some people say that mobile text should always be short and easy to snack on.

The Pew Research Center report in May 2016 looked at 117 million mobile phone interactions on content from from 30 news websites. It showed that readers spend more than twice the amount of time reading and scrolling through articles longer than 1,000 words than they do on shortform stories.

It also found that readers were more likely to consume longer content early in the morning or late at night: 'This stands out in particular, because late night attracts a smaller portion of visitors than any other daypart – just six per cent of sessions with long-form news occur in the late night hours' (Mitchell et al. 2016).

This supports a common view that longform journalism does just as well as short articles on mobile devices. One American Press Institute report issued the same year, for example, analysed more than 400,000 stories and found that stories longer than 1,200 words got 23 per cent more engagement, 45 per cent more social referrals and 11 per cent more page views (Edmonds 2016).

The reality is that news organisations deploy a range of lengths. There is snackable content that will appeal to those on the Monday morning commute into work and those users who are reading from the sofa at home. BuzzFeed's Janine Gibson, for example, notes both the trend towards live-ness, as well as another, contrasting, trend towards investigative and in-depth features that require long-term planning and have 'weight and meaning and impact beyond the transitory ... When we started Guardian US we said we were going to do very, very live and almost documentary long-form and cut out all the stuff in the middle' (Posetti 2014).

## Telling stories with data

With so much of modern life being digitised, there is an increasingly large amount of data that can be used as the basis for storytelling. This is not limited to statistics and spreadsheets: data have been used to tell stories about everything from fashion and music (see polygraph.cool, for example) to sex and relationships (see the book *Dataclysm*).

The term 'data journalism' refers broadly to a range of practices involved in gathering data, finding stories in them and communicating the results. It is perhaps most associated with the practice of data visualisation, but there are at least five other ways of communicating data stories, too: text-based narration; case study-driven broadcast formats; creating data-driven tools; personalisation; and hosting communities around data (Bradshaw 2011).

Text-driven narratives can adopt any traditional storytelling structure, from news stories in the inverted pyramid format (key new facts at the top, then fleshed out with quotes, details and background context), to longform narratives outlined above. In broadcast, data stories often lead on a case study that illustrates the numbers being reported.

Data visualisation tends to use charts, graphs and maps. Choosing the right type is important – as different charts are designed for different types of story.

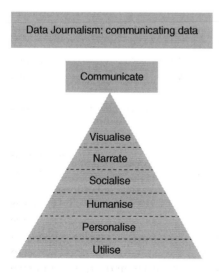

*Figure 5.2* Six ways of communicating data journalism
By Paul Bradshaw, 2011

Identifying whether your story is trying to compare different things, or talk about the composition of something (the two most common types of data story), will help you choose a chart which does just that: a pie chart, for example, is not the best chart to *compare* things – it's designed to show the *composition* of a whole. Likewise a bar chart is good for comparing many things, but not the composition of one thing. And if you want to compare things over time, a line chart is what you need.

Less common story types involve *relationships*, or showing the *distribution* of things. Scatter charts can tell both types of stories, but you can also show distribution using a histogram, and if the distribution is geographical you can use a map. You can also show relationships between people or organisations using a network graph.

It is important to be clear what the *purpose* of the visualisation is in the story. There are at least three typical ways that visuals are employed:

- **Complementary**: the visualisation *illustrates*, or adds further detail to, a story – typically this type of visual sits alongside a text narrative, for example.
- **Explanatory**: the visualisation *tells* the story on its own – typically this sort of visual has minimal introductory text, or is designed to be consumed natively on social media or chat platforms.
- **Exploratory**: the story that the visualisation tells is not immediately clear, and is to a large extent decided by what the user decides to do. An example might be an interactive map (showing incidents of crime, or fire, or food hygiene ratings), where the user might choose to look at places of interest to them

Maps are particularly relevant to talk about in this respect, as they are perhaps the most misused type of visualisation: people often choose to use a map because the data is geographical, but it is always worth asking if the story might be more clearly told using a simple chart: after all, if you are comparing different regions is it not easier to compare using a bar chart? Maps are good for showing north–south or east–west divides, but if there is no such pattern – no *distribution* story to tell – then it may not be helpful.

Maps are useful, however, if your intention is exploratory: where you are not seeking to tell one story but rather to allow the user to explore the map in their own way. You can find many map creation tools online, including BatchGeo, Carto and Google Fusion Tables.

Personalisation can add an extra dimension to visualisation: charts can be dynamically redrawn to reflect information that the user provides – for example, showing where they sit in relation to the 'typical' person, or how a particular issue affects them. The BBC's data-driven feature 'The world at seven billion', for example, include an interactive tool that allows users to find out 'What number are you?' and share that with their friends on social media. The story becomes both personal and social.

Considering how that interactivity and visualisation works on mobile is an important dimension to any data journalism project. Some news organisations, for example, opt to strip out some visualisation for faster mobile delivery, while others consider how to make interactive data articles resemble apps when viewed on mobile, with search features at the top of the interface. Ultimately the decision will be guided by the editorial priorities of the story, and which elements work best – and fastest – on mobile devices.

## Horizontal storytelling and the 'Stories' format

For most of the history of online journalism, stories have been overwhelmingly presented in a vertical format: users were required to scroll down a single webpage until they reached the end of the article, even if the article was split across multiple pages.

Mobile consumption and publishing, however, prompted a rethink of the vertical-by-default approach, with an increasing number of apps and publishers beginning to implement a navigation system whereby users could advance horizontally by swiping right-to-left across, or tapping on the right of, the screen.

From Snapchat, Instagram and Facebook Stories, to Twitter's Moments, Instagram's Carousel and Medium's Series feature, horizontal navigation is now found on almost every major social platform, while Google's AMP Stories (ampproject.org/docs/design/visual_story) has brought it to the web, and it has become a part of news apps from NowThis's Tap For News, the *Telegraph* and *Guardian* apps to the BBC's daily vertical video roundup.

This horizontal approach is not merely a superficial change to the way information is presented: where the default mode for vertical storytelling has been the text narrative, horizontal storytelling is overwhelmingly visual – and storytellers now have to think about the order in which they take and combine images and what meanings those sequences create in the user.

Considering sequence has some knock-on effects too. Ordering elements means you also have to think about variety. In traditional television terms that means aiming to include a variety of shots (close up, wide shot and so on), but on a platform like Twitter or Instagram that also means variety of media: still image, video, gif, text.

You might think of this as the element of surprise: repeat the same type of content too often, and the story becomes predictable; there is less narrative tension. More variety, in contrast, keeps the user engaged.

Stories also often have what Todd Brison calls resumability (Brison 2017): the ability for users to resume consuming a story at the point where you last stopped. This makes it easier to tell stories in 'episodic' formats, publishing part-by-part throughout the life of the story rather than releasing the story in its completed form, with the possibility to heighten narrative tension through using the technique well.

*Review of storytelling techniques*

Story: *Lego parliament: tracking the UK election brick by brick*

Source: *Mashable*

URL: *mashable.com/2015/05/07/lego-parliament/#7Ml10L4QKPqy*

How do you cover the 2015 UK general election in a way that is both innovative and different? The election saw lots of online data visualisations and interactive tools, but Mashable knew these techniques wouldn't appeal to its young audience. So they created a Parliament building made out of Lego building blocks and photographed it! Scroll through the timeline, and you can relive the drama of election night as the Lego Parliament takes shape. Blue, yellow and red building blocks symbolise the size of the main political parties. The output was shared widely on social media throughout election night. This was an early output from the company's in-house interactive storytelling 'collective' which advises Mashable journalists on interesting storytelling techniques.

Story: *Get up, stand up: social media helps Black Lives Matter*

Source: *Wired*

URL: *wired.com/2015/10/
how-black-lives-matter-uses-social-media-to-fight-the-power/*

This longform piece of journalism combines text, pull quotes, stunning photojournalism and video to create a compelling narrative. The 2,000 words of feature text appear in a double-spaced white serif font and run over a black background, which gives the article a moody and intense feel. The article highlights how civil rights protest groups such as Black Lives Matter have harnessed technology to interact and promote their aims.

## Conclusion

The proliferation of formats, platforms and media options in journalism has also meant a proliferation of choices for the professional storyteller. But innovation around new forms of storytelling has also been accelerated through the opening up of those platforms to a non-professional public. It was citizen journalists, not those with a press card, that pioneered the use of raw media for reporting breaking news events; liveblogging emerged first on blogs, not on news websites; and curation has been popularised by startups such as Tumblr, Flipboard and Pinterest. Journalists are no longer the only ones deciding how we tell news (Westley and Rulyova 2017), and so in order to communicate effectively with a modern audience, you must be in the habit of consuming a wide variety of media to keep your storytelling techniques and media literacy up to date. A major development in this respect has been the rise of *visual journalism*, a development so significant that we devote the next chapter to it.

## Further reading

*The Living Handbook of Narratology* at www.lhn.uni-hamburg.de.
It covers a range of narrative techniques and concepts.
Bradshaw, P. (2016) *Snapchat for Journalists.*. Leanpub.
Explains techniques to use in vertical storytelling and the 'stories' format.

## References

After The Flood (2014) BBC explainers guide. After The Flood, Available at http://aftertheflood.co/projects/explainers-videos/.

Bradshaw, P. (2011) *The Online Journalism Handbook*. Routledge.

Bradshaw, P. (2016) Curation is the new obituary: 8 ways media outlets marked Bowie's life and death [now 16]. Online Journalism Blog. Available at: https://onlinejournalismblog.com/2016/01/11/curation-is-the-new-obituary-8-ways-media-outlets-marked-bowies-life-and-death/.

Bradshaw, P. (2017) *The Online Journalism Handbook*. (2nd ed.), Routledge.

Bradshaw, P., and Miers, C. (2012) *8000 Holes: How the 2012 Olympic Torch Relay Lost its Way*. Leanpub.

Branch, J. (2012) Snow fall. *New York Times*. Available at: www.nytimes.com/projects/2012/snow-fall/.

Brison, T. (2017) Medium's 'series' are *way* more than a copycat feature–here's why. Available at: https://medium.com/@ToddBrison/mediums-series-are-way-more-than-a-copycat-feature-here-s-why-118d404d2e49#.z0rsbfvwr.

Browne, M., Cirillo, C., Griggs, T., Keller, J., and Reneau, N. (2017) Did the Turkish President's security detail attack protesters in Washington? What the video shows. *New York Times*. Available at: www.nytimes.com/interactive/2017/05/26/us/turkey-protesters-attack-video-analysis.html.

Corcoran, L. (2015) Three things to know about engagement on native Facebook video. NewsWhip. Available at: www.newswhip.com/2015/05/three-things-to-know-about-engagement-on-native-facebook-video/.

Csutoras, B. (2015) Videos on Facebook: Native vs YouTube. Which wins? Search Engine Journal. Available at: www.searchenginejournal.com/videos-facebook-native-vs-youtube-wins/134389/.

Dowling, D., and Vogan, T. (2014) Can we 'Snowfall' this? *Digital Journalism*, 3(2), 209–224. http://dx.doi.org/10.1080/21670811.2014.930250.

Edge, A. (2014) Advice for 'adaptive storytelling' from the *Washington Post*. Journalism.co.uk. Available at: www.journalism.co.uk/news/advice-for-adaptive-storytelling-from-the-washington-post-/s2/a557052/.

Edmonds, R. (2016) Shorter isn't better, photos aren't always alluring and deep digging pays off, recent report concludes. Poynter, Available at: www.poynter.org/news/shorter-isnt-better-photos-arent-always-alluring-and-deep-digging-pays-recent-report-concludes.

Elliott, C. (2016) Inside the *Guardian*: how the live blog has changed the face of news reporting. *Guardian*. Available at: www.theguardian.com/membership/2016/feb/04/inside-the-guardian-how-live-blog-changed–ews-reporting.

Ellis, J. (2015) The upset alert in your pocket: USA Today's new sports app wants to help cure your fear of missing out. NiemanLab, Available at: www.niemanlab.org/2015/02/the-upset-alert-in-your-pocket-usa-todays-new-sports-app-wants-to-help-cure-your-fear-of-missing-out/.

Garber, M. (2011) Mother Jones web traffic up 400+ percent, partly thanks to explainers. NiemanLab. Available at: www.niemanlab.org/2011/03/mother-jones-web-traffic-up-400-percent-partly-thanks-to-explainers/.

Gentzel, K. (2013) Thinking device first: time for adaptive journalism. Digiday UK, Available at: https://digiday.com/media/adaptive-journalism-in-a-device-first-world%E2%80%A8/.

Haik, C. (2013) Adaptive journalism. Cory Haik. Available at: web.archive.org/web/20131006133728/https://coryhaik.tumblr.com/post/49802508964/adaptive-journalism

Henley, J. (2014) Firestorm. *Guardian*. Available at: www.theguardian.com/world/interactive/2013/may/26/firestorm-bushfire-dunalley-holmes-family.

Jenkins, H. (2006) *Convergence Culture: Where Old and New Media Collide*. NYU Press.

Knobel, M., and Lankshear, C. (2007) Online memes, affinities, and cultural production. In M. Knobel and C. Lankshear (eds), *A New Literacies Sampler*. Peter Lang, pp. 199–228.

Koc, E. (2015). *Review of Interactive Storytelling at the New York Times*. Future NYT. Available at: http://futurenytimes.org/reviews/interactive-storytelling/.

Kovach, B., and Rosenstiel, T. (2007) *The Elements of Journalism: What Newspeople Should Know and the Public Should Expect*. Three Rivers Press.

Krug, R. (2014) *Cool Infographics: Effective Communication with Data Visualization and Design*. John Wiley & Sons.

Manel, J. (2016) Body on the moor. BBC News. Available at: www.bbc.co.uk/news/resources/idt-e8c6cbab-da44-4a3c-8f9b-c4fccd53dd24.

Marsh, P. (2014) 5 tips for news writing with mobile eyes in mind. INMA. Available at: https://inma.org/blogs/ahead-of-the-curve/post.cfm/5-tips-for-news-writing-with-mobile-eyes-in-mind.

Marshall, S. (2014) 6 types of explainer at the *Wall Street Journal*. Sarah Marshall. Available at: http://sarahmarshall.io/post/97985821273/6-types-of-explainer-at-the-wall-street-journal.

Medium (2016) *How we Curate: Guidelines and Principles*. Your Friends @ Medium. Available at: https://medium.com/@yourfriends/how-we-curate-guidelines-and-principles-fdcf43e049c5.

Mitchell, A., Stocking, G., and Matsa, K. E. (2016). *Long-Form Reading Shows Signs of Life in our Mobile News World*. Pew Research Center. Available at: www.journalism.org/2016/05/05/long-form-reading-shows-signs-of-life-in-our-mobile-news-world/.

Moses, L. (2016) Uh-oh, some publishers see a drop in Facebook traffic. Digiday UK. Available at: https://digiday.com/media/publishers-just-saw-decline-facebook-traffic/.

Moses, L. (2017) Publishers are seeing another big decline in reach on Facebook. Digiday UK. Available at: https://digiday.com/media/publishers-seeing-another-big-decline-reach-facebook/.

Newman, N. (2016) *News Alerts and the Battle for the Lockscreen*. Reuters Institute for the Study of Journalism. Available at: https://reutersinstitute.politics.ox.ac.uk/sites/default/files/News%20Alerts%20and%20the%20Battle%20for%20the%20Lockscreen.pdf.

Parton, G. (2015) *Five tips on writing content for a mobile audience*. Econsutancy, Available at: https://econsultancy.com/blog/66669-five-tips-on-writing-content-for-a-mobile-audience/.

Patel, S. (2016) 85 percent of Facebook video is watched without sound. Digiday UK, Available at: https://digiday.com/media/silent-world-facebook-video/.

Posetti, J. (2014) Guardian's Janine Gibson: storytelling is going real-time or long-form. Mediashift. Available at: http://mediashift.org/2014/05/guardians-janine-gibson-storytelling-is-going-real-time-or-long-form/.

Przybylski, A. K., Murayama, K., DeHaan, C. R., and Gladwell, V. (2013) Motivational, emotional, and behavioral correlates of fear of missing out. *Computers in Human Behavior*, 29(4), 1841–1848. http://dx.doi.org/10.1016/j.chb.2013.02.014.

Scott, C. (2016) Why storytelling 'is still everything', despite new journalism tools. Journalism.co.uk. Available at: journalism.co.uk/news/why-storytelling-is-still-every thing-despite-new-journalism-tools-and-technology/s2/a634299/.

Scott, C. (2017) The *Guardian* is reaching new audiences on Facebook with video series for people who dip in and out of news. Journalism.co.uk, Available at: www.journalism. co.uk/news/the-guardian-is-reaching-new-audiences-on-facebook-with-video-series-for-people-who-dip-in-and-out-of-news/s2/a701870/.

Shepherd, M., and Watters, C. (1998) The evolution of cybergenres. In R. H. Sprague Jr (ed.), *31st Hawaii International Conference on System Sciences*. IEEE Computer Society Press, 97–109. Available at: https://web.cs.dal.ca/~shepherd/pubs/evolution.pdf.

Spasojevic, N., Li, Z., Rao, A., and Bhattacharyya, P. (2015) When-to-post on social networks. Lithium Technologies/Klout. Available at: https://arxiv.org/pdf/1506.02089v1.pdf.

Thiruvengadam, M. (2013) How journalists can create better explainers. Poynter. Available at: www.poynter.org/2013/how-journalists-can-create-better-explainers/202622/.

*Washington Post* (2016) Feels. www.washingtonpost.com/graphics/politics/facebook-messenger-elections-feels-bot/.

Weinstein, A., and the Mother Jones News Team (2012). The Trayvon Martin Killing, Explained. Mother Jones. www.motherjones.com/politics/2012/03/what-happened-trayvon-martin-explained/#newvideo.

Westley, H., and Rulyova, N. (2017) Changing news genres as a result of global techno-logical developments. *Digital Journalism*. DOI: 10.1080/21670811.2017.1351882.

# 6    Visual journalism, video and audio

**This chapter will cover:**

- Considering composition in visual storytelling
- Meme journalism, GIFs and emojis
- Telling stories for social and mobile with video and audio
- Live video
- Making audio for mobile
- Immersive visual journalism: VR, AR, drone journalism and 360 degree video
- Risk assessment and legal issues in video

## Introduction

The second wave of social media platforms at the start of the 21st century's second decade was overwhelmingly visual: the launches of Instagram and Pinterest in 2010 were followed by those of Snapchat in 2011, Vine in 2012, and Meerkat and Periscope in 2015. Older social platforms quickly adapted: Facebook bought Instagram, tried to buy Snapchat and launched its own live video service; Twitter acquired Periscope and Vine before either service was even officially launched (Vine was shut down in 2017).

At the same time publishers were discovering that visuals, including GIFs, had a major role to play in optimising the performance of updates on Twitter and Facebook (Rogers 2014; Corliss 2012): journalists were told to include images with social media updates wherever possible.

The *Washington Post*'s graphics director Kat Downs has described this period as seeing 'The rise of images as the currency of the digital world' (Cairo 2017), while research on changing news genres in this period notes the development of 'a greater emphasis on the visual due to the many technological affordances for visual recording and distribution' (Westley and Rulyova 2017). But there is more to that change than simply more people using images and video than was previously the case. The publisher of Mic (mic.com), Cory Haik, argues that the real change has come in shorter 'new mixed-media formats in social video' and the horizontal tap-to-advance formats explored in the previous chapter. Specifically, she says, these formats are 'less an evolution of video itself and more of an evolution of the hundreds and thousands of pieces of text-based journalism that are produced and consumed digitally' (Haik 2017), particularly in the way that text has become increasingly distilled, and used, on screen.

Alongside mixed-media social video formats the same period has also seen the rise of live video. Kicked off in 2015 with the launch of the Meerkat app, the baton was quickly picked up by Twitter's new Periscope app and then by the launch of Facebook Live. The following April Facebook – traditionally a social network dominated by text and images – announced the company would be adopting a video-first strategy. At the company's annual F8 conference founder Mark Zuckerberg predicted that in a decade 'Video will look like as big of a shift in the way we all share and communicate as mobile has been.' In anticipation of that shift he announced plans to place video 'at the heart of all of our apps and services' (Zuckerberg 2016; watch the keynote in full at developers.facebook. com/videos/f8-2016/keynote).

The announcement echoed another four years earlier, when Zuckerberg had highlighted the importance placed on smartphone devices over desktop, and announced a mobile-first strategy. Times were changing quickly, and Facebook promptly threw more than $50 million at media organisations and celebrities to create video for the platform (by the end of the following year it had stopped paying) while tweaking its algorithm to favour video.

The combination of text, still images, moving images, live video, audio and other elements, such as emojis and stickers, is what makes visual journalism more than the sum of its parts. In this chapter, then, we outline some of the key techniques that visual journalism borrows from its various antecedents, and the new tools and techniques that have emerged and continue to develop.

## Still images

One of the most obvious impacts of the spread of visual social media platforms has been an increase in the quantity and quality of visual material produced by audiences and those involved in news events, routinely relied upon by publishers and agencies (Patrick and Allan 2013) and used by activist media. One piece of research into community photojournalism, for example, argues that it 'constitutes an important step towards a more analytical brand of journalism with different news values' (Baroni and Mayr 2016), while research on news imagery on social media concludes that it has had 'the unanticipated effect of rescinding the uniformity of collective visual consciousness and the traditional formation of iconic imagery' (Dahmen and Morrison 2015).

One interesting effect of this diversity of visual styles appears to be a mixing of visual languages: research on journalists' use of Instagram in 2015 noted that journalists and non-journalists were trying 'to simulate the … conventions and discourses of the other in an attempt to get closer either to the sense of amateurish authenticity or to professional neatness' (Borges-Rey 2015).

## Composition and other photojournalism techniques

Photojournalism is just one of those sets of 'conventions and discourses' which visual journalists can learn from. One primary way that photographers tell stories in images, for example, is through attention to the composition: the 'rule of thirds' is widely used in photography to divide an image vertically and horizontally into thirds. The focus of a shot typically goes where those divisions intersect (for example, off to the side and slightly above the middle), drawing the eye away from the centre – but you can create more movement in a shot by using more than one of those intersections, drawing the eye from one to another as the viewer explores the picture.

Most mobile phones allow you to overlay a 'rule of thirds' grid when taking images: check your camera settings and look for a 'Grid' option, or search online for this feature and your particular phone model.

Lighting is important in visual storytelling – not just to make an image clear, but also to direct attention within it. Filters can be used in a similar way: most mobile phones now include some filtering options in their cameras, and they are also offered in an increasing number of social apps from Instagram and Snapchat to Twitter. But it is also worth experimenting with dedicated photo editing apps such as Adobe Photoshop Express (photoshop.com/products/photoshopexpress), VSCO (vsco.co), Camera360 (camera360.com), Darkroom (darkroom.co) and Litely (lite.ly)

*Figure 6.1* These two stills from Snapchat stories show how CBS News (left) uses the rule of thirds to compose a shot effectively, while USA Today does not, resulting in a much less effective image

By Paul Bradshaw, 2016

More specific effects can be found in apps like Photo Splash (make a photo black and white, with a spot of colour to direct attention), PicsArt (picsart.com – create collages and draw on top of images), AfterFocus (afterfocus.en.softonic. com – adjust focus) and Slow Shutter (cogitap.com – capture light trails and motion blur).

It is also important to consider whether images are to be used alone, or in sequence as part of a gallery. If it is the latter then a variety of subjects, settings and shot (wide, close, medium) also becomes an important consideration, in order to assemble an effective narrative – one assessment of news websites galleries was highly critical of the lack of 'concern for rhetorical structure, image quality, or even the number of images in a gallery' (Caple 2014).

## Meme journalism, GIFs and emojis

Memes are broadly defined as 'an idea, piece of information, or behavior that is passed from one person to another by imitation' (Observatory on Social Media 2017), a concept that dates back to Richard Dawkins' 1976 book *The Selfish Gene*. However, when memes are discussed in journalistic circles we are normally referring to something slightly different – *internet* memes: a 'particular idea presented as a written text, image, language "move," or some other unit of cultural "stuff"' (Knobel and Lankshear 2007).

The use of internet memes and meme techniques in journalism has moved from young publications such as BuzzFeed and the Huffington Post into the very mainstream: the homepage of the *Daily Mail*, for example, routinely employs GIFs to draw readers into its stories.

> The *New York Times* used autoplaying looping videos to create the appearance of GIFs in its story 'Did the Turkish President's security detail attack protesters in Washington? What the video shows'. View it here: nytimes. com/interactive/2017/05/26/us/turkey-protesters-attack-video-analysis. html (Browne et al. 2017).

Internet memes have an obvious appeal for publishers in at least three ways: first, as a *subject* of reporting: memes are often inherently newsworthy as 'trend' stories and/or simply entertaining. The popularity of The Star Wars Kid video in 2002, for example, led to widespread media interest, while more than one outlet in the UK decided to devote an article to curating the best '2017 election memes'.

Secondly, memes can be appealing commercially: a successful meme can 'go viral', generating lots of traffic for the organisation associated with it. News organisations might adopt memetic techniques in an attempt to increase their audience or brand awareness.

But finally, memes represent a new literacy (Knobel and Lankshear 2007). And so, in order to communicate with an audience, journalists often need to be able to understand the shared language, tools and platforms that underpin internet memes.

The website I Can Has Cheezburger? (icanhas.cheezburger.com), founded in 2007, helped popularise some of the most widely known internet memes and meme formats, and provides tools which help users quickly create their own (typically placing black-bordered text in the Impact font on top of an image). Know Your Meme, launched as an offshoot of video podcast Rocketboom a year later, provides a database of widely shared internet memes, and Imgur, founded in 2009, similarly serves as a platform for users to create, find and share popular photos and videos. Regular use of sites and apps like these can help develop an understanding of – and literacy around – recurring themes and techniques.

GIFs and emojis have become important parts of this shared language. Emojis – icons for everything from facial expressions to objects that can be accessed from a mobile phone keyboard (or using a keyboard shortcut on a laptop) – are particularly useful when characters are limited, such as Twitter updates or mobile phone lockscreen notifications. As with any type of literacy, however, it is important to consider the audience that you are communicating with, and the type of message being delivered. The *Financial Times*, for example, only uses emojis in its WhatsApp channel. 'Because it's a chat app, it feels personal,' Alana Coates, the *FT*'s audience engagement editor, explained in 2017. 'People use emojis for visual cues, so we do the same. It's a shortcut for people to understand what's happening, and it seems to work in this context' (Southern 2017).

Some news Twitter accounts will use emojis to illustrate updates: in one tweeted 'emoji factfile' on Eurovision singer Lucie Jones, for example, the @ BBCWales account used the birthday cake emoji, house emoji and dog emoji to illustrate the text for biographical details relating to 'birthday', 'home' and 'pets', while the Press Association's Stephen Jones summed up a night of local election results for the four main parties with different face emojis (Labour's was 'sad', UKIP's was 'grimacing').

Emojis can also be combined in a sequence that tells a story or creates a 'clue': Vox used emojis for its end of year review '2014: The Year In Emoji', while a month later the *Guardian* converted Barack Obama's State of the Union address into emoji form (Bajak 2014). Much of this reflected an early curiosity and experimentation with the form which has since faded into more routine use, particularly in mobile lockscreen notifications on less serious stories: one report found editors open to the use of emojis where there was 'more latitude for creativity and humour with feature content, lifestyle, entertainment, and sport' (Newman 2016), for example.

GIFs are often used in a similar way to emojis, to express the emotions of the person sending them – but they can also be used to explain, illustrate and summarise key events. Strictly speaking GIF is an image format (it stands for Graphics Interchange Format), but most usage of the term 'GIF' now refers to its animated form, that allows users to combine multiple images with the resulting effect replicating the use of frames in video. An 'animated GIF' is played automatically, and loops once it has reached the end, making it well suited for short clips.

The format has become so embedded in online communication that many platforms now make it easy for users to select and add GIFs without having to leave the app. Twitter, for example, added support for GIFs in 2014, and the next year over 100 million GIFs had been shared on the platform (Reddy 2016). By 2016 the company announced that it was partnering with GIPHY and Riffsy to add GIF search. Chat app Telegram integrated GIF search in 2014 and WhatsApp followed in 2017. Choosing GIFs in this way raises its own ethical problems: one Teen Vogue article titled 'We Need to Talk About Digital Blackface in Reaction GIFs' highlighted the practice of 'digital blackfacing', for example, arguing: 'Overrepresentation of black people in GIFing everyone's daily crises plays up enduring perceptions and stereotypes about black expression' (Jackson 2017).

Aside from choosing GIFs from libraries such as GIPHY (giphy.com), there are also numerous online tools which allow you to create your own GIF by recording your screen, or by selecting a brief sequence from a YouTube video. Making GIFs from a video raises copyright issues if you do not have permission to do so: in 2015 BuzzFeed was criticised for a story that used 12 GIFs from one Lifehacker video about bad breath – the site later reduced the number of GIFs and embedded the original video (Sirucek 2015).

GIFs can be also be created from sequences of still images: the Reuters Twitter account did this to illustrate a tweet about a story on food shortages, while Vox used the technique to juxtapose images of the crowd at Donald Trump's inauguration with those at other events in the same place, and Channel 4 News's nine-month-long Tumblr-based GIF experiment '4NewsWall' (4newswall.com) used it to animate story headlines (one word per frame). GIFs are also increasingly used to animate multiple examples of data visualisation (explored below).

## Telling stories with video and audio

Techniques for telling stories with video and audio range from the 'piece to camera' and narrated footage, to captioned video sequences, audio-as-video, livestreaming and longform documentary formats.

### Packaged video on YouTube and Vimeo

YouTube and Vimeo – launched in 2005 and 2004 respectively – may be the old kids on the online video block, but they remain major players in the sector, not least because both have well developed infrastructures for making sure highly successful video creators get paid. YouTube in particular remains a giant in online video and is the main competitor for Facebook in the video arena, but they work in different ways. Trushar Barot, Mobile Editor, BBC World Service, says: 'YouTube is a "destination" for video, while video on Facebook is usually "bumped into" when a user is going through their news feed. As a result, videos are consumed for a longer duration on Youtube, while most videos on Facebook need to take into account that the user is probably watching with the sound turned off' (Corcoran 2016b). In recent years both YouTube and Vimeo have begun to support vertical video.

YouTube's approach is all about getting big audiences and selling advertising to them: the YouTube Partner Programme – available after your channel has surpassed 10,000 views – allows YouTube to show adverts against a channel's videos, and share the revenue with the creator. The channel will also need to comply with the Partner Programme's policies and Community Guidelines.

YouTube also offers differing levels of support, depending on how many subscribers you have: those on the top 'Silver level' of over 100,000 subscribers get their very own 'partner manager', for example. Very few YouTube channels make enough money to support their creators: depending on the value of your audience even a million views per month may not be enough to generate a living wage.

Vimeo's approach is focused on quality over quantity: it may not have anything like the scale of YouTube, but its community of users is passionate about video, and its commercial options reflect that: Vimeo On Demand – available to users subscribing to a Pro account – allows you to sell directly to audiences.

YouTube offers creators the opportunity to sell videos, too, as well as rentals, and subscriptions – but you must be in the YouTube Partner Programme and already have 1,000 'active' subscribers before you can do the latter. But as these are not a core part of YouTube's business model, it does not actively promote or curate content in the same way that Vimeo does.

Aside from the core built-in commercial models above – advertising, rental, subscription and direct sales – many professional video creators have additional revenue streams too, such as merchandise, events, affiliate schemes, writing, appearance fees, sponsorship, endorsement and product placement. If you are to explore the last options you should ensure you are familiar with the laws regulating advertising, many of which are explained on the Advertising Standards Authority website (asa.org.uk). In 2014, for example, the ASA ruled against five vloggers over YouTube videos featuring the Oreo 'lick challenge'. Although the vloggers had each said 'Thanks to Oreo for making this video possible', that 'did not clearly indicate that there was a commercial relationship between the advertiser and the vloggers' (ASA 2014), and any disclaimer should also have appeared at the start of the video.

Aside from their different commercial frameworks, you will also find different approaches to video production on the two platforms. Vimeo is perhaps best known for documentaries and broadcast-style production. YouTube, on the other hand, is better known for vlogging and a style of production associated with successful YouTubers that has begun to feed back into TV production: presenter-led formats with a breezy presentational style, jump cuts, close framing with particular types of composition and good lighting. If you are to make video for either platform it is important to familiarise yourself with the visual language and conventions used there, and read about the unseen production practices that different creators use: for example, most will plan videos carefully with storyboards, scripts and rehearsals, as well as production schedules that include research, guests, location filming and content diaries that ensure a regular output.

### Live social video

Live video has very quickly become one of the most popular formats for publishers, largely because of Facebook's decision to prioritise live video in its algorithm and its high engagement levels, but also because of its cost (low compared to more packaged formats), and suitability for breaking news events. The focus here is specifically on social media platforms' live video services – Facebook Live, Twitter's Periscope, Instagram Live and YouTube Live – rather than those such as Ustream (www.ustream.tv) and Bambuser (bambuser.com) which are platform-neutral.

Each social video service has its own advantages and disadvantages: Facebook's main strength is, of course, its sheer scale: BuzzFeed famously set a Facebook Live record in April 2016 when over 800,000 viewers watched as they attempted to make a watermelon explode with rubber bands. And because Facebook Live can be used on Facebook pages, it works well for news brands that have existing 'brand' pages (for programmes or sections, for example) that users can be directed to. BBC's *Newsnight* programme, for example, used its Facebook page to broadcast a day of Facebook Live programming in the wake of the UK's EU referendum vote.

Twitter's main strength is that the network is built for breaking news, so stories that tap into that urgency may perhaps suit Periscope better, whereas content that performs well on Facebook tends to be softer and have a longer shelf life. Twitter is perhaps also better for interaction: not only is it is technically easier to respond to commenters, and for users to chat with each other, but users may also be more likely to do so if there is not an overwhelming number of them.

Functionally there are differences between the platforms: Facebook provides more detailed analytics for its live video, and videos can be added to a playlist, whereas Periscope video expires after a certain period of time (although you can download the video for republishing elsewhere). Both offer audience reactions. Facebook also introduced a split screen option in 2017 which makes it easier to use the platform to conduct interviews.

Also useful for conducting interviews is YouTube Live. YouTube's major selling point is monetisation, and subscriptions. It's also better for search engine optimisation, as people can find your videos through normal search. And once finished, video can be edited without having to be downloaded.

Instagram added its own live video at the end of 2016, focusing on ephemerality – broadcasts disappear from the app once they have finished, and are only accessible on mobile. This urgency is perhaps is biggest strength, as users know if they don't tune in they will miss out – but this is also its biggest weakness: videos cannot be embedded elsewhere, so need to be very much 'of the moment'. Planning ahead and giving notice of live video plans will help increase your chances of getting an audience that is ready when you are.

Planning ahead is good practice in general when it comes to any sort of live coverage: those who are poorly prepared can easily make any number of easily avoidable mistakes, from 'dead air' when nothing is happening, to the phone ringing while you are live. Some basic things to consider, then, include:

- Device: what are you going to livestream from? As well as a phone, you can also stream from a tablet or – depending on the platform – a laptop.
- Memory: if the device has very little free memory it is more likely to crash. Make sure that you have freed up as much memory as possible by deleting video and other large files.
- Battery: livestreaming can drain battery power quickly, so make sure that the device is fully charged, and is plugged in if possible. Having some sort of battery pack gives you extra backup.
- Signal: you will need a reliable and good wifi signal to broadcast. Remember that if lots of other people are also accessing it (at a live event, for example), then that will make it less reliable. If possible bring your own independent mobile wifi.
- Turn flight mode on and notifications off: you don't want to be interrupted by calls, so make sure flight mode is on (but turn wifi on too), and notifications from social media services are turned off.
- Tripod: you need a steady shot, so use a tripod. You can get grips or frames that will attach a phone to a traditional tripod – make sure these are solid (the cheap ones tend to lose grip), or you can also use flexible 'gorillapods' that can be wrapped around nearby objects. If you really want a smooth shot you might want to invest in a gimbal too.
- Tap the screen to lock focus and exposure every few seconds.
- Clean your lens (dust will compromise your video).
- Sound: invest in a microphone and an adapter (such as the iRig Pro) if needed for the device – otherwise viewers won't get clear audio. Shoot in a quiet room and be aware of background noise.
- Film a variety of shots and different angles. Smartphones are bad in low light, so avoid that if possible.
- Hold your phone horizontally unless your content is for social media sites that use vertical video (such as Snapchat). In horizontal mode, ensure your phone's home button is on the right-hand side. This will prevent you from accidentally shooting upside down!
- Cross-platform promotion: most engagement for Facebook Live videos takes place while the event is happening (Kant 2016; Corcoran 2016a), so using other social accounts – both before and during broadcast – can make a significant difference

Shaheryar Popalzai, a journalist based in Pakistan, advises journalists not to start broadcasting without thinking about what your viewers will want to see, or what they care about. By way of example, when livestreaming one of Pakistan's most prominent religious processions, Popalzai's team decided not to start recording in a crowd but instead found somewhere which would provide good audio and a 'bird's-eye perspective' (Popalzai 2016).

Once you are live Popalzai also recommends not broadcasting for hours at a time. 'A front camera video showing a reporter talking for an hour is a surefire way to lose viewers (unless it is a breaking news situation).' He recommends having at least two people in the video, one of whom is able to engage with viewer comments.

In addition, you may want to consider third-party software: aside from platforms' own live video offerings there are numerous services which offer extra functionality on top. Companies such as Switcher Studio (switcherstudio.com), for example, offer technology which livestreams video to more than one plat-form at the same time, can add graphics and effects, and switch between mul-tiple cameras – in effect, replicating a broadcast studio setup. Open Broadcasting Software (OBS – obsproject.com) also offers extra features such as the ability to broadcast pre-recorded material.

### The spectre of streaming

Social media trainer and former BBC journalist Sue Llewellyn points out a series of ethical issues to consider when livestreaming. She refers to it as the easy to remember 'S-P-E-C-T-R-E of streaming' (Albeanu 2016):

- S = Safety

  Your livestreams should not endanger those around you and yourself. Llewellyn says that unlike many broadcast film crews, mobile journalists operate alone, so they need to be aware of their surroundings.

- P = Privacy

  Filming of minors (children) needs consent. But even shooting celebrities in the street can raise legal issues.

- E = Ethics

  Streaming raises many ethical issues that need dealing with live.

- C = Copyright

  If there is music or video playing in the background there may be copyright issues. You usually can't broadcast ticketed events, such as a football matches or gigs, from your seat in the stands!

- T = Trolling

  Your live feeds may allow comments and this may attract abusive comments.

- R = Reputation

  Poor-quality live content can damage your reputation as a journalist and that of the media provider you work for.

- E = Emotional trauma

  Be wary of broadcasting material that is likely to cause trauma to the viewer (see the section on vicarious trauma).

Livestreaming isn't just for broadcasting, it is also a great research tool. Facebook Live Map (facebook.com/live/discover/map) and Persicope Map (periscopemap. live) came into their own during the 2016 Turkish coup d'état attempt when hundreds of ordinary citizens broadcast live coverage from the streets.

However, livestreaming has limitations. Jonathan Albright writes: 'The problem with news coverage of a crisis event ... is that people are shown what is happening but given little context around how and why. The connection between the developing narrative and an organizing (storytelling) strategy is key' (Albright 2015).

---

**Staying up to date**

All platforms are adding new features regularly, so make sure to follow the industry press and official blogs at Periscope's Medium blog (medium.com/ @periscope), Facebook Media (media.fb.com), the Instagram Blog (blog. instagram.com) and the YouTube Official Blog (youtube.googleblog.com)

---

### Narrated and piece-to-camera social video

Generally in online video the advice is to remove the presenter wherever possible: presenter-led packages perform badly on services such as the BBC's iPlayer, and short clips do much better. 'Online, there is often no need for the reporter as an intermediary', noted Alfred Hermida, 'as a user will have already read the story' (Hermida 2010).

However, social platforms such as Snapchat, and the rise of live video, have seen a partial return of the presenter, as journalist-led social media accounts create a narrative role for the reporter themselves – either as narrator (talking over the video footage that they are filming), or as presenter. These formats can work well in behind-the-scenes coverage where the journalist is the person who can best explain an experience, or the narrative is a discussion between reporters, rather than stories involving interviewees (viewers have little patience for watching reporters asking questions), and it might be argued that such personality-driven reporting, which often mixes the personal and the public, acts to 'construct celebrity by appearing to offer a peek behind the Curtain' (Olausson 2017).

The BBC, for example, used Snapchat Stories to 'walk' viewers through the 'Jungle' immigration camp in Calais, with the reporter recording a number of clips explaining what was around him. *Telegraph* video reporter Alastair Good filmed the same story from behind the camera, but narrated it as he filmed instead of appearing on camera.

Magazine formats like reviews and agony aunt columns also fit presenter-led formats well. The *Toronto Star's* Snapchat account used emojis to 'rate' celebrity fashion in one Snapchat story, for example, while one Huffington Post reporter used a series of snaps to answer user questions in their 'sex and love Q&A' story – the integration of social interaction through the app being a particularly important consideration (Bradshaw 2016).

### Packaged social video

Ultimately, video is normally used because there are interesting people and places that the journalist wants to introduce us to. Some of the most engaging video, therefore, centres around interviews in interesting locations.

At the most basic, that might be a sequence of 'vox pops' with people at an event, or with regard to a topical issue – these can work well within the ten-second limitation of Snapchat Stories clips, for example (Bradshaw 2016). But finding people who are inherently interesting – people who have been in the middle of a news story, experts on a current issue or who might be responsible for that issue – and interviewing them can be much more effective. You can also split longer video interviews into short chunks, one per answer, or create a video format that focuses on just one question.

### Caption-driven social video

Some social video is actually one or more still images and/or video clips with captions overlaid to add animation, and there are a number of mobile apps created specifically for that. The Legend app (legend.im) is a typical basic example: users upload an image or a video clip (it will be trimmed to six seconds) type a caption, choose how that caption will be automated over the image or clip, and then choose a filter if desired. The BBC's Suzanne Lord used the app to create brief updates during the 2015 UK election, while Robin Brant used it for a series of six-second explainers under the title 'What will UKIP do with your money?'

Similar apps include Ripl (ripl.com) – which allows more images – and Adobe Spark Post (spark.adobe.com), which has more functionality but takes more time to learn. Apple's own Clips app (apple.com/uk/clips) – seen as an attempt to take on Snapchat – also allows you to animate text over images or video, or create other combinations. RTE journalist Patricia O'Callaghan, for example, used Clips to create a caption-driven video report showing scenes (both still and video) at Ibiza Airport when the cleaners went on strike, while colleague Pat McGrath used Clips' dictation feature to automatically generate captions on top of his narrated video of a post-fire scene.

## Audio for mobile

It may sound like an odd section in a chapter on visual journalism, but in a multiplatform world audio is visual too. Not only do radio programmes regularly use video and images on their social platforms, but they also have to think of visual ways of presenting audio content. At the most basic, this means choosing a good image to go with their audio clip (and strong accompanying text), but other options are open to the multiplatform audio creator too.

### Mobile audio apps

Popular recording and editing tools for recording audio include Voice Recorder Pro, Ferrite, Twisted Wave's TW Recorder and Hindenburg Field Recorder. Most offer the ability to check levels while recording, perform basic editing and even do multi-track editing. Other tools focus more on publishing and distribution: Clyp and Audioboom, for example, both make it easy to instantly share short recorded audio via social media. All have the ability to add an image to your audio.

A separate generation of apps is focused on some form of podcasting or pseudo-podcasting. Anchor is perhaps the most ambitious and powerful of these, with the ability to directly record and edit audio, combine clips, draw on a library of background tracks or pull in music from your own phone, and even use your phone to record interviews directly into the app. There's also a feature allowing you to host a 'call-in' whereby other users can submit audio recordings and you can choose whether to include them in your 'show'. The results can be published to podcast directories on iTunes and Google Play and you can generate video versions too.

The service also offers background tracks and segue effects like 'awkward crickets' and 'This is an exclusive'. The Audioboom app can also be used for podcasting – although it has less functionality it does boast a well established userbase thanks to content from established broadcasters and personalities including the BBC and Russell Brand. SoundCloud and MixCloud are widely used as platforms for distributing audio content, but do not offer mobile recording functionality at the time of writing.

A further group of apps focuses on live audio, allowing the user to instantly stream to users of the app, as well as embed a live player on their own site. Spreaker and Mixlr both fall in this category, allowing you to chat with users while on air just as you can on live video tools such as Periscope. At the higher – and more expensive – end LUCI Live (luci.eu) and LUCI Live Lite are aimed at broadcasters using mobile devices for live broadcasts.

Then there are more experimental audio tools. Story Spheres for Journalism (storyspheres.com), for example, allows you to add audio 'hotspots' to 360 degree images.

It's worth remembering that most chat apps – including WhatsApp, Telegram and Line – include the facility to send audio clips, and these can be useful ways of creating or sharing audio content to audiences using chat platforms. Many journalists use Evernote (evernote.com), a note-taking app, for audio recording and submission for editing. It is free and available across desktop and mobile platforms.

Note that audio and video services launch and close regularly, so make sure you back up your content and explore new services to see what other options are available should your favourite service go under.

### Audio-as-video

In trying to find ways to help audio to perform better on social media some publishers have decided to turn their audio clips into video 'versions'. In 2016 for example the radio station WNYC, inspired by New York Magazine's audio Instagram updates, created 'audiograms': automatically generated video showing the waveforms of an audio clip moving over a logo background, while the audio track played. WNYC's social media director Delaney Simmons said: 'We think shorter, more snackable content is the way to go' (Owen 2016) and the organisation later open-sourced the Audiogram Generator on GitHub (github.com/nypublicradio/audiogram).

Easier ways to convert audio clips into social video include the app Voice Recorder Pro's 'Save in Photo Album' option, which can export a clip from the app as an mp4 file (you need to set an image for the audio clip first, which is then used as a background) and the social audio service Anchor, which includes a tool that automatically generates a video clip based on captions that have been automatically transcribed from the audio. The Talkee app works the other way around: starting from an image and allowing you to record a voice-over. More broadly, you can also import an audio track into video editing software and add a still image, or a sequence of images, to achieve a similar effect. Or you can use audio as the basis of some sort of animation …

### Video animation and explainer tools

Video explainers warrant a category all of their own: the interest in creating animation-driven video has led to a number of tools that make it relatively easy to make your own, among them PowToon (powtoon.com), Biteable (biteable.com), Wideo (get.wideo.co), Animaker (animaker.com) and VideoScribe (videoscribe.co). Most have a number of templates that you can use to animate particular transitions that can be adapted with custom captions to explain a process or concept.

## Immersive visual journalism: 360, AR and VR

Augmented reality (AR), virtual reality (VR) and 360 degree video deserve special consideration on their own. Each allows the video creator to add extra information for the viewer, and each adds particular opportunities, problems and considerations as a result.

Before we do so it is worth distinguishing between the terms VR and 360: these are often used interchangeably, and some will argue that they are the same thing. It might be argued that consumers see them as the same thing (because they are consumed in the same way), but producers use them differently, to distinguish between 360 degree virtual environments (that do not exist in reality) and 360 degree video of environments that are not virtual. Virtual reality might be used to take viewers to places no camera can go (such as inside your brain, or on Mars), or to simulate an experience (such as 'riding the stock market rollercoaster'), while non-virtual 360 video might allow you to experience the sights and sounds of an event that happened last week – or is happening now.

For that reason it is often used for large news events such as protests, marches and election rallies. These suit 360 coverage particularly well: being able to gauge the scale of the crowd at a protest or demonstration, or to step behind the scenes of a political rally, all offer unique opportunities for a 360 experience. These might be described more broadly as news scenarios where multiple things are happening within the same time and space, and the viewer then needs to choose where to direct their attention. As well as hard news events, it also suits colourful public cultural events like parades, festivals and performances, travel and sports events: the VR YouTube channel of Swiss news website Blick (youtube. com/channel/UCA5qlP_iECKBtUBSDFz87PA) has sections dedicated to sports, aviation, cars and 'Swiss Views', while launch partners for GoPro's Fusion 360 VR camera, for example, included Fox Sports, AccuWeather and travel blogger Louis Cole.

Augmented reality, in contrast, focuses on the place where you are right now – but adds (augments) an extra visual layer on top that typically presents extra information. While AR has been around for some time, it went mainstream with the popularity of Pokemon Go in 2016. The gaming app uses the player's GPS to locate and battle virtual creatures which appear on screen as if they were in the same real-world location as the player, but the same technology can be used to place location-based journalistic information on the screen, too.

You might be looking at a city high street, but the AR also tells you what the food hygiene rating is of that restaurant, or how many people were victims of pickpocketing on that street this year, or which tourist attractions get the best ratings on TripAdvisor, or what the street looked like 100 years ago. It can do this because it uses the phone's geolocation functionality to understand where you are – and what you are looking at.

Alternatively, AR can use something that is on-camera (such as a QR code printed on a magazine cover) to understand what is in front of it, and then use that information to superimpose extra visuals on top (such as an animated version of that cover, to create the appearance that it is moving). Perhaps the most widely used example of this is Snapchat's face filters, which use facial recognition to understand where the 'face' is, before applying some sort of transformation to it.

Editorially, then, AR is typically either approached as a way of presenting information that is tied to specific geographic points (fundamentally a data-driven storytelling form), or as a way to transform a smaller object for entertainment, engagement or educational purposes.

### Mounted, moving or point of view?

360-degree cameras and their virtual equivalents can be used as a mounted camera, an action camera, or a point of view camera for different editorial effects. A mounted camera, for example, allows the user to take a look around without necessarily being directed to look at one thing over another: it is editorially 'passive', and the default position of the viewer is exploratory. However, direction can be added: for example, the default position of the camera (the direction it points to begin with) is an editorial choice, and you can also add 'hot spots' that the viewer can interact with (for example by clicking) in some way, or text overlays on screen. You can also add a presenter either talking directly to camera, or narrating what is being shown, or audio from an interview. Editing together multiple shots can also add movement to a story.

Choosing to use a 360-degree camera to 'follow the action' means that you are taking a more direct editorial role, moving the viewer from one place to another. This may frustrate them if they do not wish to be taken away from something interesting, but it can also open up more narrative possibilities.

Finally, a point of view approach suggests you are trying to convey a more personal experience, not looking merely outward but also 'inward' to consider what it might feel to be someone in that situation. This is the approach taken by the *Guardian*'s VR project 6×9, which places viewers in a prison cell as a vehicle for exploring the broader issue of solitary confinement.

Some 360 video uses more than one approach. The *New York Times*' 360 VR feature 'The Fight for Falluja', for example (youtube.com/watch?v=_Ar0UkmID6s), uses a moving 'follow the action' shot from a moving vehicle for the first minute, before switching to a mounted camera inside the vehicle, all narrated by the filmmaker. 360-degree text is used to introduce different parts of the video, and at some points we are looking more from the 'point of view' of the creator, while at others we are focused on interviewees. Another *New York Times* video, 'The Displaced' (youtube.com/watch?v=ecavbpCuvkI), runs interview audio and subtitles over 360-degree footage of the interviewees as they do other things.

Many of these examples use traditional documentary-making techniques, but expand the canvas to take in everything that is around the camera. The composition of the shot becomes less important, because there is no frame (although the placement of the camera still plays a role in limiting the possibilities), but a consideration of all elements that are in sight of the camera, including the production team and any private material (textual material, for example, which may need to be hidden or blurred) becomes more important.

More simple examples merely document what is happening at a particular place and time in one shot. 'Scenes at Place de la République' (youtube.com/watch?v=2eWMIpKKc3w) and 'Scenes outside the Bataclan' (youtube.com/watch?v=jR-nE38r9kU), filmed by BBC News's Matthew Price four days after the Paris terror attacks in 2015, takes the viewer around a monument covered with tributes, while a voice-over (recorded separately) adds occasional context. Many of the techniques are borrowed from broadcast reporting, but the pace is slower, and the length longer, to allow more exploration.

AR, in contrast, rarely tries to tell a story or direct the viewer's attention: instead they are given the opportunity to explore elements in view that are of interest to them. Exceptions, of course, exist too: augmentations could direct the viewer to look in a particular direction, or AR might be used within a 'treasure hunt' narrative where viewers must find certain elements, as in the AR game Pokemon Go.

---

## Locating 360 content

It may sound obvious, but it is worth viewing 360 video on a mobile phone or tablet. The experience is tied to your phone's accelerometer and the video is viewed by physically moving your phone around. It just won't work on a desktop computer! The YouTube 360 Channel (youtube.com/360) is one of the best places to track down content.

---

### Hardware and software

The technologies have been around for over a decade, but modern mobile phones have made AR, VR and 360 video accessible to a much wider audience than was previously the case: the Wikitude app, for example, uses AR to superimpose information from review sites over what your mobile phone camera is seeing (using geolocation). The Layar app augments pages in magazines and newspapers with interactive content; and Star Walk places constellation descriptions over the part of the night sky you are directing the camera at.

In 360 and VR Google's Cardboard device, costing less than the price of a DVD, turns most phones into a VR headset, or for a higher quality experience you can invest in the Gear VR. Once in the device, users can download the Google Cardboard app, or dedicated VR showcase apps such as Within, Jaunt VR, NYT VR and Discovery VR. You can also view 360 degree video on YouTube, Facebook, WordPress, Twitter – or the Google Street View app. If you have a high-powered VR-ready computer you can also use Oculus Rift to access VR content.

The Google Street View app can also be used to create 360-degree photos (tap the photo button in the app and it will direct you to take photos in different spots), while the mobile app Splash allows you to create very short 360 video. These are useful for initial exploration, but a dedicated 360 degree camera is likely to be needed for good-quality footage. These are changing all the time with perhaps the best known including Ricoh's Theta range, Samsung's Gear 360 camera, the GoPro and Kodak's PIXPRO range.

Some 360 cameras use dual-lens technology and stitch the results to create 360-degree results, while other, single-lens cameras don't require stitching, typically creating better results. Where footage is stitched that point is called the 'stitch line': *New York Times* contributor William Widmer notes that aiming this point toward the light source ensures 'a better exposure than having only one lens face the light source' and also suggests trying to prevent your subject crossing through that stitch line 'if they're too close to the camera [as it] causes distortion of the subject as they pass between lenses' (Cullen 2017).

Most cameras connect to your mobile phone to allow you to control the camera or transmit the footage live – and some are actually attached to the phone camera in the same way as you attach a camera lens. Most come with an app, too, and you will want to check the features offered in that too (some, for example, may require you to convert the video before uploading to YouTube).

When it comes to image resolution, remember that there will always be a trade off between quality and speed: higher quality footage creates larger files which take more time and bandwidth to transmit if timeliness is important. Other considerations to bear in mind include battery life, removable batteries, memory, what the camera can be attached to (e.g. selfie sticks) and whether you need your camera to work in extreme conditions or under water.

### The future of AR and VR

Most news organisations are still experimenting with the possibilities of these technologies for storytelling – and the economic factors that make them feasible within a newsroom, such as the most cost-efficient workflow and equipment. Of course, this isn't just about whether it can be used to produce compelling journalism. There need to be strong monetisation possibilities. How will users respond to ad breaks in content? Will there be possibilities for native advertising?

The key question facing them all is the shape and size of user takeup: will high-end virtual reality headsets become the way that most people experience this content – or will it be a mobile-first experience? It may be both, or it may remain a minority pursuit.

The *New York Times*' VR app was downloaded more times in its first four days than any Times app before, and viewers spent an impressive average of nearly 15 minutes using it, according to data from *Advertising Age* (Kaye 2015). But individual success stories do not necessarily mean the basis for widespread change in working practices: arguing that VR would 'not go mainstream in its current form', *The Economist* used a leader in the same year to remind readers how the technology had 'flopped in the 1990s' (*The Economist* 2015).

Apple CEO Tim Cook is similarly critical of VR while positively gushing in praise about AR: 'I regard [AR] as a big idea like the smartphone,' he told the *Independent* in 2017. 'I think AR is that big, it's huge. I get excited because of the things that could be done that could improve a lot of lives. And be entertaining.' (Phelan 2017).

VR, on the other hand, was more problematic, he said: 'Most people don't want to lock themselves out from the world for a long period of time and today you can't do that because you get sick from it' (Phelan 2017).

### Drone journalism

Unmanned Aerial Vehicles (UAVs), more commonly known as drones, can be combined well with 360-degree video to create striking footage. Holton et al. note that they have been used to 'provide glimpses of natural disasters that would otherwise be too hazardous for journalists to obtain, and to offer unique perspectives that enrich news storytelling' (2015). This can be as dramatic as flying over a fire in a dogs home, or as simple as flying through the tunnels of transport projects or cathedrals.

As early as 2014 *The Economist* magazine was describing striking news footage produced by the technology: 'fires burn on the streets of Kiev; scorched banners flutter on buildings; madding crowds stumble through the chaos below. It is also strange: although aerial, it does not look as if it was shot from a helicopter. The

*Figure* 6.2 The DJI Phantom Drone with camera
By Pexels

camera flies right up to burning buildings; people on the ground so near that you can pick out the colour of their clothes' (*The Economist* 2014).

Drones do have their limits, however. Wind speeds over 20 mph, strong rain and extreme temperatures can all cause problems for UAVs, while battery life limits range, and legal requirements mean you must be able to see the drone while flying. Often two operators are needed: one to control the drone and another to control the camera.

Perhaps the biggest limits are legal ones. In many countries you will need permission to fly a drone (in the UK it is the Civil Aviation Authority; in the US the Federal Aviation Administration), and that also means understanding what you cannot do: for example, in the UK drones cannot be flown over congested areas without authorisation, and cannot fly within 50 metres of any person, vessel or structure not controlled by the pilot. Insurance is vital: invasion of privacy, being hacked and crashes can all lead to unexpected costs (Collins 2015): the BBC recommends insuring against damage up to at least £5 million.

Legal restrictions severely limit how journalists can deploy drones to cover breaking news. So in practical terms, you will almost certainly need a helicopter to film large-scale events, such as protests or concerts. However, a drone was used to dramatically show the scale of flooding in Chertsey, Surrey, in 2014. The local news site Get Surrey featured the video (getsurrey.co.uk/news/local-news/aerial-video-shows-scale-chertsey-6714381).

Laws are changing quickly in this field, so make sure that you check the latest guidance on drones on the Civil Aviation Authority website, the Professional Society of Drone Journalists in the US (dronejournalism.org) and the BBC's online Safety Guidelines on the use of Unmanned Aerial Systems.

## Risk assessments and legal issues

Aside from the technicalities of the various forms of video, it is also important to also consider health and safety issues and legal and ethical considerations. Health and safety is actually also a legal consideration itself. The Health and Safety at Work Act 1974 lays out the requirements on employers 'to ensure, so far as is reasonably practicable, the health, safety and welfare at work' of employees. That includes making sure that staff are adequately trained in health and safety, and ensuring the safe operation and maintenance of the working environment.

The working environment for journalists using video can range from a TV studio to a site of armed conflict, so it is important to undertake risk assessments for any project. What's more, those environments also involve non-journalists, so an assessment needs to be made for risk to those where relevant, too.

Hazards can range from lifting heavy objects and driving a vehicle, to the dangers presented by power leads and weather conditions. 'Risk', strictly speaking, is the likelihood that a person may be harmed or suffer adverse health effects if exposed to a hazard: icy weather may be a hazard, but the risk of that weather varies depending on what precautions are taken, and how the task is approached. A good risk assessment identifies any hazards involved in a project, assesses the risks associated with those and outlines strategies for reducing those risks – including alternative arrangements that do not involve those hazards at all. The BBC Academy has extensive guidance on health and safety (bbc.co.uk/academy/work-in-broadcast/health-and-safety) and the BBC myRisks website (bbc.co.uk/safety) publishes a range of materials, including a Journalism Safety Guide online, with sections devoted to everything from farms to psychological trauma.

Legal considerations when using video will vary depending on the context. If you are filming on private land, for example, such as a shopping mall, you'll want to ensure that that is cleared in advance if you don't want your filming to be interrupted by a security guard asking if you have permission to film. And if you are streaming live video on a controversial subject, you may want to brief contributors on issues around libel and defamation. If anything defamatory is said on air, you will need to be able to react quickly to mitigate the legal risks surrounding the statement, and make a decision whether to remove the video after streaming has finished. Video which risks contempt of court because it relates to ongoing proceedings will need particular care.

Privacy is an increasing concern, particularly when your device is indistinguishable from a mobile phone: anyone in the environment should be aware that filming is taking place, and consent forms should be signed by any contributors. 360-degree video raises particularly new challenges in this respect, because the camera is filming in all directions at once. This means you need to adopt a similar perspective: watch out for private documents which are visible in the environment, or individuals who are 'in shot' but may not know it.

## Conclusion

As journalism has become increasingly mobile, and mobile platforms have become increasingly visual, journalists themselves have had to become visually literate as well – regardless of whether they work in organisations that have historically revolved around print, audio or moving pictures.

That visual literacy might be something as simple as knowing how to use emojis in tweets or mobile notifications, or being able to adapt a well-worn meme – or it might involve turning your audio clip into an animation, making a caption-driven video, or crafting an eye-grabbing GIF

New forms of video are also changing the way that news reporting is experienced. Live video allows us to report on breaking news events in a way that is social, mobile (typically vertical), and interactive – and virtual reality, augmented reality and 360-degree formats allow the user to immerse themselves in the story, raising new editorial challenges around composition and direction, and new legal and ethical challenges too.

As journalists get to grips with these new technologies, it helps to look back to core principles of visual storytelling such as composition, sequence and the importance of sound – but we will also be discovering new rules along the way. It will be important to follow industry developments as those rules become discovered through experimentation, and codified in industry practice.

## Further reading

Burum, I., and Quinn, S. (2015) MOJO: *The Mobile Journalism Handbook: How to Make Broadcast Videos with an iPhone or iPad.* Focal Press.

A book dedicated to how to produce professional-quality video with a mobile phone.

Lancaster, K. (2013) *Video Journalism for the Web.* Routledge.

Shoot better video and tell better stories on the web.

## References

Albeanu, C. (2016) The spectre of streaming: 7 issues to consider before going live from your phone. Journalism.co.uk. Available at: www.journalism.co.uk/news/the-spectre-of-streaming-7-issues-to-consider-before-going-live-from-your-phone/s2/a633195/.

Albright, J. (2015) The revolution will not be ... periscoped? Medium. Available at: https://medium.com/d1g-est/the-revolution-will-not-be-periscoped-285e93f95434.

ASA (2014) *ASA Adjudication* on Mondelez UK Ltd. ASA. Available at: www.asa.org.uk/rulings/mondelez-uk-ltd-a14-275018.html.

Bajak, A. (2014) Is there such thing as emoji-journalism? Storybench. Available at: www.storybench.org/emojis-in-journalism/.

Baroni, A., and Mayr, A. (2016) 'Shared photography': (photo)journalism and political mobilisation in Rio de Janeiro's favelas. *Journalism Practice*, 11(2–3), 285–301. www.tandfonline.com/doi/full/10.1080/17512786.2016.1218786.

Borges-Rey, E. (2015) News images on Instagram. *Digital Journalism*, 3(4), 571–593. DOI: 10.1080/21670811.2015.1034526.

Bradshaw, P. (2016) *Snapchat for Journalists.* Leanpub.

Browne, M., Cirillo, C., Griggs, T., Keller, J., and Reneau, N. (2017) Did the Turkish President's security detail attack protesters in Washington? What the video shows. New York Times, Available at: www.nytimes.com/interactive/2017/05/26/us/turkey-protesters-attack-video-analysis.html.

Cairo, A. (2017) Nerd journalism. Unpublished thesis. Available at: www.dropbox.com/s/umr3r11v8dc088x/nerdJournalismDISSERTATION.pdf?dl=0.

Caple, H. (2014) Anyone can take a photo, but. *Digital Journalism*, 2(3), 355–365. www.tandfonline.com/doi/abs/10.1080/21670811.2014.882074

Collins, M. M. (2015) News drones: risks and rewards. NetNewsCheck. Available at: www.netnewscheck.com/article/46302/news-drones-risks-and-rewards.

Corcoran, L. (2016) How much engagement on Facebook live videos happens while they're live? NewsWhip. Available at: www.newswhip.com/2016/09/important-to-promote-your-facebook-live-videos-while-theyre-live/.

Corcoran, L. (2016b) New report: what publishers should expect from social media in 2017. NewsWhip. Available at: www.newswhip.com/2016/12/2017-predictions-report/.

Corliss, R. (2012) Photos on Facebook generate 53% more likes than the average post [new data]. Hubspot. Available at: https://blog.hubspot.com/blog/tabid/6307/bid/33800/Photos-on-Facebook-Generate-53-More-Likes-Than-the-Average-Post-NEW-DATA.aspx.

Cullen, G. (2017) Lessons learned in 360 video from a New York Times contributor. Journalism360. Available at: https://medium.com/journalism360/lessons-learned-in-360-video-from-a-new-york-times-contributor-47548f856c4f.

Dahmen, N. S., and Morrison, D. D. (2016) Place, space, time: media gatekeeping and iconic imagery in the digital and social media age. *Digital Journalism*, 4(5), 658–678. DOI: 10.1080/21670811.2015.1081073.

Haik, C. (2017) We're in the early stages of a visual revolution in journalism. Recode. Available at: www.recode.net/2017/8/7/16106862/pivot-video-digital-revolution-journalism-advertising-visual-media-storytelling-business-model.

Hermida, A. (2010) Lessons from the BBC on online video that works. Reportr.net. Available at: www.reportr.net/2010/09/20/lessons-bbc-online-video-works/.

Holton, A. E., Lawson, S., and Love, C. (2015) Unmanned aerial vehicles: opportunities, barriers, and the future of 'drone journalism'. *Journalism Practice*, 9(5). http://dx.doi.org/10.1080/17512786.2014.980596

Jackson, L. M. (2017) We need to talk about digital blackface in reaction GIFs. Teen Vogue. Available at: www.teenvogue.com/story/digital-blackface-reaction-gifs/amp.

Kant, V. (2016) News feed FYI: taking into account live video when ranking feed. Facebook Newsroom. Available at: https://newsroom.fb.com/news/2016/03/news-feed-fyi-taking-into-account-live-video-when-ranking-feed/.

Kaye, K. (2015) How Mini, GE, Google and the NY Times created a watershed moment for virtual reality. AdAge. Available at: http://adage.com/article/media/mini-ny-times-created-a-watershed-moment-vr/301334/.

Knobel, M., and Lankshear, C. (2007) *A New Literacies Sampler*. Peter Lang.

Newman, N. (2016) *News Alerts and the Battle for the Lockscreen*. Reuters Institute for the Study of Journalism. Available at: https://reutersinstitute.politics.ox.ac.uk/sites/default/files/News%20Alerts%20and%20the%20Battle%20for%20the%20Lockscreen.pdf.

Observatory on Social Media (2017) Frequently asked questions. Available at: http://osome.iuni.iu.edu/faq.

Olausson, U. (2017) The celebrified journalist. *Journalism Studies*. DOI: 10.1080/1461670X.2017.1349548.

Owen, L. (2016) Hoping to make audio more shareable, WNYC introduces 'audiograms' for social media. NiemanLab. Available at: www.niemanlab.org/2016/03/hoping-to-make-audio-more-shareable-wnyc-introduces-audiograms-for-social-media/.

Patrick, C., and Allan, S. (2013) 'The camera as witness': the changing nature of photo-journalism. In K. Fowler-Watt and S. Allan (eds), *Journalism: New Challenges*. CJCR. Available at: https://microsites.bournemouth.ac.uk/cjcr/files/2013/10/JNC-2013-Chapter-10-Patrick-and-Allan.pdf.

Phelan, D. (2017) Apple CEO Tim Cook: as Brexit hangs over UK, 'Times are not really awful, there's some great things happening'. *Independent*. Available at: www.independent.co.uk/life-style/gadgets-and-tech/features/apple-tim-cook-boss-brexit-uk-theresa-may-number-10-interview-ustwo-a7574086.html.

Popalzai, S. (2016) What you need to know to get started with Facebook Live. IJNet, Available at: https://ijnet.org/en/blog/what-you-need-know-get-started-facebook-live.

Reddy, S. (2016) Introducing GIF search on Twitter. Twitter Blog. Available at: https://blog.twitter.com/official/en_us/a/2016/introducing-gif-search-on-twitter.html.

Rogers, S. (2014) What fuels a Tweet's engagement? Twitter. Available at: https://blog.twitter.com/2014/what-fuels-a-tweets-engagement.

Sirucek, S. (2015) BuzzFeed will steal your video and chop it into tiny little GIFs. deathandtaxes. www.deathandtaxesmag.com/253447/buzzfeed-steal-lifehacker-video-bad-breath/.

Southern, L. (2017) Why the *Financial Times* is going vertical on WhatsApp to drive subscribers. Digiday UK. Available at: https://digiday.com/media/ft-going-niche-whatsapp-drive-subscribers.

*The Economist* (2014) Eyes in the skies. *The Economist*. Available at: www.economist.com/news/international/21599800-drones-often-make-news-they-have-started-gathering-it-too-eyes-skies.

*The Economist* (2015) Awaiting its iPhone moment. *The Economist*. Available at: www.economist.com/news/leaders/21662548-virtual-reality-promising-technology-will-not-go-mainstream-its-current.

Westley, H., and Rulyova, N. (2017) Changing news genres as a result of global technological developments. *Digital Journalism*. DOI: 10.1080/21670811.2017.1351882.

Zuckerberg, M. (2016) Mark Zuckerberg's Keynote @ Facebook F8 2016. The Zuckerberg Files. Available at: https://dc.uwm.edu/zuckerberg_files_transcripts/172/.

# 7 Publishing directly to social media

**This chapter will cover:**

- The rise of 'distributed content' and 'native content'
- Why publishers output content directly to social platforms
- Differences between different social platforms – and how to make the most of their qualities
- Publishing using Facebook Instant Articles
- The rise of chat platforms
- Measuring success: the use of analytics and metrics in publishing on social
- Generating revenue on social media
- Tracking audience sentiment: using trends tools

## Introduction

In September 2015 media reporter Peter Kafka was interviewing BuzzFeed founder Jonah Peretti for the *Re/code Decode* podcast. Kafka was 30 minutes into the podcast and asking about the organisation's approach to social media platforms when Peretti reached into his pocket to check something on his phone that would help him illustrate a point. 'I think I have some rough unvetted figures', he said.

The figures illustrated just how much of BuzzFeed's audience was consuming its content *outside of its website*: 31 per cent of BuzzFeed's content, for example, was being consumed directly on its Facebook accounts – most of it native video, with a small percentage of native images. That was the same proportion of content that was being consumed directly on Buzzfeed's website.

And it still left another third of content consumption happening elsewhere: a further 21 per cent of their content was being consumed within Snapchat; 14 per cent on YouTube; and 3 per cent on other platforms (Kulwin 2015). By 2016 the proportion of views off-site was 80 per cent according to one analysis (Liscio 2016).

The message was clear: when it came to distribution, the organisation's own website was not where most people were consuming their content. We had entered an age of 'distributed content'.

Do you run your own blog? If so, you'll want to check your site's analytics to see where traffic is coming from. For many bloggers, social media referrals have increased considerably in the last few years, overtaking referrals from Google searches. As a result, you may well have considered publishing your content 'social media first' or even closing your blog entirely.

Facebook-owned WhatsApp and Instagram have also grown rapidly in the past few years and offer different types of social activity and engagement opportunities which publishers may wish to test.

As Cory Haik (2016) puts it: 'The battle for audiences will be fought and won off-platform, on distributed platforms where published content is presented and consumed away from a publisher's own controlled user interface platform (app or website) … there is no shame in wanting that reach.'

Apps such as Facebook, Twitter and the like provide a curated and personalised news feed for the user. It also saves the user a huge amount of time as they don't need to spend hours visiting each separate app to get their news fix.

But there are risks for publishers. Each platform has its own technical requirements, monetisation possibilities, user retention and speed of evolution. So there are pros and cons to consider when publishing directly to social media. We encourage an experimental approach and to diversify so you don't become reliant on one social media company.

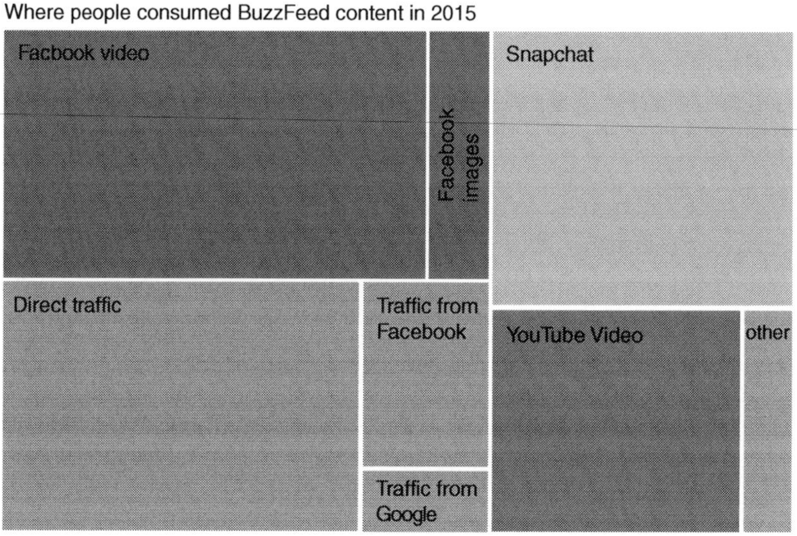

Where people consumed BuzzFeed content in 2015

*Figure 7.1* BuzzFeed content views in 2015 by platform
By Paul Bradshaw

## Distributed content: from social-first to social-only

'Distributed content' is a strategic approach to publishing whereby social media platforms are used not to 'drive traffic' to the publisher's own website, but instead to host content that only, or primarily, exists within that platform. Content produced this way is typically called 'native' content: in other words, it is native to Facebook, Twitter, Snapchat or whichever platform it has been published to, rather than having been first published elsewhere.

The term 'distributed content' appears to have been coined by BuzzFeed itself, when in August 2014 it announced the creation of BuzzFeed Distributed: a dedicated team of 20 staff who would make original content 'solely for platforms like Tumblr, Imgur [image sharing], Instagram, Snapchat, Vine [video, now defunct] and messaging apps' and 'scale BuzzFeed's deep understanding of the social web and why people share across other platforms' (BuzzFeedPress 2014).

They were not the first news organisation to adopt a platform-based strategy – YouTube in particular had been adopted as the primary platform for a number of video operations, while it could be argued that platforms like Tumblr and Medium blurred the boundaries between operating your own website and using a platform and network built by others – but BuzzFeed was the first big news organisation to make a noisy, and well funded, move in this direction.

Others followed. Fusion TV created its own team dedicated to distributed content in November 2015. NowThis News closed its website entirely and announced it would only publish on social media. Within a year the site had more than doubled its audience to a billion monthly video views. 'I'm paraphrasing Sarah [Frank, editor of NowThis], and she says that killing the homepage was the best thing we've ever done,' managing editor Versha Sharma told Journalism. co.uk (Ciobanu 2016).

New youth lifestyle publication Obsessee launched entirely on Facebook, Instagram, Snapchat, Periscope and Tumblr, while social news startup Reported.ly decided to focus on Medium, Twitter, Facebook and reddit. 'We don't try to send people away from their favorite online communities just to rack up pageviews,' they explained in an announcement (Carvin 2014).

In addition some outlets used the strategy as a way to spread risk and avoid government censorship: the Turkish citizen journalism project 140journos, for example, launched on Twitter and spread to 15 platforms where it could engage directly with its audience and the content that they were producing.

BuzzFeed Distributed head Summer Anne Burton saw the platform publishing strategy as a form of future-proofing, proposing that over the coming decade the internet would become a place where people would 'consume media within the places where they're also networking with their friends' (Benton 2015). Their team's objective was to understand that behaviour and the type of content that worked best – and establish an audience before their competitors.

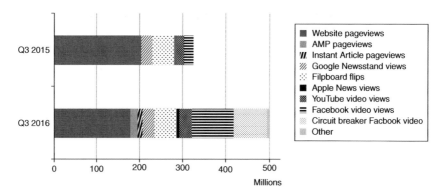

*Figure 7.2* The Verge is just one of a number of platforms to see a significant proportion of new views happening off-site on social platforms

By Nic Newman, 2017

Audience data appeared to support her predictions: metrics shared by the Verge website showed that all of the growth between 2015 and 2016 had come from distributed consumption (Newman 2017).

Three major technology launches had contributed to this: Facebook's launch of Instant Articles in 2015, followed by Apple News the same year, and then Google's Accelerated Mobile Pages (AMP) project – also used by Twitter. All three launches also made it possible for publishers to more easily make money from distributed content: publishers could keep 100 per cent of advertising if they sold it themselves; or 70 per cent if Facebook or Apple sold it (Google didn't take any cut, but required publishers to use Google partners to sell advertising).

In July 2017 *Fortune* magazine reported that Facebook was testing a paywall system that would 'direct users of the social network's Instant Articles feature to sign up for digital news subscriptions after reaching a threshold of monthly articles' (Huddlestone 2017). The move makes sense as some publishers have complained that they are unable to generate enough revenue through Instant Articles and Facebook hadn't done enough to help them do so.

They also performed better on two key metrics: speed, and engagement: a Chartbeat report in 2017 found that AMP loaded four times faster than 'the standard mobile site experience', while Instant Articles loaded so quickly that in the majority of cases it was not possible to record a load time. Engagement time with AMP content was also a third longer than standard mobile web content (Chartbeat 2017).

In many ways we had been here before: many news websites in the earliest days of web publishing served merely to 'drive traffic' offline, to the publisher's newspaper or broadcast, containing only teasers of the full content. It was only as online advertising began to boom that publishers started to look at the Web as a place to publish 'native' content. Once they made that decision, they needed

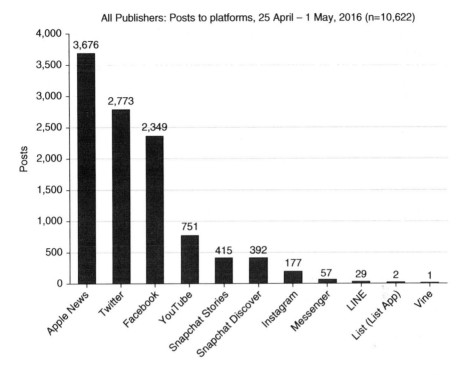

All Publishers: Posts to platforms, 25 April – 1 May, 2016 (n=10,622)

*Figure 7.3* Numbers of posts by publishers to social platforms in 2016
By Emily Bell, 2016

to find out what content worked best at attracting and retaining audiences on this new medium. And the same thing was happening all over again with mobile publishing, where social media apps had become just as important as the browser.

## Key challenges in creating content for many platforms

But this isn't just *one* new platform – it is dozens. Producing native content for Facebook is not the same as telling the same stories on Snapchat, Instagram or Twitter, and most of the teams dedicated to distributed content reflect this, with different individuals allocated to different platforms.

Deciding how many platforms to create content for, and what resources to allocate to each, is just one of the challenges of a distributed content strategy. One study of nine media organisations by the Tow Center for Digital Journalism in April 2016 found as many as 21 different platforms were being used, and by February the following year that was up to 22 – but the majority of effort was being expended on just five: Apple News, Twitter, Facebook, YouTube and Snapchat (Bell 2016).

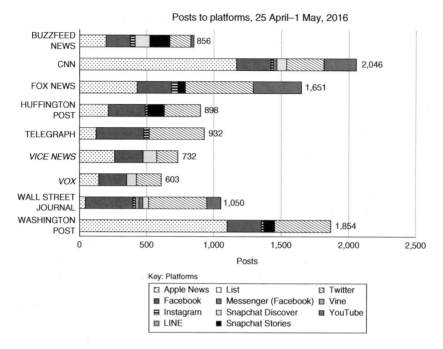

*Figure 7.4* Posts to platforms by publisher
By Emily Bell, 2016

When broken down by publisher, however, a more complex picture emerged. The *Wall Street Journal*, for example, was focusing most of its efforts on Facebook while CNN and the *Washington Post* published more content to Apple News. Snapchat played a bigger role for the Huffington Post, while YouTube was a major focus for CNN and Fox News.

Choosing which platforms to focus on depends on a range of factors. Chief among these is audience: a publication targeting a young audience may choose to invest more resources on creating content for Snapchat than a publication looking to target an older audience, for instance.

Often the nature of the story is taken into account when choosing which platform to use: BuzzFeed uses a ranking system to decide which platform to use for each of its stories: breaking news events might focus more on platforms which suit that best, such as Twitter and push notifications, whereas lifestyle content might be focused on platforms such as Instagram and Snapchat.

The resources and culture of the organisation itself is a factor too: a broadcaster like Fox News or CNN is likely to have access to more video creators and production facilities, and possess a more audiovisual culture, than competitors with a history in print. It is no surprise, then, that those organisations lean more towards video platforms like YouTube, but this does not stop publishers including the *Washington Post* and *Wall Street Journal* from building or expanding existing video production resources – especially when advertising for video sells at a much higher rate.

The money factor is important: YouTube might not be as fashionable as newer social networks, but one study of 19 publishers showed that it accounted for more distributed content than any other (O'Reilly 2017). Likewise, platforms like Snapchat were boasting some impressive statistics on engagement from users: the vice president and editorial director of digital at Hearst Magazines, Kate Lewis, said in 2015 that 72 per cent of users were clicking through every story after they opened the *Cosmopolitan* magazine on Snapchat Discover (Sloane 2015).

Commercial relationships are significant, too: when Facebook launched Instant Articles it had already lined up a number of media partners, and Snapchat's Discover feature is only accessible to media organisations who have signed a deal with the company. The 'first mover advantage' of being involved from the early days of a platform's new feature offer additional benefits for the publisher, such as access to early information on what types of content works, at what time and for what audience. It also allows the publisher to build an audience on the platform before its competitors, and build some buzz around itself. The *Washington Post*'s announcement that it would publish 100 per cent of its articles on Facebook's Instant Articles, for example, was as much (if not more) about positioning itself as a bold industry innovator as it was about building audiences.

## Risks

Behind the decision to begin creating social-native content was a fear of three things:

- Losing audiences on those platforms to competitors
- Losing advertising on those platforms to competitors
- And losing expertise on the best ways to avoid doing both of these

Publishers also feared that their website audiences might begin to decline as consumption behaviour shifted towards social platforms.

But adopting a distributed content strategy brings its own risks too. Chief among these is a loss of visitors to the publisher's own website: by anticipating a change in consumption patterns towards native content, publishers might actually be creating a self-fulfilling prophecy, facilitating that change in behaviour as more content is created to feed it.

However, publishers reminded themselves that their core objective was not necessarily to increase website visits – the core objective of a media business is to make money. Website visits are just one way to do that, and early evidence suggested that they might not be the best way to do so: one leaked study of 19 organisations by premium publisher trade body Digital Content Next (DCN) suggested ad rates against distributed content were seven times higher than the rates that publishers could charge on mobile visitors to their websites, largely due to the fact that most distributed content advertising was video advertising (which commands higher rates) (O'Reilly 2017). For those with a public service remit, such as BBC News, the objective was even clearer: to engage with audiences, wherever they might be.

Income is not the same thing as revenue, however: a publisher must also take costs into account. Research into mobile news consumption noted the increased complexity associated with such a move: 'The production process is complicated if it must account for different consumption patterns and potentially different audiences across these platforms' (Molyneux 2017).

That complexity can also have an impact on the type of content that it is possible to produce. The co-founder and president of Evolve Media, for example, noted that platform publishing had led the publisher 'to sacrifice budget for longer-form content published directly to our site' (Moses 2016).

Perhaps the risk most prominent in publishers' minds was the loss of control that came with using someone else's platform. This took a number of forms:

- Losing some control over editorial priority (for example, the positioning of stories)
- Losing some control over advertising
- Losing some control over user data
- Losing some control over branding

Losing control over user data and branding also means a loss of control over the user relationship. When you run your own website you can measure how many users visit that website, when and for how long. Further information about who those users are can be gathered, too, especially if users have to register to access content.

Platforms like Facebook, of course, have access to a huge amount of data on users and their behaviour, and one of the appeals of Instant Articles was being able to use that data to more specifically target ads. But which parts of data publishers can access depends on Facebook's systems and its willingness to open those up to publishers. At the time of writing, for example, Facebook's Instant Articles format allows publishers to embed 'in-house analytics tools or third-party measurement services', including Google Analytics (Facebook for Developers 2017), but advertising is limited to formats supported by Facebook's systems, and is managed using its Audience Network. There's also a limit to the number of adverts publishers can include in each article. By April 2017 many publishers were complaining about the service:

> Facebook hasn't designed their ad products to really let publishers sell their own inventory, and it'll be months, if not years, if not never, when this is truly supported. Which makes sense because of their own self-interest.
>
> (Benes 2017)

Similar complaints were heard when Facebook introduced a feature allowing publishers to sell subscriptions through the platform: the process didn't integrate well with publishers' own subscription systems, and subscribers were left with a disappointing user experience.

But perhaps of biggest concern is the reliability of metrics from third-party sites. In September 2016 the *Wall Street Journal* reported that Facebook had been exaggerating average video viewing time for over two years – because it didn't include video views lasting under three seconds. The following month the site announced that it had conducted a review of over 220 metrics and found more errors, including inflation of seven- and 28-day organic reach for Instant Articles. And in December Facebook admitted that it had been miscalculating the likes and reaction emojis for live videos too.

The lack of control over analytics was further highlighted in February 2017 when Facebook removed measurements for video views lasting for 30 seconds or longer, instead providing metrics for the number of views longer than ten seconds.

The advertising offerings of Apple News and Snapchat have also been criticised for a lack of variety, a lack of performance metrics or both, with both platforms promising to add more features and more information.

Alongside this is a concern that using formats like Facebook's Instant Articles contributes to a loss of branding. Research in 2017, for example, found that only 37 per cent of consumers who encountered news via a social platform were able to recall the original publisher two days later (Kalogeropoulos and Newman 2017), compared to 81 per cent of consumers who accessed the story directly. Users were more likely to remember the platform where they found the content than the organisation which authored it. Notably, the study explicitly omitted native content and focused only on consumption of stories via clicks through to a news website on desktop computers: at the time of writing it is not clear whether the effect is more pronounced on mobile, and/or when the user does not end up on the news website at all.

Furthermore, when publishers allow advertising to be sold by a third party – which also happens on news websites where it is arguably a bigger problem – there is the potential for the brand to be damaged by the placement of adverts next to content which is at odds with the brand values of the publication.

But it is the lack of editorial control which perhaps affects all the other factors listed above: if a change in a social platform's algorithms lead to a publisher's content becoming less visible to users, then views are going to drop, along with the accompanying ad revenue. And platforms' decisions to take action – or not – on content can be politically or commercially motivated: the Indonesian platform publisher Rappler, for example, pointed out that Facebook took down 30,000 fake accounts during the French election: 'If they had done that for the Philippines, maybe the results here would've been different' (Wang 2017).

## Platforms and media publishers – best of frenemies?

> It's their world. I see them as a partner. We call them a frenemy, and I don't even know if that's totally accurate.
>
> (Bell 2016)

Distributed publishing is a tacit acknowledgement of a modern reality: publishers once used to controlling their own distribution are now at the mercy of large corporations who dominate the networks of media consumption: Facebook, Google, Apple and Amazon.

Whether they like it or not, publishers have decided they must deal with these new competitors. The tensions in that relationship have been summed up in the portmanteau 'frenemy': a competitor (enemy) who is also a partner (friend).

In order to do that, many organisations have had to create positions dedicated to managing those relationships: in 2016 the *Wall Street Journal* reported that Conde Nast International, Vox Media and CNN were among those creating new roles 'to help coordinate and deepen its relationships with social media and video platforms, messaging apps and even hardware manufacturers' (Marshall 2016), but not everyone has had the same access. Research conducted by the Tow Center for Digital Journalism found smaller publishers complaining of 'having less access to, or access to lower-ranking, partnership managers at platform companies. Indeed, neglecting the needs of local publishers in particular is a problem that Facebook has acknowledged publicly' (Brown 2017).

The broader challenge was to to try to identify where the social platforms were going – and whether publishers wanted to head in the same direction. The advice from the World Association of Newspapers and News Publishers was to consider the corporate goals of each platform, and how that might impact on publishers' own objectives (Pfeiffer 2015).

By 2017 most platforms had moved into content production and commissioning themselves, putting themselves in direct competition with their 'customers' in the media. Facebook spent over \$50 million commissioning video for its site, making the waters even muddier: Vox Media, BuzzFeed, ATTN and Group Nine Media were among the companies being paid to create video for the platform, raising questions about editorial impartiality and transparency on both sides.

In April that year the UK industry publication *Press Gazette* launched its 'Duopoly' campaign to call for Facebook and Google to be broken up 'in the name of media plurality' (Ponsford 2017), and by July the balance of power had shifted so far across the Atlantic that the News Media Alliance – a US-Canadian organisation representing almost 2,000 news organizations – called on Congress to allow publishers to negotiate collectively with dominant online platforms. Publishers, they said: 'are forced to surrender their content and play by their rules on how news and information is displayed, prioritized and monetized' (News Media Alliance 2017). The group argued that those rules had 'commoditized' the news and contributed to the rise of fake news.

## Social media sites examined

Social media platforms differ from each other in a range of ways, including:

- The size of its audience – and whether that is growing quickly
- The demographics of the audience (and appeal to advertisers, for example)
- Audience behaviour on that platform (for example, how, and how often, they use it)
- Availability of metrics
- Commercial opportunities such as the ability to sell advertising or share revenue
- Technological affordances – what you can do on the platform

Facebook has been by far the most widely used social media platform for some years now: a survey of media use across 36 countries in 2017 found 70 per cent of online users had accessed Zuckerberg's social network in the last seven days, followed by YouTube (61 per cent). Just under a quarter had used Instagram in that period, and one in five Twitter.

The proportion using those services for *news*, however, varied: more Facebook users than those on Twitter had used the service for news in that period, while just a third of YouTube users and a quarter of those on Instagram had done so (Newman et al. 2017).

Having a large userbase is just one metric – but platforms are also continually looking for ways to get their users checking in more often. On this score Facebook dominates again: more than three-quarters of its US users check the service daily, compared to only half of US Instagram users, two in five Twitter users and a quarter of Pinterest users (Greenwood et al. 2016).

And the direction that those numbers are heading in is equally important. In its *Digital News Report* for 2017, the Reuters Institute for Journalism noted that growth in the use of social media for news outside the United States and United Kingdom seemed to be flattening out. 'In most countries growth has stopped and we have seen significant declines in [others]' (Newman et al. 2017). The report noted, however, that Facebook's decision to change its algorithm to prioritise friends and family updates over professional content may have contributed to this.

### The rise of messaging and chat apps

Consumer behaviour has shifted significantly towards chat apps in recent years: in 2016 use of the top four messaging apps (WhatsApp, WeChat, Viber and Facebook Messenger) overtook use of the top four social platforms (Facebook, Twitter, Instagram and Snapchat) for the first time (BI Intelligence 2016) – and by 2017 WhatsApp and Facebook Messenger were used by more people than all social media platforms apart from Facebook and YouTube. A quarter of people were using such platforms for news.

But here again geographical usage varies significantly. WhatsApp, for example, is used by three-quarters of internet users in Brazil, Spain, Chile, Hong Kong, Malaysia, Singapore, Mexico and Argentina, and around two-thirds in Spain, Austria, Switzerland and the Netherlands, compared to only a third of users in the UK and the US and one in five in Australia. Viber is much more popular in Croatia and Greece, Line is big in Taiwan and Japan, Kakao Talk is number one in South Korea, and in Hong Kong 46 per cent of people use WeChat.

In Russia, Telegram has a major presence, and interviews with publishers show a range of ways of using the platform, including writing differently than for social media. 'On Telegram, there is a sense that the subscriber will actually read the message, not just scroll away from it. It has way less distraction than social media,' says one editor (Valeeva 2017), who also notes the importance of not annoying readers by sending messages too late.

### Communication modes: the affordances of platforms

Marshall McLuhan's tetrad (set of four) of media effects invites us to look at any new technology in four ways:

- What does the medium enhance?
- What does it make obsolete?
- What does the medium retrieve that had been obsolesced earlier?
- What does the medium flip into when pushed to extremes? (McLuhan 1992)

This is a useful framework for considering the advantages and disadvantages of any social or chat platform for journalistic use. Chat platforms, for example, enhance the privacy of communication (or at least the appearance of privacy), and the professional chat platform Slack specifically seeks to make email obsolete as a form of organisational communication. The use of stickers and emoji on platforms like Snapchat retrieve a playful form of communication that we normally abandon in early childhood, while Pinterest explicitly retrieves the fun of the old-fashioned scrapbook, and so works particularly well for lifestyle publications and subjects, and much less so for news. Facebook can flip from something personal, private and affable into a hostile, impersonal and public experience when someone's post goes unintentionally 'viral'.

In addition, it is important to highlight that many platforms now offer multiple ways ('modes') of communicating, and ever-expanding functionality. Snapchat, for example, began as a self-destructing messaging service before adding its 'Stories' feature, and then Snapchat Discover. Each assumes a different type of audience (singular, multiple friends and mass audience), and has different functionality.

Twitter likewise has over the years added its own 'Twitter Moments' feature, along with the ability to add live video and GIFs to updates, while message limits have been altered, and while Instagram at first forced users to adopt a square ratio for image updates, Snapchat has always been vertical-first. When it comes to chat apps not all platforms are equal: WhatsApp in particular has frustrated many publishers with the platform's limits on mass messaging and the use of bots.

---

### What is Twitter Moments? (twitter.com/i/moments)

Moments was released in October 2015 and aimed to promote Twitter's role in breaking news. It brings together the latest news stories that are buzzing around into a curated news feed of tweets. However, because the feed is curated and edited by humans it is often slow to update during busy breaking news events when tweets are being posted every few seconds. In 2016, the company opened it up to anyone to curate content. Because of the time needed to properly curate a 'moment' the service works best as a way to create a permanent record of a group of related tweets before they disappear underneath later updates, rather than as a form of live coverage.

---

Each platform has its own cultural history, too: Twitter's focus on short real-time updates has created a strong association with breaking news and gossip, while Facebook is more strongly associated with human interest stories and quizzes, and WhatsApp users are more accustomed to using the tool for conversational communications, leading some organisations to frame their updates as informal communications from individual journalists rather than news brands (Valeeva 2017; Kramer 2017).

The choices that news organisations have made around the organisation of staff producing 'native' content demonstrate how these qualities, and audiences, are interpreted strategically. At NowThis News, for example, Twitter video is primarily produced by the real-time or trending news team, reflecting its role for users in providing breaking news. In contrast, the 'emerging media team' creates content for Snapchat, Vine, Instagram, Tumblr, YouTube, Weibo and WeChat. Facebook video production is organised based on subject, with different teams producing content for different Facebook pages (Ciobanu 2016).

### *Quality of engagement: what data are supplied by owners?*

Platforms vary in the amount of information available to publishers on how users interact with their content – this information is referred to as 'metrics' (see below). Facebook's Insights tool, for example, provides a range of information including the demographics of people liking a particular Facebook page, how many people see a particular update and whether they took some sort of action such as sharing or liking the update. Twitter Analytics similarly allows you to download a spreadsheet of any month's data showing, for each tweet, the number of people who saw that tweet and how many engaged with it in some way.

In contrast, data from Instagram and Snapchat have historically been much sketchier. In a Snapchat story you can see how many people saw each 'snap', and how many took a screenshot, but there is little information beyond that. Both began introducing more detailed metrics for commercial clients in 2017, while third-party services have also attempted to fill the gap in the market, but the information still falls short of that provided by more established services.

## Media metrics in detail

Platform publishing invariably involves some sort of measurement of performance – after all, how do you know if a distributed content strategy is working if you are not measuring its impact?

Any form of measurement needs to start with a clear sense of objectives: a metric is only meaningful if it relates to what you are seeking to achieve. A public service organisation like the BBC, for example, is likely to have an objective around reaching a wide audience, or attracting hard-to-reach audiences. Because its TV and radio programmes tend to attract a particularly old audience, it uses social platforms to reach younger ones. And in some parts of the world it will use chat platforms to interact with audiences who might not use other channels to communicate with the corporation.

Commercial news organisations will be led by their business model: objectives might centre around building *engagement* in the audience, because that will allow them to charge more for advertising, or drive more subscriptions. Sometimes the strategy is about *branding*.

A good objective should be SMART: this stands for Specific, Measurable, Achievable, Realistic and Time-limited. An example might be 'Increase the average engagement by 10 percentage points by the end of three months'. Note that this objective has a deadline (three months), is specific (10 percentage points) and measurable. So which measurement are we using?

Typical measurements in traditional online publishing include the number of page views or page impressions that a story receives, and the number of unique visitors to a site. An equivalent metric on social platforms is *reach*: this refers to the number of *people* who have been reached by your content or page within a certain period (one day, or one week, or one month, for example). This is different to *impressions*, which refers to the number of *times* that content was seen in total: this figure can be higher because one person might have watched your content multiple times (if it was really good!).

On Facebook in particular reach is also categorised in four different ways: organic, viral, unpaid and paid. *Paid reach* refers to people who saw your *sponsored* content (content where you have paid Facebook for extra promotion). If you haven't paid to promote your content then you won't have any paid reach. *Viral reach* is the number of people who saw your content because a friend shared it, while *organic reach* is those who saw it in their news feed or ticker without a friend's intervention. Note that users can be reached by your content both organically and because a friend shared it. *Unpaid reach* is essentially the total of all the people who saw your content or page minus the number who saw it because it was sponsored content.

Note that reach is different to the number of *followers* of your Facebook page, or social media account. The number of followers is not a particularly useful metric for two reasons: first, because you cannot guarantee that followers will always see your content, and secondly because you cannot guarantee that they are even real people: one study estimates that as many as 15 per cent of Twitter accounts are bots, for example (Varol et al. 2017). The site Twitter Audit (twitteraudit.com) offers to provide an estimate of the number of your followers who are likely to be fake.

Reach is not the only metric that publishers and advertisers use – indeed, over time publishers and advertisers have realised that a better measure of an audience's value is often *engagement*. This is because they noticed that users who engaged in some way with the content – posting a comment, voting in a poll, reading all the way to the end, sharing it with a friend, clicking on a 'like' button – tended to also be the users who returned more often, subscribed or bought the products that were being advertised.

Engagement metrics take a number of forms. On Twitter it is broken down into categories such as 'retweeted', 'liked', 'viewed media' (i.e. they viewed the video in the tweet) and 'replied'; whereas on a Snapchat story the key metric of engagement is someone taking a screenshot.

RELATIVELY CLEAR DEFINITIONS/MEASUREMENTS

LESS CLEAR DEFINITIONS/MEASUREMENTS

| Interest | REACH | ENGAGEMENT | LOYALTY | IMPACT |
|---|---|---|---|---|
| Definition | The number of people exposed to content in a given period of time | Time someone spends with content during a session or a given period of time | Frequency with which someone seeks out a given brand's site, app, or social media content | Whether the content made a difference in people's life (individual or societal) |
| Measurement | Unique users (website) User sessions (apps) Impressions (off-site social media use) | Session time (website) Time in app (apps) Engaged time (time spent actively interacting with content) Number of pages/visit | Return visits (website) User sessions (apps) | No agreed upon metrics |
| Data issues | De-duplication from devices to people App/browser proliferation Access to off-site data | Aggregation of individual users' engagement across devices, apps, and browser use Integrating on-site/app engagement with off-site engagement | Aggregation across devices, apps, and browser use Integrating on-site/app use with off-site use | No agreed upon sources of data |

*Figure 7.5* A matrix of how news organisations employ user metrics
© Reuters Institute for the Study of Journalism

## Monetisation

As already mentioned, one of the attractions of distributed content for many publishers has been the additional targeting and higher pricing available on social platforms. One analysis of BuzzFeed's distributed content strategy, for example, describes the move as 'increasingly prescient as falling ad prices and the rise of ad blockers threaten the core advertising businesses of many traditional media companies' (Liscio 2016). Conversely, many publishers decided to withdraw from Facebook Instant Articles when initial metrics suggested that it was more lucrative to link back to their own sites.

Some useful acronyms to understand in this respect include:

- ARPU (average revenue per user, or sometimes per unit)
- CPM (cost per thousand impressions)
- CPC (cost per click)
- CPA (cost per action)

ARPU is the total revenue you get – from advertising on a particular platform, for example – divided by the number of users you have. CPM is the amount that you charge an advertiser for every thousand impressions that their advert gets. A platform like Facebook or Twitter, for example, can often charge a higher CPM because they are able to target more specifically than traditional media services. From an advertiser's perspective, they might spend more money – or the same amount of money on less advertising – because they believe it will be more effective.

CPC and CPA are rates charged to advertisers only when someone clicks on their advert, or takes some sort of action (like calling an advertised number). In these cases advertisers might be even more confident that the advertising has been effective, and willing to pay higher rates as a result.

However, it may be that one of the biggest sources of monetisation for distributed content is not traditional advertising at all. A 2017 report into platform publishing concluded that subscriptions and display advertising played a 'small role' in the commercial models surrounding the strategy:

> Most current and planned business models are based around a combination of other sources of revenue, including native advertising and sponsored content, coupons, partnerships, or the sale of services.
>
> (Anderson 2017)

### *Generating revenue on social media in the future*

News consumption is moving away from publishers' own sites and towards social media mobile apps. This is an area where Facebook is the most dominant player. While having your stories appear on Facebook may generate impressive reach and engagement, translating it into revenue (AKA cold hard cash!) has proved challenging, to say the least.

In 2013 Cory Bergman, general manager of Breaking News, warned of the 'tremendous' gap between revenue generation on desktop versus mobile. 'It's not just all incremental traffic,' he says. 'You are going to see that as people shift behaviour to mobile, desktop consumption will decrease and because of that we'll see revenue impacts at news organisations which are not able to ramp up quickly enough on mobile and sell mobile effectively enough to compensate' (Marshall 2013).

So how should journalists and media publishers respond? Henrik Ståhl, Product Owner and Digital Strategist, Bonnier News, says that publishers must 'surrender the War of the Banner Ads, because it has already been won by Google and Facebook, and prepare to face even tougher financial challenges, and even more aggressive advances from the social networks' (NewsWhip 2016).

There is some evidence that the social media platforms are providing better advertising opportunities and revenue share to those publishers who go to the efforts of publishing natively. The fact that Facebook has launched a service whereby publishers can charge subscriptions, a key demand of magazine publishers, is a key sign of this.

## Making editorial decisions based on data versus traditional news values

The increasingly widespread use of metrics in publishing has led to concerns about the impact on editorial independence. This is not a new concern, of course – publishers have always been accused of spicing up stories to sell papers or increase viewing figures, and overlooking important stories because they weren't 'sexy' enough – but the granularity of the data, which allows publishers to see which specific stories are performing best, and with whom, has only heightened those fears. And when Gawker announced in 2008 that payments to writers would be based in part by the popularity of their work, concerns were raised that it would lead to a 'race to the bottom'.

Despite those concerns, metrics have become a fixture of the modern newsroom: statistics on the best performing stories are shown on screens inside the newsroom, they are shared in weekly and monthly internal emails, and accessible to journalists at any time through internal dashboards. In the morning news conference metrics are likely to inform decisions about which stories to cover – and how to cover them.

Trinity Mirror's regional newspapers have had newsroom targets since 2013 and team targets since 2015. David Higgerson, the digital publishing director, has written widely about the role of analytics in the organisation, and is at pains to emphasise that audience analytics don't dictate the stories that they write. 'It's more about looking at data and making sure we're producing content in the right way, and asking ourselves why content we might consider crucial to what we are, isn't doing that well, and how we make it more popular' (Dyson 2014). Examples

RUDIMENTARY ANALYTICS  ∘  GENERIC ANALYTICS  ∘  EDITORIAL ANALYTICS

| Some data, but little organisation and culture, and no systematic link to decision making and few attempts to update to an evolving environment | Multiple standard tools and organisation and culture in place for short-term optimisation | Tailored tools, organisation, and culture supports both short-term and long-term data-informed decision-making in the newsroom and evolve over time |

*Figure 7.6* A continuum of forms of analytics used in newsrooms
© Reuters Institute for the Study of Journalism

include live blogging council meetings and staying for longer than if reporters had decided to write articles after the event, and the increasing use of analysis and explainers accompanying news articles, 'because they are often very well read' (Higgerson 2016).

A report interviewing over 30 audience development editors and newsroom analysts across Europe and the US found similar sentiments being expressed about analytics being used to inform, not lead, editorial strategy, an approach that the authors describe as 'editorial analytics'. These are distinct from more generic approaches to metrics because they are:

> [A]ligned with the editorial priorities and organisational imperatives … informing both short-term day-to-day decisions and longer-term strategic development, and … continually evolving to keep pace with a changing media environment.
>
> (Cherubini and Nielsen 2016)

The authors also note that commercial objectives such as reaching larger audiences are complemented by editorial and branding objectives such as maintaining the reputation of the brand for in-depth reporting or holding power to account.

A significant piece of research by Tow Center Fellow Caitlin Petre, however, highlighted the potential for analytics to be poorly used by individual reporters. Her ethnography of Gawker Media, the *New York Times* and analytics company Chartbeat found that it was 'not uncommon for journalists to become fixated on metrics that rank them or their stories, even if these are not the sole criteria by which they are evaluated' (Petre 2015), and that busy journalists tended to use metrics in an ad hoc way rather than in relation to strategic journalistic goals.

Perhaps most relevant to our purposes, she also concluded that news organisations should consider the business model and the values of the company providing analytics. In terms of web publishing, this meant operators such as Chartbeat (chartbeat.com), Omniture (adobe.com/uk/marketing-cloud.html) and the free Google Analytics (analytics.google.com). But when it comes to social platforms, often there is only one vendor of analytics: the platform itself. And even third-party services are themselves largely reliant on what the platform makes available.

## Platform analytics tools and dashboards

In order to obtain metrics on your performance on a particular platform you will need to use the relevant analytics tool. Dwyer (2017) includes these tools as part of a broader ecosystem of 'metadata' services: news analytics companies (including Google Analytics, Omniture and Chartbeat); social management companies (such as Hootsuite and Gigya); community intermediation services such as ICUC, which monitors social media discussion; and bookmarking and link-shortening services such as Bit.ly and TinyURL.com.

In most cases the platforms provide their own analytics dashboards: Facebook's is at facebook.com/analytics and Twitter's at analytics.twitter.com. You can also access Facebook Insights from any Facebook page you control by clicking on the 'Insights' button across the top of the page.

Third-party tools tend to provide access to similar information, but in a more customised or integrated way (for example, comparing multiple platforms). Hootsuite (Hootsuite.com), for example, is available as a free social media dashboard that allows you to post (or schedule updates) to multiple Twitter, Facebook, Instagram, LinkedIn, Google Plus, YouTube and WordPress accounts from the same place. The same dashboard allows you to generate analytics reports too. Paid-for plans provide the ability to add more accounts, more customised reports and access support and training.

Buffer (buffer.com) is a similar service built around scheduling content to a range of social platforms: the idea is that the service will space out ('buffer') your updates so that you don't have to post them all at the same time, and it will also try to do so at the 'optimal' times. These times are based on analysis by the company of large datasets – one analysis of 4.8 million tweets by the company, for example, suggested that early morning hours are the best time to get clicks on tweets, while evenings and late at night were when tweets received the most favourites and retweets (Lee 2016).

However, it is important to highlight that these findings tend to be based on a broad variety of updates. News consumption patterns might vary from these, and your own audience might have a different behaviour. For that reason it is important to test a number of different approaches yourself and work out the best times and content approaches for your own market.

The analytics tools NewsWhip (newswhip.com), Socialbakers (socialbakers.com) and Crowdtangle.com (owned by Facebook), for example, all offer to 'benchmark' your stories' performance on social media against your competitors.

---

**Spike from NewsWhip (newswhip.com)**

Spike is a powerful tool which allows publishers to identify what it calls 'pre-viral' content – its social media monitoring tools use data to predict the likely engagement a story will get. To make it easy to work out the life-span of engagement on articles, each one is given a handy 'Velocity' score showing how and when it was most popular. Unfortunately, this is a paid-for product which individual journalists or students are unlikely to be able to afford. However, many larger media companies use it.

---

It may be that other publications are using more effective strategies around timing, choice of angle, or the way that they have told their story on social media. Likewise SocialFlow (socialflow.com) is used by some publishers to identify the right content and time to publish for their particular audience and business objectives, and Cortex (meetcortex.com) offers a similar service.

Increasingly, analytics tools designed around websites also offer to track performance on social media. Chartbeat and Google Analytics, for example, can also be integrated into Facebook Instant Articles and Google AMP pages.

*Figure 7.7* Spike from NewsWhip predicts the likely shares of individual stories on social media

By NewsWhip

## Tracking audience sentiment: trends tools

As well as analytics tools focused on measuring the performance of your own content, there are also many tools offering to identify how other people's content is performing – and highlight topics or individuals that you might want to be looking into.

Services like BuzzSumo, for example, focus on trending topics and identifying 'influencers'. The Social Media Editor at the *Telegraph* Richard Moynihan used it to compile a list of 'sports influencers they could work with (to co-create content), as well as people who could share it with their followers' (Cleary 2017).

Twitter has inspired a range of sites which identify trending terms and hashtags on the site. Trends24 (trends24.in), for example, allows you to identify trends at a global, country or large city level, and across timescales ranging from the last hour to 24 hours ago. Trendsmap (trendsmap.com) presents trends data against a map: users can pan or zoom to find particular locations, and use a slider to change the timescale covered. Twitter itself also displays trends in the inside column when viewed on desktop – these are customised based on your location and who you follow, but you can click on 'change' to specify a different location, for example.

The email newsletter tool Nuzzel (nuzzel.com) offers to deliver a regular email with links to the stories that have been shared most often by the people you are following on Twitter and/or Facebook, providing a useful insight into the 'buzz' within a particular community.

Facebook launched its own trends service, Signal (signal.fb.com), which also covered Instagram, in September 2015. The service, which was only available to journalists, offered to track posts which were trending, as well as which public figures were being mentioned most on the platforms.

Google Trends is one of the longest-running trends services around: this provides information on the most searched-for terms within a specific country or region, and timescale. Although this does not relate directly to social platforms many of the searches will be driven by social media behaviour.

As with other analytics tools, metrics provided by trend monitoring services should be approached strategically and sceptically: a subject which may be trending worldwide or within your social circle may not have the same level of interest for your publication's audience. And if a story is trending an important question to ask is, first, can you add anything new to it, and secondly, will that still be of interest by the time you have written it – or will interest have moved on? News organisations typically adopt a dual role: not just following the news agenda, but setting it too by unearthing stories of interest that others haven't spotted. While trend monitoring can help reporters to 'feel the pulse' of an audience, it has limited ability to help them see things that their audience isn't already talking about.

*Table 7.1* Advantages and disadvantages of publishing content as Facebook Instant Articles (by Steve Hill)

| Pros of Instant Articles | Cons of Instant Articles |
| --- | --- |
| Very fast on mobile | Reduced referral traffic to publisher's own website or blog |
| Highly convenient for the user – better reach and engagement (e.g. shares). | Weaker bond between publisher and audience |
| Rich storytelling – easy to embed video, photos, maps etc | Facebook algorithm controls presentation of content |

## Publishing using Facebook Instant Articles

Facebook Instant Articles allow you to host your content on Facebook's servers. There are a few good reasons why you may want to do this. As we have seen, one reason why some companies publish first to social media is that it brings them improved reach and better engagement. In short, this means more people are viewing our journalism.

Facebook Instant Articles help in two key ways: It optimizes our content for mobile on iOS and Android using the latest HTML5 technology (this is discussed later in the book). The fact that Facebook hosts our articles on its own servers and content is shown within the 'walled garden' of the Facebook app means that our content is also delivered very fast. Previously publishers shared links that would point to their external website.

Implementing Instant Articles technology is surprisingly straightforward and you don't need any technical knowhow. Simply set up a Facebook Page (you may well have this already) and, if you use WordPress, download a free Facebook Instant Articles for WP plugin (wordpress.org/plugins/fb-instant-articles) which converts your articles to the correct format.

## Conclusion

In truth, digital publishers have always used platforms – the World Wide Web itself is just a platform built on the infrastructure of the internet. But the shift from desktop to mobile consumption has also seen a shift from the open platform of the Web to platforms that are more closed, and whose technologies are more proprietary. The first wave of these mobile platforms, which crossed both desktop and mobile apps, was social; a second wave has seen mobile-native messaging platforms overtake those. And it could be argued that bots – used on both messaging platforms like Facebook Messenger and social platforms such as Twitter – represent a format which has yet to be fully explored.

Often overlooked, however, are other platforms. Games consoles, for example, already provide a platform for interacting with social media and on-demand video content, and some news publishers have experimented with consoles as a distribution network too. The arrival of virtual reality (VR) – facilitated by channels such as the Facebook-owned Oculus store – has been described by ex-*Guardian* and *New York Times* executive Aron Pilhofer as having the potential to be 'the most distributed form of journalism that we've seen yet' (Anderson 2017). And augmented reality (AR), which provides a visual overlay on top of what the user is seeing through their glasses or mobile camera, turns our very environment into a platform for content too.

Voice-driven platforms promise to be an interesting wave of platform development over the coming years: publishers are already building ways for users to interact with their content on platforms such as Amazon's Alexa, Google Home and Apple's Siri – not just in connected devices in our home and our cars but in our clothing, and ultimately our bodies – too.

With so many platforms the challenge will be not just how to create the best ways to engage with audiences, and the best platforms to do that, but having the best strategies behind those, the ways to measure their effectiveness and deciding when to change approach.

## Further reading

Bradshaw, P. (2017) *The Online Journalism Handbook*. (2nd ed.), Routledge.
This contains a chapter dedicated to writing for social media and chat platforms.
Anderson, K. (2017) *Beyond the Article: Frontiers of Editorial and Commercial Innovation*. Reuters Institute for the Study of Journalism, Available at: http://reutersinstitute.politics.ox.ac.uk/sites/default/files/Beyond%20the%20Article%20-%20Frontiers%20of%20Editorial%20and%20Commercial%20Innovation.pdf.
This provides insights into how different parts of the industry are responding to the challenges of platform publishing.

## References

Anderson, K. (2017) *Beyond the Article: Frontiers of Editorial and Commercial Innovation*. Reuters Institute for the Study of Journalism. Available at: http://reutersinstitute.politics.ox.ac.uk/sites/default/files/Beyond%20the%20Article%20-%20Frontiers%20of%20Editorial%20and%20Commercial%20Innovation.pdf.

Bell, E. (2016) Who owns the news consumer: social media platforms or publishers? *Columbia Journalism Review*. Available at: www.cjr.org/tow_center/platforms_and_publishers_new_research_from_the_tow_center.php.

Benes, R. (2017) Publishers say Facebook can save Instant Articles with better data, subscription tools. Digiday. Available at: https://digiday.com/media/save-facebook-instant-articles/.

Benton, J. (2015) A wave of distributed content is coming – will publishers sink or swim? NiemanLab, Available at: www.niemanlab.org/2015/03/a-wave-of-distributed-content-is-coming-will-publishers-sink-or-swim/.

BI Intellligence (2016) Messaging apps are now bigger than social networks. Business Insider. Available at: http://uk.businessinsider.com/the-messaging-app-report-2015-11.

Brown, P. (2017) Platforms and publishers: no sign of retreat. *Columbia Journalism Review*. Available at: www.cjr.org/tow_center/platforms-and-publishers-no-sign-of-retreat.php.

BuzzFeedPress (2014) BuzzFeed announces major expansion across all business lines. BuzzFeed. Available at: www.buzzfeed.com/buzzfeedpress/buzzfeed-announces-major-expansion-across-all-business-lines.

Carvin, A. (2014) Welcome to Reported.ly. Medium. Available at: https://medium.com/reportedly/welcome-to-reported-ly-3363a5fb7ea5.

Chartbeat (2017) The new speed of mobile engagement. Chartbeat, http://lp.chartbeat.com/TheNewSpeedofMobileEngagement_Download.html.

Cherubini, F., and Nielsen, R. K. (2016) *Editorial Analytics: How News Media are Developing and Using Audience Data and Metrics*. Reuters Institute for the Study of Journalism. Available at: https://reutersinstitute.politics.ox.ac.uk/sites/default/files/Editorial%20analytics%20-%20how%20news%20media%20are%20developing%20and%20using%20audience%20data%20and%20metrics.pdf.

Ciobanu, M. (2016) Distributed news: how NowThis reached one billion monthly video views on social. Journalism.co.uk. Available at: www.journalism.co.uk/news/distributed-news-how-nowthis-reached-one-billion-monthly-video-views-on-social-/s2/a612332/.

Cleary, I. (2017) The ultimate guide to using BuzzSumo. RazorSocial. Available at: www.razorsocial.com/buzzsumo/.

Dwyer, T. (2017) Sharing news online: social media news analytics and their implications for media pluralism policies. *Digital Journalism*, 5(8), 1080–1100. www.tandfonline.com/doi/full/10.1080/21670811.2017.1338527?ai=15148.

Dyson, S. (2014) *Newsroom 3.1: A Progress Report*. InPublishing. Available at: www.inpublishing.co.uk/kb/articles/newsroom_31__a_progress_report_1445.aspx.

Facebook for Developers (n.d.) Analytics for Instant Articles. Facebook for Developers. Available at: https://developers.facebook.com/docs/instant-articles/analytics.

Greenwood, S., Perrin, A., and Duggan, M. (2016) *Social Media Update 2016*. Pew Research Center, http://assets.pewresearch.org/wp-content/uploads/sites/14/2016/11/10132827/PI_2016.11.11_Social-Media-Update_FINAL.pdf.

Haik, C. (2016) Rise of the distributed domain. Tinius Trust. Available at: https://tinius.com/2016/05/18/rise-of-the-distributed-domain/.

Higgerson, D. (2016) Does a focus on audience metrics inevitably lead to clickbait? TheMediaBriefing. www.themediabriefing.com/article/does-a-focus-on-audience-metrics-inevitably-lead-to-clickbait.

Huddleston Jr, T. (2017) Facebook could be moving ahead with a subscription news service and paywall. Fortune. Available at: http://fortune.com/2017/07/19/facebook-subscription-news-service-paywall/.

Kalogeropoulos, A., and Newman, N. (2017) '*I saw the news on Facebook': Brand Attribution when Accessing News from Distributed Environments*. Reuters Institute for the Study of Journalism. Available at: http://reutersinstitute.politics.ox.ac.uk/sites/default/files/Brand%20attributions%20report.pdf.

Kramer, M. (2017) Pushing messaging platforms beyond their boundaries. Poynter. Available at: www.poynter.org/2017/pushing-messaging-platforms-beyond-their-boundaries/467182/.

Kulwin, N. (2015) This week on 'Re/code Decode': CEO Jonah Peretti explains how BuzzFeed won the internet (updated). Recode. Available at: www.recode.net/2015/9/16/11618618/this-week-on-recode-decode-ceo-jonah-peretti-explains-how-buzzfeed.

Lee, K. (2016) The biggest social media science study: what 4.8 million tweets say about the best time to tweet. Buffer Social. Available at: https://blog.bufferapp.com/best-time-to-tweet-research.

Liscio, Z. (2016) What networks does BuzzFeed actually use? Naytev Insights. Available at: http://blog.naytev.com/what-networks-does-buzzfeed-use/.

McLuhan, M. (1992) *Laws of Media: The New Science*. New ed. University of Toronto Press.

Marshall, S. (2013) Mobile-first: breaking news shifting focus to mobile. Journalism.co.uk. Available at: www.journalism.co.uk/news/mobile-first-breaking-news-developing-new-apps/s2/a552039/.

Marshall, J. (2016) The rise of the publishing platform specialist. *Wall Street Journal*. Available at: www.wsj.com/articles/the-rise-of-the-publishing-platform-specialist-1458896683.

Molyneux, L. (2017) Mobile news consumption: a habit of snacking. *Digital Journalism*. www.tandfonline.com/doi/abs/10.1080/21670811.2017.1334567.

Moses, L. (2016) The hidden (and not so hidden) costs of platform publishing. Digiday. Available at: http://digiday.com/publishers/hidden-not-hidden-costs-platform-publishing/.

Newman, N. (2017) *Journalism, Media and Technology Trends and Predictions 2017*. Reuters Institute for the Study of Journalism. Available at: http://reutersinstitute.politics.ox.ac.uk/publication/journalism-media-and-technology-trends-and-predictions-2017.

Newman, N., Fletcher, R., Kalogeropoulos, A., Levy, D. A. L., and Nielsen, R. K. (2017) *Reuters Institute Digital News Report 2017*. Reuters Institute for the Study of Journalism. Available at: https://reutersinstitute.politics.ox.ac.uk/sites/default/files/Digital%20News%20Report%202017%20web_0.pdf.

News Media Alliance (2017) News media alliance calls for legislation to address digital duopoly impact. News Media Alliance. Available at: www.newsmediaalliance.org/release-digital-duopoly/.

NewsWhip (2016) What should publishers and brands expect from social media in 2017? NewsWhip. Available at: www.newswhip.com/wp-content/uploads/2016/12/2017-Predictions-and-Advice-Report.pdf.

O'Reilly, L. (2017) A leaked report shows how much money publishers make from platforms like Facebook, Google, and Snapchat. Business Insider. Available at: http://uk.businessinsider.com/dcn-report-shows-publisher-revenue-from-google-facebook-snapchat-2017-1.

Petre, C. (2015) *The Traffic Factories: Metrics at Chartbeat, Gawker Media, and the New York Times*. Tow Center for Digital Journalism. Available at: http://towcenter.org/research/traffic-factories/.

Pfeiffer, A. (2015) The distributed content landscape: an overview for publishers – part 1. WAN-IFRA. https://blog.wan-ifra.org/2015/10/26/the-distributed-content-landscape-an-overview-for-publishers-part-1.

Ponsford, D. (2017) *Press Gazette* launches Duopoly campaign to stop Google and Facebook destroying journalism. *Press Gazette*. Available at: www.pressgazette.co.uk/press-gazette-launches-duopoly-campaign-to-stop-google-and-facebook-destroying-journalism/.

Sloane, G. (2015) Cosmo is getting 3 million readers a day on Snapchat Discover. Digiday UK. Available at: https://digiday.com/media/cosmo-says-getting-3-million-readers-snapchat-discover/.

Valeeva, A. (2017) Chat app Telegram, not much loved by the Russian government, still attracts a loyal readership for news. NiemanLab. Available at: www.niemanlab.org/2017/07/chat-app-telegram-not-much-loved-by-the-russian-government-still-attracts-a-loyal-readership-for-news/.

Varol, O., Ferrara, E., Davis, C. A., Menczer, F., and Flammini, A. (2017) Online human–bot interactions: detection, estimation, and characterization. Eleventh International AAAI Conference on Web and Social Media. https://aaai.org/ocs/index.php/ICWSM/ICWSM17/paper/view/15587/14817.

Wang, S. (2017) Facebook rules the internet in the Philippines: Rappler walks the line between partnership and criticism. NiemanLab. www.niemanlab.org/2017/07/facebook-rules-the-internet-in-the-philippines-rappler-walks-the-line-between-partnership-and-criticism/.

# 8   Publishing news to the Web

**This chapter will cover:**

- UX design
- Apple versus Google
- UX design – case studies
- The psychology of the user
- Design mistakes
- The mobile UX is different
- Responsive design
- Coding for journalists
- HTML5
- CSS
- Speed as a UX issue

## Introduction

Do journalists need to code? If we had a penny for every time we have been asked this, we could buy ourselves at least one expensive cappuccino per year.

There are arguments for and against. Do you need to know how to fix your car's ignition system or the power steering? Most of us leave it up to trained mechanics to fix things when they go wrong. Websites and apps can be complicated to code and some would say journalists don't need to understand how they work.

However, sticking with the car analogy, some would say as a responsible driver you should at least be able to change a tyre on the car or fill up the oil should you break down on the motorway. So in this chapter we look at the basics of languages such as HTML5 – Hypertext Markup Language version 5 and CSS – Cascading Style Sheets. It will help you to 'think like a developer' so you understand the strengths and limitations of the technology.

The debate over coding boils down to whether journalists need the skills to design and create interactive services, or whether they are solely content providers. In the UK it is more common for journalists to view coding as a useful, but not an essential skill.

But the concept of the 'code-friendly journalist' has gained traction in the USA. A survey by Tow-Knight Center (Stencel et al. 2016) found that the news industry's needs in the USA for coding skills fall into two categories:

- **Newsroom-friendly coders:** Those with an 'editorial sensibility to work with their journalist colleagues on everything from big editorial projects to publishing systems to new news products'.
- **Code-friendly journalists:** Those with 'development skills to build out editorial features and products on their own'. They will be working closely with the teams that control the brand's overall digital output.

Tow-Knight found that more than two-thirds (71 per cent) of the media companies said that coding and development skills were among their 'top five to 10 needs in the coming year'. This was particularly true for digital-only news operations, companies such as BuzzFeed, rather than older media companies.

Getting computer science (CS) and journalism students together in a room – as they do at 'hacks and hackers' meet-ups – is usually a rewarding experience for both sides. Journalists have the creative skills to produce multimedia content that is entertaining, educational and informative. We understand what appeals to our users.

CS students understand the possibilities and limitations of the key programming languages. As journalists we think in terms of word counts for stories and how images will look on the page. But there is a lot more to design than this. We need to think about better interactivity and personalisation on our news websites.

## UX design

User experience (abbreviated as UX) is how a person feels when interfacing with a system. The system could be a website, a web application or desktop software and, in modern contexts, is generally denoted by some form of human-computer interaction (HCI).

(Gube 2010)

If the UX is the overall feel of the website or app, then the user interface (UI) is the design and presentation. In an ideal world, you don't want users thinking about the interface at all. The best navigation mimics systems and designs that users are already familiar with from using other sites, apps and similar technologies. Another aspect of the UX is 'usability' – whether the website or app is easy to learn, efficient and pleasant to use.

Every product on the market – whether website, app or even a bottle of tomato ketchup – has a UX. It sounds strange, but ketchup is a classic example of UX product design. Heinz introduced ketchup in 1876 in a glass bottle. While relatively environmentally friendly, glass bottles had a poor UX. Getting

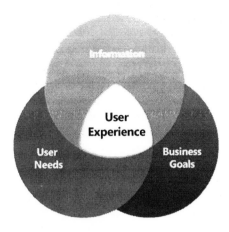

*Figure 8.1* The needs of the user compete with the business goals of the publisher
By Borys Kozielski/Wikimedia (CC BY 4.0)

the sauce to flow can be frustrating – it often involves large whacks to the base of the bottle or some serious knife poking. A century later, in 1987 to be precise, the company introduced squeezable plastic bottles. But getting the last drops of ketchup out was still tricky. In 2003 Heinz designed an upside-down plastic bottle which we use today. It squirts sauce not from the top, but its base, allowing the user to squeeze the last drops of sauce out. No whacking of the base required!

So it is possible to make design improvements even to the simplest of products. Obviously websites and apps are more complex than ketchup bottles, but you may wish to think of improvements you could make to the ones you access the most for news. Designers must also realise that by adding extra functionality to a website or app they can unintentionally make the UX worse. Websites can start with a logical and consistent design, but as new features are added over the years they can confuse the user.

Examples of a bad UX design:

A) Slow loading websites and apps
B) Websites that don't have responsive design – forcing users to pinch (zoom in) and scroll when viewing text on a mobile device
C) Apps that are plagued with annoying adverts
D) Frequently used navigation buttons placed in unusual places – like low down a page
E) News websites with either no search box (or a search that produces poor results)

*Figure* 8.2 The late Steve Jobs of Apple prioritised the user experience
By Matthew Yohe

## Apple versus Google

His many fans regard Steve Jobs, the late founder of Apple computers, as a UX guru. He stated in 2003 that people think that design is merely about appearance – the look of the product:

> People think it's this veneer – that the designers are handed this box and told, 'Make it look good!' That's not what we think design is. It's not just what it looks like and feels like. Design is how it works.
>
> (Steve Jobs in Walker 2003)

A great UX makes the user feel more intelligent because carrying out complex tasks feels easy and even fun.

Apple's focus on the user means that rivals have had to raise their game to compete in the mobile world. *The Economist* (2013) states Google has long 'had a reputation for caring far more about algorithms than aesthetics'.

## UX design – case studies

Designers talk about the 'needs' and 'wants' of the users. This is based on Maslow's hierarchy of human motivation, a theory in psychology that dates back to the 1940s. Steven Bradley (2010) states:

a design hierarchy of needs rests on the assumption that in order to be successful, a design must meet basic needs before it can satisfy higher-level needs. Before a design can 'Wow' us, it must work as intended. It must meet some minimal need or nothing else will really matter.

The aim is to create the best 'task flow' to cope with these needs. It looks at the user's objectives when they engage with a website or app – essentially what are they looking to achieve? Designers then map the steps that the user will need to take.

At this stage, it is worth considering a range of media experiences you may be familiar with. In each case it is worth looking at:

1.   What demographic is targeted? Typical age, gender, location and social class.
2.   What are the likely *needs* of the user? Define a single basic thing they want to achieve.
3.   What are the user's *wants*? What would make the experience more enjoyable or pleasant?
4.   What are the business needs of the publishers? The need to monetise content through adverts often leads to a poor UX and an unpleasant appearance.

Take a look at UX of a range of media products, not just news websites, to consider the likely *wants* and *needs* of a typical user.

## A) OK! – *a print magazine*

OK!, a celebrity magazine, was founded in 1993 and has a circulation of just under 200,000 copies a week (ABC circulation figures, Ponsford 2017). The magazine consists of full-page photos of celebrities – their homes and weddings – and is aspirational in tone. A print magazine is a tactile experience where the quality of paper matters. Upmarket magazines tend to be printed on thicker paper. Unlike websites, a print magazine is a linear experience, i.e. designed to be browsed in a leisurely way, usually from front-to-back.

## B) Match.com – *a dating site*

Match was founded in 1995 and is a global online dating website with three million users based in the UK (Munbodh 2018). It's an example of a database-driven interactive site. Users come to the site with a single specific *need* – i.e. they wish to meet a partner. A successful interaction on Match.com is never having to use the site ever again! Although users *want* the browsing of profiles to be a fun and rewarding experience.

## C) Gov.uk – *UK government site*

'The Paul Smith of websites' is how the judges at the Design of the Year Awards described this unexciting government website (BBC 2013). Gov.uk won the top prize for its 'understated design' and 'subtly British look' that reminded them of Paul Smith, the famous British fashion designer. But applying for a passport or paying taxes is never a pleasure and always a chore. Gov.uk has also been criticised for its complex navigation and endless requests for user feedback.

## The psychology of the user

Whatever media outlet you work for, try to get into the mind of your user. If you have designed a website or app yourself, chances are its navigation and layout will make complete sense to you. But a key aspect of taking a user-centred approach is to consider how first-time visitors are likely to see your site. Some key questions include:

- What is their motivation to visit our site?
- How quickly can they find what they want?
- What habits are created if they do this action over and over?
- What do they expect to see when they click particular links?
- Are you assuming they know something that they haven't learned yet?

### Testing, testing, 1, 2, 3 ...

The only way to achieve a great UX is to continually test our sites and apps. This may involve using special software, doing online surveys or running focus groups with our users.

Software that can help:

- **Google Analytics (analytics.google.com)**

  This tracks a user's location, device (e.g. mobile/Mac etc), how they found us (e.g. search engine or social media) and our most popular stories.

- **Google Webmaster Tools (google.com/webmasters)**

  From 2013 Google has been penalising slow to load websites and those which or work poorly on mobile devices. But install the free Webmaster Tools and it will suggest usability improvements to your site which will help you improve your search ranking and deliver a better experience.

- **Hotjar (hotjar.com)**

  **CrazyEgg (crazyegg.com)**

  **Chartbeat (chartbeat.com/)**

  These three tools come under the category of 'content intelligence'. They provide tools that allow us to explore what people are looking at on our sites to establish visitor motivation and desires. You can see what people are clicking or tapping on in real time. Chartbeat include heat maps – which show which parts of each web page are looked at most and the areas of the site that are getting few visitors.

## Design mistakes

Print journalists are trained to regard the front page as being prime real estate and a very important selling tool. Hours are spent selecting striking images and writing attention-grabbing cover lines for magazines. Similarly, in print newspapers much emphasis is still placed on the front-page splash – ideally, you want it to be an exclusive story that will stand out in the shops and sell papers.

But it is a massive mistake to view a web page or app as having a UX even remotely similar to a print product.

Espen Sundve (2017), a developer, states:

> We create pieces of [web] content meant for everyone, and manually curate our front pages. This works very well when everyone is on the same level and are interested equally in the same content – but they're not. People consume continuously and have different prior knowledge, interest, context and user modes.

In this respect it is easy to see how media publishers have taken the traditions of content publishing in print and moved them online.

1. Old print user experience – moved to a desktop user experience
2. Desktop user experience – now ported to responsive mobile web pages
3. Mobile web pages – ported to apps

This process is often a simple re-engineering of content from one platform to the next. Although there are publishers who are breaking the porting of content cycle, with BuzzFeed, the *Guardian* and *The Economist* deserving special mention for their innovative approaches.

We will often browse a printed newspaper or magazine from front-to-back. We access news online at a much more granular level – i.e. by following a link to an individual story which has been found via a search engine or shared with us via social media. We bypass the front page of a website entirely. So what is the point of website homepages?

A study by Parse.ly calculated the percentage of article referrals generated by the homepage. It found:

> For over half of publishers, this number was less than 10 per cent, indicating that they rely more heavily on social or search referrals than homepage referrals.
>
> (Bennett 2017)

Users rarely engage with website home pages – unless the news has very strong brand loyalty such as the BBC News site.

The Parse.ly survey found that when people accessed homepages they tended to focus on news that appeared at the top. They were very unlikely to scroll down. Dramatic images and headlines would improve click-through rates for top-placed stories.

### Online advertising as a cause of bad UX

No director has ever set out to create a bad movie and no designer goes out of their way to create a terrible website or app with a frustrating UX – it just happens. A frequent problem is that those all-important needs and wants of users conflict with the business needs of the publisher. We've said that generating revenue from journalism online is challenging, News websites can make money through online banner advertising or sponsored content, although both can be bad for the user experience.

Advertising, by definition, is designed to interrupt the content consumption process in some way. Commercials on TV interrupt the viewing experience when they come on. So viewers will take the opportunity to make a cup of tea or use the bathroom. Readers of printed newspapers and magazines are used to seeing display adverts and don't find them too troubling.

But we have all had to cope with annoying online adverts. It is very irritating to have to manually close a pop-up advert that appears on our mobile screen. And don't get us started on autoplay video adverts, which suddenly blast out music from our computers. These adverts really annoy users as they can't be controlled and often appear unexpectedly.

Users are taking revenge on annoying online adverts by installing ad-blocker software. AdBlock Plus (adblockplus.org) is a popular tool. At the time of writing, Google has said it will include ad-blocking software in the latest version of its Chrome browser and, worryingly for news sites, it will be switched on by default. Sridhar Ramaswamy, Google's senior VP of ads and commerce, states:

> It's far too common that people encounter annoying, intrusive ads on the web – like the kind that blares music unexpectedly, or forces you to wait 10 seconds before you can see the content on the page.
>
> (Sulleyman 2017)

Ad-blocking software presents a major threat to the commercial viability of news websites. So what are news sites to do? In Sweden, publishers experimented with the rather drastic step of collectively blocking all content from people who use ad-blockers and slowed down their viewing of online videos. Jason Kint, of Digital Content Next, states:

> Collectively frustrating your consumers who are clearly demonstrating there is a problem in the ecosystem doesn't seem like a smart way out of this mess.
>
> (Southern 2016)

Another way news sites attempt to generate much needed revenue is through sponsored or branded content. This is content that is partly funded by advertisers and has been a key revenue source. However, this too raises UX issues. Sponsored or branded content must be identified in such a way that users understand that it is paid for by a company and is different to normal editorial content. Having too much sponsored content can undermine the credibility of the news site.

Annoying the user is *always* bad news and mobile adverts can be especially irritating. The needs and wants of users often conflict with the business needs of the publisher leading to a poor experience.

## The mobile UX is different

Mobile design is an exciting and emerging field. There are few established design conventions and this means that users often have to learn new ways to navigate.

Smartphones and tablets are different to desktop computers. 'There's an emotional reaction with a personalised mobile device that you don't get with a mouse and a keyboard', explains Jon Wiley (*The Economist* 2013), a search designer who is part of an initiative to revamp Google's design philosophy.

We personalise our phones in a bewildering range of ways from the apps we choose to install, the wallpaper and even the case of the phone. The touchscreen of a phone makes the experience very tactile. We have learned to navigate by tapping, pinching and swiping rather than by using a mouse.

We use mobile devices on the sofa at home, but also on the go in environments that are noisy. There may be multiple distractions, poor connectivity to their mobile network provider and low lighting. We often glance at and scan our

*Figure* 8.3  Navigating a phone using a touchscreen is a tactile experience
By Stevepb/Pixnio

mobiles rather than reading content in detail. This means that our websites and apps must be simple to navigate and fast to load.

### Designing for mobile

Lyndon Cerejo (2012), a user experience strategist, writing in Smashing Magazine, lists 12 key elements of the mobile user experience:

1. Functionality
2. Information Architecture
3. Content
4. Design
5. User Input
6. Mobile Context
7. Usability
8. Trustworthiness
9. Feedback
10. Help
11. Social
12. Marketing

It is well worth reading the full article by Lyndon Cerejo, 'The elements of the mobile user experience' (smashingmagazine.com/2012/07/elements-mobile-user-experience).

### Interaction and personalisation

We like news apps that provide a interactive and personalised experience; sadly many news apps are read-only. News apps could learn from Netflix which is constantly learning about the types of TV shows we like to watch and provides a personalised and interactive recommendation system.

People take little notice of the platforms they use to consume content. Rather they enjoy moving seamlessly between desktop, tablet laptop, TV, mobile and radio throughout the day. They use the device that is most convenient at any given moment without giving it much thought.

### Navigation bars

App navigation bars have to be clear and it is worth studying a range of apps on your phone to examine their primary and secondary navigation systems. It is easy to get 'lost' when using an app. Lyndon Cerejo (2012) advises:

> Provide navigational cues to let users know where they are, how to get back and how to jump back to the start. Mobile breadcrumbs are often

implemented by replacing the 'Back' button with a label showing users the section or category that they came from.

He writes that for mobile websites conventions include using a 'home' icon to link back to the start screen. This is especially important when navigation isn't repeated on every screen. On mobile websites menu systems can automatically condense into a non-descriptive three-lined button. Designers refer to it as a 'hamburger' or 'navigation draw' due to its layered appearance.

Raluca Budiu (2015) a usability expert writes:

> Making navigation important and accessible is a challenge on mobile due to the limitations of the small screen and to the need of prioritizing the content over the UI elements. Different basic navigation patterns attempt to solve this challenge in different ways that all suffer from a variety of usability problems.

BBC Mobile Accessibility (n.d.) states: 'Ensure that material that is central to the meaning of the page precedes material that is not.'

### Obey principles of online journalism

Ensure text on the page obeys the key rules of online journalism writing. Are the most important headlines in the largest text size? Use chunking techniques to break up long articles. Chunking involves using short paragraphs and subheads (titles within the text) to divide up longer articles.

Keep your sentences short in news articles – around 15–20 words is good practice. The reader feels as if they are progressing through your text faster when you use shorter sentences.

Bullet point lists often work well on small smartphone screens. The *Daily Mail* website uses this technique. Video stories should include the option of captions. This is essential for deaf and hard of hearing users. But it also means that people don't need the sound up to understand video content. Facebook can add captions automatically, although do check spellings.

### When designing apps, follow guidelines from Apple and Android closely

Dave Feldman (2014) writes:

> Great design is a synthesis of art and science, of aesthetics, usability and a deep understanding of user needs and behaviours. To succeed, we need a balance. Beauty that isn't part of holistic, effective product design will be wasted.

Apple (developer.apple.com/design) provides designers with strict interface guidelines for designing for its mobile operating system iOS. Here is a sample of its advice (Apple n.d.):

*Clarity:*

> Throughout the system, text is legible at every size, icons are precise and lucid, adornments are subtle and appropriate, and a sharpened focus on functionality motivates the design. Negative space, colour, fonts, graphics, and interface elements subtly highlight important content and convey interactivity.

In a section on 'deference' it says that 'translucency and blurring' often hint at more. Limit the use of gradients, and drop shadows to keep the interface 'light and airy'. The aim is to highlight the key content.

Android (developer.android.com) also sets out rules for designers of apps.

## Provide a text editor

Unlike shopping sites, news sites usually don't demand the user inputs text into forms. If a user has to type text on a phone it is well worth providing a text editor that allows auto-completion, a spellchecker and predictive technology. As anyone who has ever had to file an article longer than, say, 300 words from a mobile phone knows, typing on a touchscreen is a frustrating experience and it's easy to make mistakes.

## Real-world usage

This aspect takes into account how people use mobile devices in the wild (i.e. in real life). As we have mentioned before, people use their mobiles when they are bored e.g. when they are waiting for the train or bus. We would like to see news apps exploit location-based functionality, where a user wants to find out what is going on around them, e.g. a recommended movie. Google's location-based service Google Now, has filled a gap in the market where news apps should be.

## Ease of use and usefulness

Usability is the engineering science that looks overall at how usable and useful a website or app is to achieve specific objectives. 'We don't figure out how things work. We muddle through' writes usability guru Steve Krug (2000) in his classic text *Don't Make me Think: A Common Sense Approach to Web Usability*.

## How trustworthy?

Most news apps aim to appear trustworthy. If your app collects personal data (e.g. location) you need the user to have tapped the button to say they agree with this. Aside from the quality of the journalism, does the design of the app suggest trustworthiness? A consistent selection of fonts, colours and images can improve this.

*News alerts*

Feedback is information sent from a website or app back to the user. It could be a vibration of the phone – known as haptic feedback – which signifies the user has pressed a button on their touchscreen. We can use 'alerts' that pop up on the screen of a smartphone, tablet and on smartwatches to tell users about breaking news. Users often like this form of feedback, but it should be used sparingly. Alerts need to be relevant, brief and clear. Be aware of times that the user is likely to be sleeping – alerts sent through smartwatches can be very disruptive if people are in bed. So give users the ability to silence alerts at night or when they are busy.

*Contact us*

This is not so much an issue for news providers, but users should be able to contact both the editorial team and the web development team to provide feedback and get help with using the app.

*Social*

You can embed social media into apps easily. APIs (application programming interfaces) are a set of a set of functions and procedures that link apps to the database of the social media provider and are discussed in Chapter 9 on apps.

## Responsive design

Most media publishers will need a responsive website that works on mobile devices, even if they also have a dedicated mobile app. Responsive websites are designed in HTML and CSS in such a way they automatically adjust their layout, image and text sizes to the screen size of the user's device, operating system and how the device is held (the orientation).

Web designer Ethan Marcotte came up with the concept of responsive design in 2010. You can read his original blog post – Responsive Web Design (alistapart.com/article/responsive-web-design).

In the past, designers assumed that most people would view our sites on desktop and laptop computers and a width of 960 pixels (PX) was a standard size. The rise of the iPhone changed all this. Viewing a site designed for desktop with fixed widths on a small mobile screen involves lots of pinching (zooming in and out) and scrolling – so a poor user experience. Responsive designs uses percentages of screen size as a measurement tool – meaning that the sites are easily viewable on small phone screens.

Responsive design demands more work than fixed width web design as you cannot predict precisely the user experience. Designer Dan Scott (2014) states:

> There are literally hundreds of different possible scenarios of how a user could be using your website. This comes down to the number of smartphones

and tablets out there with their varying screen sizes, resolutions and input types. They could even be using their televisions.

The good news is that most modern professionally designed WordPress themes (the website template) are designed to be responsive. However, you will want to test your site on a smartphone and tablet just to be sure. You can also test your site to see how mobile friendly it is using a free Google tool (google.com/webmasters/tools/mobile-friendly).

---

### Know your widths

Designers have to be aware of the viewport – this is the visible area of a web page and of course this will vary with different screen sizes and devices. The website MyDevice (mydevice.io) lists device sizes, viewports and resolution for a vast range of smartphone and tablet devices and suggests appropriate CSS to include in your page.

---

### Case study: WordPress powers large news websites

Once considered a rather basic blogging platform, today WordPress CMS (content management system) powers some very large newspaper sites. The *Sun* (thesun.co.uk) newspaper in the UK switched to it in 2016 as it provided much better story SEO (search engine optimisation) than its more expensive CMS rivals.

*Metro* (metro.co.uk), the free newspaper, moved to a responsive WordPress design. Martin Ashplant, then head of digital at *Metro*, said the move transformed its traffic and it soon became fastest growing UK national newspaper website.

Ashplant states that while *Metro* has a desktop website, it worked very poorly on mobile and 'the page views per visit were horrendous and the dwell time was horrendous as well'. He adds: 'My preference would always be [to] focus on mobile because that's where the growth is, that's where the audience is, that's where it's going to increase in the next few years' (Ponsford 2014).

---

### Coding for journalists

Most CMSs have a design or visual editor which takes a WYSIWYG approach to layout or What You See Is What You Get. So there is no need to get your hands dirty with code. It is in this part of the CMS where online journalists spend most of their working days.

But occasionally you'll find your articles are not showing as well as they should on your smartphone or tablet or text or images are not formatted correctly. At this point it helps to view the raw HTML code. To do this in WordPress you switch from visual editor to the text or code editor in the CMS. So it helps to be able to understand code, even if you never actually design a site yourself.

Responsive websites are created using a combination of:

- HTML – hypertext markup language
- CSS – cascading style sheets

HTML is the framework of the web page and CSS provides the design elements. This is so essential to understand, that we will repeat this:

- HTML = framework (the structure)
- CSS = design (the presentation)

It is possible to design web pages in HTML, but this method is considered old-fashioned and inefficient.

## Hypertext Markup Language (HTML)

Here comes a random bit of HTML:

```
<h3><span style='font-weight: 400;'>Emily* is an 18-year-old girl who
loves Facebook and Instagram. She's been on social media for most of her
teen years, and enjoys scrolling Instagram for funny videos and photos her
friends post. </span></h3>
```

The great thing about HTML is that it has common sense logic to it. In other words, you may be able to guess what the above HTML does.

The H3 HTML 'tag' means Heading 3. The HTML <span> tag is used for grouping and applying styles to inline elements. Tags have to be opened and closed – note the use of the forward-slash (/) to close tags. The font-weight CSS describes how thick or thin characters in the text should appear.

Published in 2014 after ten years in development, HTML5 was created to improve how websites run on mobile devices, which are relatively low-powered compared with laptops. It was an important development for us as journalists, as it improves the way that multimedia material, particularly video, was embedded into web pages.

The website of HTML5: The Web Platform (platform.html5.org) shows precisely what it can do.

### HTML5 and video

Watching online video on a phone used to be a frustrating experience. Before HTML5, Flash was a common way that animation and videos were embedded into web pages. The late Apple boss, Steve Jobs, hated Flash so much he even banned it from running on Apple devices! Jobs said it was battery hogging, crash-prone and presented security issues. Many Flash videos behave inconsistently when reduced in size on small mobile screens. Banning Flash on Apple devices was a problem at the time as YouTube displayed videos in Flash and, for a brief period, it didn't work on Apple devices.

Eventually Adobe, the company that created Flash, threw in the towel and admitted that HTML 5 was 'the best solution for creating and deploying content in the browser across mobile platforms' (Winokur 2011).

An HTML5 page with video looks like this:

```
<!DOCTYPE html>
<html>
  <head>
  <title>Adding HTML 5 Video to a Web Page</title>
  </head>
  <body>
  <video   width='400'   height='300'   loop="   controls="   preload="
      poster='images/dog.jpg' src='video/dog.mp4'></video>
  </body>
</html>
```

So what does the code mean?

<!DOCTYPE> – an instruction to the web browser that the web the page is written in HTML.
<html> – this is the start of the HTML code.
<head> this is a container for metadata (data about data. The <title> element defines a title in the browser tab and displays a title for the page in search engine results.
<body> – is the content of the document…

Now onto the video bit:

<video> specifies a movie clip or video stream e.g an .MP4 file.
<audio> can link to audio files in .MP3,.WAV or similar audio formats.
Loop – Video should replay once it has ended. Looping is sometimes used in online adverts and can be quite annoying.
Controls – when used, it says that the video should have its own controls for playback.

Preload – This attribute tells the browser what to do when the page loads
Poster – this is a still image that will show when the video is downloading.
Src – is where the video can be found on the web host.

It may sound strange, but we don't recommend hosting video unless you have
a large budget for a good server. Instead, upload your videos to your YouTube
channel and then embed the video onto your website page. Once your video
file is uploaded to YouTube it can be imported as an inline frame. The <iframe>
tag is used to embed your video within your website page. Here is an example:

```
<iframe    width='560'    height='315'    src='www.youtube.com/embed/
FrLequ5dUdM' frameborder='0' allowfullscreen></iframe>
```

Having your videos hosted on YouTube, but showing on your web page, will give
your video extra visibility as many people will see your video on YouTube rather than
your news site. Users can still play the video off your web page, even in full screen.

### Semantic elements of HTML5

HTML5 introduced semantic elements – these are bits of code that describe their
meaning not only to the browser (e.g. Google Chrome, which must read the
page), but also to the creator.

Designers are encouraged to divide up their page using new semantic elements
that describe the kind of content to anyone who needs to know – be they human
or machine. Examples of semantic elements introduced by HTML5 are <form>,
<table> and, most importantly for journalists, <article>. These were designed to
have self-explanatory names and this makes HTML5 code easier to understand.

## Cascading Style Sheets (CSS)

HTML and Cascading Style Sheets (CSS) are a double act – they work together
to produce attractive web pages. You can implement 'inline CSS' to set up rules
about how the content of an element should be displayed. A straightforward way
to learn CSS is to start small by designing short email newsletters which use
inline CSS for design.

However, most large sites use 'external CSS' rules – these provide instructions
on how things like headlines, text and navigation and many other page elements
are designed. You may be able to view the CSS for your own WordPress site by
accessing the theme section.

It is common to have to change some element of design on your WordPress
news site, so you may find yourself tinkering with the CSS. It aims to save the
designer time. In the past, if you wanted to change say the font style or size of a
headline you had to go through every page on a website manually. On large news

sites this process was slow and laborious. With external CSS rules you can change the look of an entire news website just by changing the CSS once.

CSS styles are usually applied to specific HTML elements on a page – so text in an article will be styled up differently to that in a navigation bar for example.

There are many different types of CSS 'selectors' that allows you to target rules at specific elements on a web page. MDN Web Docs provides a handy list (developer.mozilla.org/en-US/docs/Web/CSS/CSS_Selectors).

CSS also helps with responsive design as rules can cleverly take into account the visible area of a web page, the viewport. Designers use percentages of the visible screen for widths, rather than fixed pixels.

Designers can add things called 'breakpoints' where certain parts of the design will behave differently on each side of the breakpoint, e.g. when a browser width reaches a certain small size you could change the text's column width.

Peter Gasston (2013) states designers should act 'mobile first':

> start with a set of styles that's served to all devices – such as colour, typography, iconography, and so on – as well as the minimal layout rules required for a small-screen device … For anyone using an even larger device, add extra rules and so on, until you've catered to a core set of devices.

Here we have only given the briefest introduction to HTML and CSS for responsive design on mobile. For those who want more detail, there are many excellent free resources online:

- **Code Academy** (codecademy.com) – free online courses in HTML and CSS.
- **W3Schools** (w3schools.com)
- **CSS Cheat Sheet** (onblastblog.com/css3-cheat-sheet/)
- **Responsive Design Weekly** (responsivedesignweekly.com) – a newsletter

One of the best ways to learn is by viewing the code of a story you have written in a CMS. Does it make sense? Is there any code that can be deleted that will speed up delivery of the page? You can also view the CSS in the themes section, but take care when making changes here. A slight change in the CSS can radically change the look of an entire site for the worse!

## Speed as a UX issue

Who enjoys waiting for a website to load on their phone? Answer: nobody! Data from Chartbeat, a website intelligence company, show that more than half of us spend 15 seconds or less looking at the average web page. So it is perhaps unsurprising that users are unwilling to wait more than three or four seconds for a page to load (Haile 2014).

So what causes slow speeds?

### Bad mobile networks

There are two key issues here – availability of internet access and speed.

A digital divide, a gap between the information-rich and information-poor, exists in some parts of the UK, with those living in rural areas (particularly in south-west England, central Wales and north Scotland) struggling to get high-speed mobile data connections.

'The average overall 4G availability across the UK is 65 per cent meaning mobile users can only access 4G nearly two-thirds of the time. This puts the UK at just 54th in the world, behind Estonia and Peru' (Woollaston 2017). South Korea has some of the fastest average 4G connections (Wong 2017).

4G is rolling out across Africa, but there is a disparity between countries, with Egypt, Nigeria and South Africa together accounting for around a third of the total subscriber base (GSMA 2016).

Pingdom (tools.pingdom.com) allows you to see how your site is responding when accessed in various cities throughout the world.

### Badly designed websites

While we have little control over mobile speeds, we can improve our sites and apps. Usability guru Jakob Nielsen (2010) states:

> Even a few seconds' delay is enough to create an unpleasant user experience … Instead of big images, today's big response-time sinners are typically overly complex data processing on the server or overly fancy widgets on the page (or *too many* fancy widgets).

There are many reasons for poor website and apps:

A) **Cheap hosting** – Two things really matter when choosing a host (the servers your site resides on) – uptime and speed. The good news is that even cheap hosting providers offer good uptime these days, i.e. your website will at least be available to view most of the time. But some cheaper hosting providers jam pack too many websites onto their hosting servers, which can slow all their sites down.

B) **Too many social media widgets** – Despite improved speeds of broadband, websites are actually getting slower. Third-party connections (known as plugins, that offer extra functionality) that need to connect to Google, Facebook or Twitter etc can slow things down. Use social media plugins sparingly.

C) **Large images** – Mobile users hate downloading large images as it takes up their data. So journalists should crunch down their image sizes in Photoshop *before* uploading to the CMS.

D) **Minify your CSS**

Special plugins for WordPress will remove all unnecessary characters from your CSS and HTML code. You could also cache your site using a CDN (Content Delivery Network), a decentralized group of data centres.

E) **Test, test and test your site again**

Google PageSpeed Insight (developers.google.com/speed/pagespeed/insights) allows you to check your speeds and can improve even the most sluggish of news websites.

Google, Facebook and Medium provide tools to optimize news content for mobile delivery.

### Google AMP

**What is it?** Google's Accelerated Mobile Pages, or AMP for short, reformats your content to the faster AMP HTML. The free plugin for WordPress – AMP for WP – will make your site AMP compatible.

**The good:** Your website pages are cached by Google to allow it to be delivered faster to the user.

**The bad:** It places strict limitations on advertising and tracking technology which slow up sites.

### Facebook Instant Articles

**What is it?** Facebook hosts your content on your behalf, in a format that's made for faster display in the Facebook mobile app. The plugin – Instant Articles for WP – will make your WordPress content compatible.

**The good:** Rather than loading an article using a web browser, which Facebook says takes over eight seconds on average, Instant Articles loads it using the faster Facebook app.

**The bad:** Unlike AMP, this only works with Facebook. It won't speed up how your site works on the mobile web. Critics say Facebook is using Instant Articles to secure its dominance in news.

### Medium

Medium (medium.com) is a free, easy and popular way to publish news content and there is no coding required. There are many benefits – articles appear very fast on mobile as it automatically formats content for both AMP and Instant Articles. The Medium is responsive by default – so your articles will be easy to read on mobile devices.

The price of keeping your site fast and easy? It only allows limited design or advertising options. This is off-platform publishing, so your content is in the hands of a third-party company.

## Conclusion

We advocate an approach that is user-centred. This means both editorial (our journalism) and design (the presentation and layout of articles) is targeted to a clearly defined user. You should establish the needs and wants of your user. When in doubt, just ask them by inviting them to take part in a survey. You can also learn much from analysing data from Google Analytics.

The main advice in this chapter is simple – don't annoy the user. This all sounds very obvious, right? So why do so many new apps get such poor reviews? Users are not necessarily like journalists or designers. They may be older and less technically literate than the journalists who are creating the content. So UX design requires that we go out of our way to deliver the type of content they find useful and in an appropriate format that makes sense to them.

The business needs of the media company often take priority over the needs and wants of users. Most people hate autoplay video ads, but newspaper websites are notorious for including them as they do generate revenue.

The damage a poor UX does to trustworthiness and reputation of the brand can be immense. Users vote with their feet and will avoid visiting poorly designed websites and apps a second time.

## Further reading

BBC Global Experience Language (bbc.co.uk/gel).
It offers plenty of tips for improving trustworthiness through a consistent design.
Creative Blog (creativebloq.com).
Design news website from Future Publishing.
Smashing Magazine (smashingmagazine.com).
Has numerous guides to mobile design.

## References

Allsopp, J. (2000) A Dao of web design, A List Apart the full. A List Apart. Available at: https://alistapart.com/article/dao.

Apple (n.d.) Overview – iOS human interface guidelines. Available at: https://developer.apple.com/ios/human-interface-guidelines/overview/themes/.

BBC Mobile Accessibility (n.d.) User experience. BBC. Available at: www.bbc.co.uk/guidelines/futuremedia/accessibility/mobile/user-experience.

BBC News (2013) Gov.UK wins design of the year award. www.bbc.co.uk/news/entertainment-arts-22164715.

Bennett, B. D. (2017) What is the value of the homepage? The Drum. Available at: www.thedrum.com/news/2018/01/02/parsely-bites-what-the-value-the-homepage.

Bradley, S. (2010) Designing for a hierarchy of needs. Smashing Magazine. Available at: www.smashingmagazine.com/2010/04/designing-for-a-hierarchy-of-needs/.

Budiu, R. (2015) Basic patterns for mobile navigation. Nielsen Norman Group. Available at: www.nngroup.com/articles/mobile-navigation-patterns/.

Cerejo, L. (2012) The elements of the mobile user experience. Smashing Magazine. Available at: www.smashingmagazine.com/2012/07/elements-mobile-user-experience/.

Feldman, D. (2014) Think your app is beautiful? Not without user experience design. *Smashing Magazine*. Available at: www.smashingmagazine.com/2014/09/think-your-app-is-beautiful-not-without-user-experience-design/.

Gasston, P. (2013) *The Modern Web: Multi-Device Web Development with HTML5, CSS3, and JavaScript*. No Starch Press.

GSMA (2016) Number of unique mobile subscribers in Africa surpasses half a billion, finds new GSMA study. Available at: www.gsma.com/newsroom/press-release/number-of-unique-mobile-subscribers-in-africa-surpasses-half-a-billion-finds-new-gsma-study/.

Gube, J. (2010) What is user experience design? Overview, tools and resources. *Smashing Magazine*. Available at: www.smashingmagazine.com/2010/10/what-is-user-experience-design-overview-tools-and-resources/.

Haile, T. (2014) What you get wrong about the internet. *Time magazine*. Available at: http://time.com/12933/what-you-think-you-know-about-the-web-is-wrong/.

Krug, S. (2000) *Don´t Make me Think: A Common Sense Approach to Web Usability*. Circle.com Library.

Munbodh, E. (2018) Best online dating websites in the UK. *Mirror*. Available at: www.mirror.co.uk/money/best-online-dating-websites-2018-5220768?service=responsive.

Nielsen, J. (2010) Website response times (no date). Nielsen Norman Group. Available at: www.nngroup.com/articles/website-response-times/.

Ponsford, D. (2014) News on the move: how BBC is going mobile-first ... Metro's online success story ... Why *Times* is reader-first, not digital-first. *Press Gazette*. Available at: www.pressgazette.co.uk/news-move-how-bbc-going-mobile-firstmetros-online-success-storywhy-times-reader-first-not-digital/.

Ponsford, D. (2017) UK magazine ABCs: winners, losers and full breakdown as circulation declines average 6 per cent. *Press Gazette*. Available at: www.pressgazette.co.uk/uk-magazine-abcs-winners-losers-and-full-breakdown-as-circulation-declines-average-6-per-cent/.

Rao, R. (2016) Between the lines: coders and developers. Tow-Knight. Available at: http://towknight.org/research/superpowers/between-the-lines-coders-and-developers/.

Scott, D. (2014) The five golden rules of responsive web design. Econsultancy. Available at: https://econsultancy.com/blog/64823-the-five-golden-rules-of-responsive-web-design.

Southern, M. (2016) Sweden's publishers are joining forces to simultaneously block ad-block users. Digiday. Available at: https://digiday.com/uk/swedens-publishers-gearing-block-ad-blockers/.

Stencel, M., et al, (2016) Between the lines: coders and developers. Tow-Knight. Available at: http://towknight.org/research/superpowers/between-the-lines-coders-and-developers/.

Sulleyman, A. (2017) Google confirms controversial Chrome ad blocker plans. *Independent*. Available at: www.independent.co.uk/life-style/gadgets-and-tech/news/google-chrome-ad-blocker-launch-date-advertising-experience-report-2018-revenue-marketing-a7769441.html.

Sundve, E. (2017) Next generation publishing products. Tinius Trust. Available at: https://tinius.com/2016/05/18/next-generation-publishing-products/.

*The Economist* (2013) Don't be ugly. Available at: www.economist.com/news/business/21573160-web-giant-wants-be-known-beauty-well-brains-dont-be-ugly.

Walker, R. (2003) The guts of a new machine. *New York Times*. Available at: www.nytimes.com/2003/11/30/magazine/the-guts-of-a-new-machine.html.

Winokur, D. (2011) Adobe to more aggressively contribute to HTML5. Adobe News. Available at: https://blogs.adobe.com/conversations/2011/11/flash-focus.html.

Wong, J. (2017) The countries with the world's fastest mobile internet. Quartz. Available at: https://qz.com/915726/the-countries-with-the-worlds-fastest-mobile-internet/.

Woollaston, V. (2017) The UK's best and worst cities for 4G revealed. Wired UK Available at: www.wired.co.uk/article/4g-uk-speeds.

# 9 Building news apps

## Introduction

The aim of the Breaking News + app to be the 'fastest source for breaking news in the world' was definitely ambitious. Harnessing the power of GPS, it claimed to break news on average 14 minutes before other news brands. Those who had installed the app on their phone or smartwatch were informed of breaking news happening around them in real time. But what made it special is that the app allowed users also to report threats such as accidents, earthquakes or even terrorist attacks to its community of users.

The app was excellent, but was eventually scuppered by poor revenue. App owners NBC News Digital, the US TV network giant, closed it in 2016. The story of Breaking News highlights how it's not enough simply to build a popular and innovative app, it has to make money.

This chapter looks at how to launch a news app or magazine digital editions on mobile devices. Many large media brands, such as the *Guardian* and *The Economist*, have both downloadable news apps and separate digital editions of their print publications. These two types of app serve different needs and wants of their users. The Apple Store launched in 2008 with just 800 apps. To date

(May 2017) there are over two million apps of which the majority are for iPad or iPhone. But there are around 10,000 for the Apple Watch and 8,000 for Apple TV, the set-top box. There are even more apps listed in the Google Play store for Android devices (Costello 2018).

If you think all the best app ideas have gone, think again. The app market is just over ten years old. New Internet of Things (IoT) devices – internet connected cars, TVs, washing machines and fridges, etc – are launching all the time. Some of these IoT devices are very suitable for the consumption of and interaction with journalism content.

In the 2013 film *Her*, the character of Theodore (played by Joaquin Phoenix) develops a relationship with an intelligent computer operating system, personified through a female voice known as Samantha (voiced by Scarlett Johansson).

Technology today isn't quite as advanced as what is imagined in *Her* – computers haven't mastered emotional intelligence, yet. However, basic artificial intelligence (AI) – that is, intelligence displayed by machines, rather than natural intelligence of humans – is becoming more commonplace. The BBC, Sky, the *Telegraph* and *Guardian* are creating content and services for a range of voice-controlled smart speaker devices from the likes of Amazon, Google and Apple. While the level of human to computer interaction is primitive, it will get better.

This chapter looks at app ideas that can harness the unique features of mobile technology to tell stories in new personalised, localised, immersive or interactive ways. That's not to say we can't have fun. We loved the creativity of the *Washington Post's* retro arcade game Floppy Candidate (wapo.st/2E7MBCk) that launched during the US Presidential campaign of 2016.

## The entrepreneurial journalist

Journalists often have developed key entrepreneurial skills. They often have to work freelance, be adaptable to change and be risk-takers.

Launching an app requires a range of creative, editorial, business and marketing skills. These are often areas of strength for those with backgrounds in journalism.

### The unique features of platforms

Convincing people to download a new app is hard. Mainstream news apps – BBC News, CNN, the *Guardian*, Sky News, etc – have built loyal followings. So news apps really need to stand out by offering something different. Why would you download a dedicated news app, unless it offered a better news consumption experience than that offered by existing news apps and Facebook?

Advantages of an app over a responsive mobile website include:

- **News alerts** –Apps work well on smartwatches, phones and tablets. Keep them short, personalised and for important breaking news only.
- **Personalisation** – Apps can algorithmically serve up related content, based on user behaviour, encouraging readers to stay longer.

- **Online and offline reading** – Apps allow content to be read without a mobile connection.
- **Location** – We take our phone and smartwatch with us wherever we go. Apps can determine where in the world a user is, although this can raise privacy concerns.
- **A tailored design** – Designers have unprecedented control over how content is accessed: a key benefit of app design versus responsive mobile websites.
- **Revenue** – Apple users are wealthier than Android users and spend more on apps.

These days apps are not significantly faster than responsive websites. Newer technologies like Google AMP and a renewed focus on website speed mean responsive websites can be fast.

Location or database-driven services can work well. Jeff Jarvis (2014) advises newspapers to build services of genuine value to serve the local community. He talks about what he calls the 'use case scenarios' of news, i.e. how news forms part of users' daily lives.

Jarvis outlines a typical scenario:

> Waking up and wanting a quick view of what's happened (the home page is a rather poor answer to this need); following and receiving alerts on stories that matter to us; getting background on a story (Wikipedia has fulfilled that function and now Vox is trying to make a business of it); connecting with members of our communities to talk or take action.

What is the use case of a printed newspaper? 'Do people truly still need a product that tells them what happened yesterday, which they likely already know?' asks Jarvis (2014).

There is likely to be more growth in full interactive TVs which will include voice control. We can't (yet!) walk into a room and ask our TV a question. Something like, 'Have the police managed to catch the killer of XXX?' or 'Is XXX appearing at the MTV Music Awards this year?' (where XXX is a person currently in the news). Obviously, this is quite a complex scenario even for modern technology to handle.

### The business of app creation

App creators, like journalists, need to understand the business of publishing. As with launching any media product, you need to create a business plan. It may consider:

- **Product** – What is the app and how will it work?
- **User** – Understand the user's wants and needs. Listen to their feedback and read reviews of rival apps.
- **Revenue** – Can you charge to download your app? If so, what price?

- **Marketing** – How will you promote it?
- **Distribution** – Via the app stores – Apple Store, Google Play and Amazon.
- **Costs** – Content creation costs time and money. Apps need regular updates.
- **Risks** – There are many risks, e.g the app stores can refuse to list your app.

You may need seed (early investment) funding.

## Seed funding

Students are often in a good position to attract funding for new ideas. Universities and students' unions may be able to provide grants or loans to those with promising new ideas. The Prince's Trust (princes-trust.org.uk) runs an enterprise programme for unemployed people aged under 30. Along with funding grants, it offers mentoring from experienced business professionals.

Crowdfunding has become a popular way to get investment. Kickstarter (kickstarter.com) and Indiegogo (indiegogo.com) are the two of the biggest names where users fund your idea in return for perks or a gift. They usually work on a principle of 'all or nothing' – if you don't reach your target investment you won't get a penny. However, the investment is not a loan and doesn't have to be paid back.

There are also business angels who are wealthy individuals who invest in good ideas and also provide business mentoring. The Dragons' Den TV show will give you some idea of how this system works. The business angels may invest, but only in return for a stake or share in your company.

Failing that, there are more traditional approaches that include 'the bank of mum and dad' – who may or may not expect their money back! Or you could get a business loan from a high street bank, peer-to-peer loan provider or use credit cards. You will need to keep an eye on the interest rate of any loan.

Make sure you understand who has the rights to the IP (intellectual property) and be wary of signing any contract that gives your rights away. Having the right IP protection helps you to stop people stealing or copying:

- the names of your products or brands
- your inventions
- the design or look of your products
- things you write, make or produce  (Gov.uk n.d.)

The pressure to come up with a new idea can be intense. For an idea to be a hit in Silicon Valley, it has to be 'disruptive' – that's to say, it should radically alter an existing market. For example, Airbnb which allows people to rent out their own home disrupted the hotel industry. Spotify, the streaming app, disrupted the music industry.

But you can be more modest in your aims. To get ideas look at apps you have installed on your smartphone, tablet or smartwatch. Can the core actions be improved? Go to the Apple Store and read reviews of as many apps as possible. Are there particular features that users like or dislike?

## News apps

There is a difference between news apps and digital editions:

- **Live news apps:** updated breaking news. Often free to download and supported by adverts.
- **Digital editions:** more of a static product – essentially the printed version of a magazine or newspaper in app form. Often subscription-based.

The likes of the *Guardian* and Mail Online and many other media brands have both types of apps listed in the app stores. Some, such as BBC News, exist only as a live news app.

Here are a few examples of interesting content-based apps.

### BuzzFeed – Tasty (Android/iOS)

Tasty is the popular cooking section of BuzzFeed. The app has a killer party trick – it communicates recipe times via Bluetooth to a smart induction cooktop known as the One Top (tastyonetop.com). This foolproof way of cooking will appeal to anyone who fancies themself as the next Gordon Ramsay. Ben Kaufman, the head of BuzzFeed Product Labs states: 'Tasty's strong brand and massive fan base give it almost limitless avenues for expansion – from cookbooks to licensing to consumer tech' (Ha 2017).

### Reuters TV (Android/iOS)

Reuters, the global news agency, has been a B2B supplier of information to newsrooms for decades. But this Reuters TV app is targeted at consumers. Tell the app how much time you have, from five to 30 minutes, and it will create a

*Table 9.1* The top news apps and digital editions for iPad and Android devices (July 2017 as listed on Apple and Google Play app stores)

| iPad – top news apps | iPad – top digital editions | Android – top news apps | Android – digital editions |
| --- | --- | --- | --- |
| 1. Twitter | 1. The Times | 1. Twitter | 1. The Guardian |
| 2. BBC News | 2. Daily Mirror | 2. BBC News | 2. Mail Online |
| 3. Mail Online | 3. The Guardian | 3. Reddit | 3. The Telegraph |
| 4. Sky News | 4. The Telegraph | 4. Sun Savers | 4. PocketMags |
| 5. The Guardian | 5. Mail Plus | 5. Sky News | 5. Pocket Casts |

personalised news broadcast. It targets 30 to 40 year old males who are moving away from traditional linear TV news.

## App users

We have said it before and will say it again, it is essential to take a user-centred approach in all aspects of mobile journalism. Persona profiling is used to create a profile of a typical user of a website or app. It is essential to give your imagined typical user a real name. The idea being that if you create an app for, say, 'Tina – a 42-year-old teacher from Surrey' – you will get closer to meeting her individual *needs* and *wants*.

The key questions you then ask 'Tina' could be:

- What media platforms does she own – phone, tablet, smartwatch, Amazon Echo, etc?
- What is the use case – when and where does she use each device? How does it fit into her average day?
- What journalism content does she seek?
- What functionality does she seek?
- What other rival media brands does Tina engage with on a typical day?

You may wish to think about doing a 'back of an envelope' persona profile of the typical user of the following media brands and imagine what they would look like:

- *Wired* (science/tech publication)
- *Cosmopolitan* (women's lifestyle)
- *Radio Times* (TV listing and review guide)

Founded in 1993, *Wired* is a technology magazine from publishers Conde Nast. It is read mostly by men (72 per cent male) with an average age of 39 (*Wired* 2017). They are relatively wealthy and tend to be early adopters of new technology. So it is worth thinking about the types of apps that are likely to appeal to this group.

Published by Hearst UK, *Cosmopolitan* has suffered falling print sales as its audience of young females move online. Younger women tend to be heavy users of mobile and social media, particularly photo sharing apps such as Instagram. *Cosmo* has a successful digital edition app and has a distributive content strategy which means it publishes to a vast range of social platforms.

At the other extreme, *Radio Times* was first published in 1923 and its readers are middle aged (the average is 56) and equally split between men and women (*Radio Times*, 2015). While its audience is less techy than readers of, say, *Wired*, the *Radio Times* has an excellent TV listings and reviews app that will bring in younger users to the brand.

How would you develop ideas for apps to appeal to each of these distinct communities of interest?

---

**Essential apps for journalists**

As a journalist you will also use apps for newsgathering and production. Here are five of the best:

- **Evernote** (evernote.com) – organises research documents and audio files.
- **iMovie** (apple.com/uk/imovie/) – video editing for iOS only. Adobe Premiere Clip (adobe.com/uk/products/premiere-clip.html) for Android users.
- **Just Press Record** (openplanetsoftware.com/just-press-record/) – record and transcribe interviews. iPhone, iPad and Apple Watch only.
- **Photoshop Express** (photoshop.com/products/photoshopexpress) – edit and share images.
- **Pocket Reporter** (pocketreporter.co.za) – excellent free app for reporters in the field (Android only).

---

## Development

Journalists have many of the creative, business and marketing skills needed to produce a great news app. The area where journalists may need to partner with someone is during the coding process. You can produce a native app (that is, one designed for a specific operating system e.g. iOS) or a hybrid app (works across many devices).

Carla White (2013) lists six stages of app development. These phases are actually overlapping and repeating. White states: 'some phases such as development and promotion never truly end'.

- **Conceptualise** – idea, discover and brainstorm
- **Design** – develop flow and story, prototype, test and output final designs
- **Develop** – code and test
- **Distribute** – submit and go live
- **Promote** – using all the offline and online tools available to you
- **Maintain** – update by working on new releases taking into account updates from Apple and Android to the operating system. Launch app on newer platforms (adapted from White 2013).

The process doesn't have to be complex. 'Instead of going nuts with features in your app, start with the bare minimum and focus on a beautiful design instead,' White advises.

Consider the following:

- What does your app need to do?
- What is the 'action' or 'event' that will take place?

- How many screens will you need to achieve the action?
- How will the action start and finish?

It is worth examining the typical user actions that are taken on news apps and other style of apps. eBay, the well-known auction app, has two distinct types of users – those who wish to buy and those who wish to sell items. It is worth exploring the actions of buying and selling from start to completion. How many screens are involved?

In doing this exercise, you are conducting a basic form of 'systems analysis' – this defined as:

> the act, process, or profession of studying an activity (such as a procedure, a business, or a physiological function) typically by mathematical means in order to define its goals or purposes and to discover operations and procedures for accomplishing them most efficiently.
>
> (Systems analysis 2018)

For your own app you will wish to sketch out on paper a flow diagram – the process by which users achieve their goals going through various screens.

The next stage is the fun part – do a wireframe design for the app. This is a visual guide that represents the skeletal framework of your app. It is likely to include the navigation system, taking into account how people will control your app using touchscreen or perhaps their voice.

Wireframe software:

- **Adobe XD** (adobe.com/uk/products/experience-design.html) is one of the most professional packages.
- **Wireframe.cc** (wireframe.cc) provides a super minimalist interface that is sufficient for most needs.

## Design, coding and testing

Now we have wireframe sketches, either on paper or using software, of what will appear on the various screens, we need to think about coding the app.

If you build a native app the key languages are:

- **Objective-C or Swift** – the main programming languages for Apple iOS devices
- **Java** – for Android apps.

There are also free low-code app development tools which take a visual, drag 'n' drop, approach. You start by selecting a generic template and those wanting to offer customised features and deeper interaction may need to look elsewhere. They often produce hybrid apps.

### Go native or hybrid?

App developers may tell you that native is always best. But the users probably won't care (or be able to tell) how your app was created, as long as it meets their needs.

If you choose to hire a developer, you will need them to maintain the app, potentially over many years. Security patches and improvements are regularly included in updates to Android and iOS. This is one reason taking a DIY approach, using a low-code environment, is growing in popularity. One advantage of using such tools is that operating systems are changing so frequently that custom app designs created by developers are struggling to keep up with the changes.

Data from analysts Gartner state that Android and iOS now account for:

> a combined 99 per cent of the worldwide smartphone operating system market. Android holds 86.2 per cent of the market, up from 82.2 per cent in the year-ago quarter. Combine that with the 12.9 per cent iOS holds, and that's 99.1 per cent of the entire market.

> (Miller 2016)

So if you are designing a native app, logic suggests that you should start with Android. Java was launched by Sun Microsystems in 1995 and is supported by Android Studio, the free integrated development environment (IDE), that is used for native app development.

iOS apps are coded in Objective-C, which was adopted by Apple for its desktop operating system (MacOS) in 1996, or the newer Swift. You will also need the Apple IDE–Xcode. Apple's Beginners Guide to App Development is an essential resource (apple.co/2BLEJ3U).

### Learning to code an app

Google and Apple are encouraging everyone to learn to code. Since 2014, Apple has been pushing a new language known as Swift, which works alongside existing Objective-C code. Apple has developed many free online training tools (developer.apple.com/swift).

App Inventor (appinventor.mit.edu) for Android was initially created by Google to train its own staff in mobile advert development. Google then donated the software to Massachusetts Institute of Technology (MIT) Center for Mobile Learning and it is now used to teach students with no experience of coding.

### MIT App Inventor

To get going with App Inventor you will need the following:

- **Computer** – It may sound obvious, but design is done on a computer and not a smartphone. App Inventor is web-based and works on both PC and Mac.

- **Google account** – You log in via Google.
- **Emulator software** – Install the emulator software from the App Inventor site on your computer. The emulator shows what your app looks like on a mocked up mobile phone screen.
- **Android phone or tablet** –You can design your app on a Mac, but to test and launch your app an Android device – smartphone or tablet – is an essential requirement. The MIT Companion App from the Google Play Store acts as a testing environment.

MIT App Inventor has two key parts – a 'drag and drop' design view and a separate coding view – known as blocks view – illustrates how your code works.

## Development jargon

There is a lot of programming jargon that comes with learning app development:

> **Components** – Components are elements you combine to create the app. Components can be visible on screen – e.g. a 'label' component shows text on the screen and 'buttons' can be clicked to achieve some action.
>
> **Properties** – These customise the appearance of the app using colour, text and sizes etc.
>
> **Methods** – You manipulate *methods* of the *components* to make things happen.

*Figure 9.1* MIT App Inventor – the design view
By MIT (ShareAlike 3.0 Unported License)

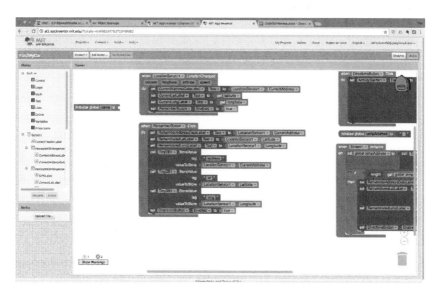

*Figure 9.2* MIT App Inventor – the blocks view
By MIT (ShareAlike 3.0 Unported License)

**Behaviours** – Behaviours can be *user-initiated* events e.g. a button is clicked and the app does something. Or they can be *external* events e.g. the app may need to respond to a text arriving on your phone.

**Debugging** – Like many IDE tools, App Inventor includes a debugger. You run the debugger to check the code is working as it should.

**Memory** – Most apps need to remember responses e.g. when a button is tapped. To personalise a news app, it can be helpful for the app to remember what content a user has looked at previously.

**Conditions** – An app can be programmed with decision-making logic, based on the data in its memory and other variables.

**Looping** – Computers are very good at repeating functions over and over again. A loop is a sequence of instructions that are continually repeated until a certain condition is reached.

**Sensors** – Apps can activate sensors on a device e.g. GPS, Bluetooth, orientation and camera.

**Control** – Navigation on smart devices is often via touch where swipes, pinches and taps have specific learned meanings. Users can also interact via speech commands e.g. Alexa or Siri.

**Compiler** – Once an app is written and debugged it goes to the Compiler. This translates the code to create an executable program. The result is the Android Package Kit (APK). This compressed file is uploaded to the Google Play store for sale.

*Pros and cons of App Inventor*

**Pros:** App Inventor is free and allows you to learn about the principles of coding in Java. Apple fans who wish to learn about app development should explore Swift (swift.org).

**Cons:** Not as quick as employing a developer or using a low-code tool.

### Low-code development platforms

If you have an idea for an app, you may wish to see if you can quickly develop it into an app. There are plenty of free low-code development tools. Top low-code picks:

- **Adobe Phonegap (phonegap.com)** – This packages content from an existing website and turns it into an app.
- **AppyPie (appypie.com)** – If speed is a priority this is a great choice.
- **Appmakr (appmakr.com)** – This is a well-known low-code tool.

**Pros:** Quick and designed to be easy. No coding required.

**Cons:** Check out prices before committing. Some charge to launch on the app stores.

## Embedding social media

MIT App Developer allows for the integration of application programmer interface (API) technology within apps. If you thought it was cool that apps can work with mobile sensor functionality – such as GPS and Bluetooth – this will blow your mind!

APIs offer the ability to get your app to communicate with external websites such as Facebook and Twitter. Deploying an API can vastly extend an app's functionality. API is the set of procedures and rules that allow this communication between apps and websites.

Facebook launched its first API in 2007 and it was actually key to the company's success in the early days. At a time when rivals such as MySpace (remember them?) were essentially standalone websites, Mark Zuckerberg wanted to make Facebook ubiquitous. This meant it encouraged websites and the apps to make close links to the site.

### Social media APIs

Facebook Connect, an API, launched in 2008 and allowed users to log in with their Facebook details to third-party websites. It became popular, as people hate having to create separate logins and passwords for all the websites they use and it meant that Facebook could spread its influence around the Web.

In 2010 Open Graph from Facebook was launched and allowed web developers to embed Facebook functionality into apps and websites. It allowed users of apps to engage with their Facebook profile and friends even when they were not on Facebook.

We can view API as providing machine-to-machine access to the content in a database. Websites and apps are constantly communicating with each other. This runs parallel with a website's human interface – the view we see.

If you have ever seen Google Maps pop up on another website or app, that is down to an API. App Inventor allows designers to create apps that link up with Amazon's database of books and a range of other APIs.

### List of useful APIs

Link your website or app with databases and services from these big names:

- **Amazon** – aws.amazon.com/api-gateway
- **Facebook** – developers.facebook.com
- **Fitbit** – dev.fitbit.com
- **Google** – developers.google.com
- **Top Ten Social APIs – For Facebook, Twitter and Google Plus** programmableweb.com/news/top-10-social-apis-facebook-twitter-and-google-plus/analysis/2015/02/17

### App stores

You've made it! You've designed, coded and tested your app and it's ready to be uploaded to an app store. As of March 2017 the number of apps in each store according to Statista was (Statista, March 2017):

1. **Google Play – 2,800,000**
2. **Apple Store – 2,200,000**
3. **Windows Store – 669,000**
4. **Amazon App Store – 600,000**

### Getting your app approved by Apple and Google

All the main app stores publish checklists of what you need to do to get your app listed. We recommend following the advice to the letter. Apple has particularly strict quality thresholds and apps are frequently rejected.

App Store Review Guidelines – developer.apple.com/app-store/review/guidelines/: This lengthy document contains rules regarding safety, performance, business, design and legal issues to with your app. For example, it states:

> Apps should not include content that is offensive, insensitive, upsetting, intended to disgust, or in exceptionally poor taste.
>
> (Apple Store Review Guidelines n.d.)

If your app contains political, religious or user-generated content you could be rejected. It warns: 'Apps with user-generated content present particular challenges, ranging from intellectual property infringement to anonymous bullying' (Apple n.d.).

The rules for getting an Android app on the Google Play store can be found at: developer.android.com/distribute/best-practices/launch/launch-checklist.html.

The aim of every app is to get into the top 20 chart in the news category – this is easier said than done. Apps with big increases in downloads may get a 'featured app' position on the store's home page, thus boosting downloads even further.

However, most apps won't get such exposure. So you will rely on users seeking out your app. Searching on the stores is often cumbersome and unforgiving to users who make simple spelling mistakes or don't know the precise name of the app. The result is that users often stick to the established names in the top 20 charts. Apps need heavy promotion when they launch on as many channels as possible – both online and offline advertising.

## Revenue

Apple, under its late boss Steve Jobs, was responsible for many significant innovations in mobile technology and the company remains a leader to this day. But while most people focus on the iPhone and iPad, the California-based tech giant also invented a new online marketplace in digital content.

Publishers had been trying to sell content prior to 2008, but they came across a significant barrier – how do you get people to pay for content that may cost as little as 99p? Apple came to the rescue with a system of micropayments through its iTunes platform and app store that was both secure and, most importantly, convenient. Today we take this system of micropayments for digital content for granted.

What will you charge for your app? You could be free to download, but include adverts. With this model, you will be reliant on a high volume of downloads which will generate advertising revenue. This is the model for most live news apps.

However, there are other revenue modules. You could make your app free to download, but charge for extra functionality or more advanced features.

*The Economist* newspaper sells a popular digital subscription for £145 a year (although it's cheaper for students) which bundles access to its website, digital edition on smartphones and tablets, email alerts and audio podcasts.

Or you could charge a one-off fee to download your app. In general, people are more willing to pay for apps that offer specialist functionality. CyberTuner, a specialist app aimed at professional piano tuners, charges £800. Apple users are more wealthy and willing to pay for apps than Android users.

### Membership fees

To list your app on one of the stores, there are fees to pay. You didn't think that the tech giants would allow you to do it for free?

*Apple Store fees (Correct in August 2017)*

developer.apple.com/support/compare-memberships/

> **Membership** – $99 (around £80) per year gives access to App Developer Program and the ability to distribute apps via the store (free for schools/ universities)
> **Revenue split** – 70 per cent to app developers. Apple takes 30 per cent of all revenue generated.

*Google Play (Correct in August 2017)*

> support.google.com/googleplay/android-developer/answer/6334373?hl=en-GBle support.google.com/googleplay/android-developer/answer/6112435? hl=en-GB
> **Membership fee:** $25 (around £20) registration fee. This is a one-off charge.
> **Revenue split** – Developer receives 70 per cent of revenue. Google takes a 30 per cent 'transaction fee'

Funds are paid after a four-week delay and there is a minimum amount of money before they pay out, which may be a concern for apps with relatively low numbers of downloads.

## Ethical issues

Smartphone apps run over the internet, but it is important to note that apps are not the same as websites. The Web (which was invented by Sir Tim Berners-Lee in the early 1990s) was designed as an open system based around HTML. It had sharing and the free exchange of knowledge at its heart.

### Are apps killing the open web?

*Wired* magazine journalist Chris Anderson (2010) wrote an influential article headlined – 'The Web is Dead. Long Live The Internet.' He writes: 'As much as we love the open, unfettered Web, we're abandoning it for simpler, sleeker services that just work.'

Users are increasingly going to apps that provide a 'walled garden'. That is to say that some social media apps do everything possible to discourage users from leaving the app by not linking out to the open web. At the time of writing, the Instagram app for example doesn't allow linking out to external news websites. which is a problem for media brands hoping to attract traffic.

Search engines cannot access app content in apps, so it is unsearchable. In this way, apps go against the open nature of World Wide Web and HTML coding language.

But the reality is more confused says Mathew Ingram (2014). He states that while

> I'm certainly not arguing with the idea that the open web needs defending, or that we should be aware of the efforts of large corporations to force increasing amounts of activity and content into their silos – that is definitely an issue with Facebook in particular, and with others.

However Ingram doesn't blame this on apps. He says that apps are just a symptom of the problem.

### Net neutrality

You may have heard about net neutrality, where the internet service providers (ISPs), the telecommunications networks who supply mobile and fixed line broadband, must treat all internet traffic equally. This may not sound very important, but it goes to the very heart of the concept of the open web.

The internet should be run on democratic principles and the traffic to and from an amateur blog or small news website is handled in exactly the same way as traffic to much larger news websites such as the BBC and CNN. In short, there should be no internet fast lane that prioritises the content of one site over another.

This may sound very sensible, but some service providers would like to charge more for access to certain sites. In particular, they highlight that the costs of delivering video in high definition means they incur extra costs that video sites should pay for. The strain on the network is already leading to bandwidth congestion. By charging companies for better access, the ISPs say they could also invest more in their network infrastructure.

Some claim that internet fast lanes have a lot going for them. The *Washington Examiner* (2017) stated that most would agree that Net traffic going in and out of a hospital should 'take precedence over bytes of 100 dudes Googling to find out whether Jennifer Lawrence is married?'

But in 2016 the EU Body of European Regulators for Electronic Communications (BEREC) ruled:

> ISPs are prohibited from blocking or slowing down of Internet traffic, except where necessary … The exceptions are limited to: traffic management to comply with a legal order, to ensure network integrity and security, and to manage congestion, provided that equivalent categories of traffic are treated equally.
>
> (Cited Toor 2016)

While net neutrality is guaranteed in Europe, a battle is on to retain it in the USA. Evan Greer (2017) states: 'I am not being dramatic when I say the Internet is at a crossroads.' He warns that if net neutrality is removed the internet will be a 'hellscape of extra fees, slow-loading apps, and censorship'.

### Apps that hook the user

Do you use your phone obsessively? Do you suffer 'withdrawal symptoms' when you are unable to access it? Mobile phone devices and social media apps are designed to be habit forming. Nir Eyal, an investor and entrepreneur, describes the importance of including 'hooks' in habit-forming products.

All of these are simple actions that are tied to an immediate reward:

- A Pinterest scroll, which might turn up an interesting photo.
- A Google search, which might teach us something new.
- A Play button on YouTube, which can capture our interest for a few minutes.

The strongest triggers, Nir says (cited Sam, S 2016), are when we feel 'Bored, lonely, confused, fearful, lost or indecisive.'

He adds that mobile devices are designed to be checked repeatedly. We look at emails, messaging apps, social media updates, etc throughout each day. In fact, this aspect of constant checking becomes a habit and routine. He states: 'we start to feel anxious or disconnected from the world around us if we don't check the phone – then the action morphs from habit into reflex' (Nir, cited Sam 2016).

Studies have examined how depressed people use apps. Silvia Li Sam (2016) states: 'If we're honest with ourselves, we all use products to modulate our mood: when someone's feeling lonely, they check Facebook; when someone's feeling unsure, they go to Google; when bored, people check YouTube, sports scores, news, and Pinterest.'

A hook can be simple and doesn't have to achieve anything specific. It is simply designed to influence a user to interact with an app and to form a habit. So if you ever feel like you are addicted to your smartphone, a developer may well have emotionally hooked you in to using their app! We are particularly vulnerable when we feel bored or lonely.

## Digital editions

Creating a native app can be costly. Developing digital editions is considerably cheaper and you may wish to do this as part of a distributive content strategy.

Magazine brands such as *The Economist*, *The Week*, *Forbes*, the *Spectator* and *Newsweek* have some of the most popular digital circulations on the app stores – it is noticeable how business and political magazines dominate the top digital edition magazine charts. *The Times*, the *Guardian* and the *Daily Mail* dominate newspaper digital edition sales.

Digital editions are replicas or closely match the layouts of a newspaper or magazine print product. The main ways people download digital editions is through the Apple, Google Newsstand and Amazon app stores.

## Readly (readly.com)

As well as downloading digital subscriptions from Apple and Google, there are also all 'you can eat' business models where a large number of magazines titles can be read for a single monthly subscription. Readly gives access to over 2,000 British and international publications, including many big name magazine brands such as *Rolling Stone*, *Time* and *Vanity Fair*. Readly works out the revenue that is sent to the publisher based on dwell time i.e. how much time members spend reading each magazine and is based on a 70:30 split – with the majority going to the publisher.

There are pros and cons of digital editions as a format. On the positive side, it really is a 'no-brainer' for legacy print publishers. They are produced using DTP software such as Adobe InDesign or QuarkXPress. Alongside sales of a magazine in print, digital editions are counted in the audited circulation figures that are collated by ABC (abc.org.uk). Media brands need to show that their circulation figures are robust, so they can retain advertisers.

Many digital editions are replicas in PDF format of the printed magazine or newspaper. However, this doesn't have to be the case and *The Times*, *The Economist* and the *Guardian* have digital editions that take into account the needs of mobile platforms in more creative ways. They embed video, audio and social media links into stories.

Digital editions provide a curated experience – journalists, acting as gatekeepers, have selected the best content. They also provide a distraction-free reading experience, similar to reading a printed newspaper. *The Times* reported that subscribers spend 30 minutes a day with its digital edition, versus just five on its website (Boyle 2013).

### Tools for designing digital editions

Getting a print magazine online could be as easy as exporting your designed PDF pages from a desktop publishing package and uploading to a magazine website. For basic magazine hosting Issuu (issuu.com) is popular.

For those looking to include deeper interaction including video and slideshows there are other tools:

### App Studio for Quark (quark.com)

App Studio is a module that outputs interactive tablet editions and embed multimedia including sound, video and images. It comes as standard with QuarkXPress and as a plugin to InDesign.

### Adobe Digital Publishing (digitalpublishing.acrobat.com)

Quark's rival in DTP also allows journalists to output content in a vast range of formats suitable for desktop, phone and tablet.

*Figure 9.3* App Studio from Quark is available as a free plugin for InDesign
By Quark Software

**Ceros** (ceros.com)

Unlike other solutions where design is done in DTP packages, you do everything on the website and it is simple to use.

**Pros:** Digital editions are cheaper to produce than apps. They fulfil a need from an audience who wishes to read their favourite magazine on their mobile device. Can be read offline, without a net connection.

**Cons:** They lack the live and dynamic experience of news apps or the web. Digital editions can look stunning on tablet devices, but text can be hard to read on smaller smartphones.

## News aggregators

Apple News, a news aggregation software, launched in 2015. It aimed to improve on the experience of digital editions and to integrate personalisation and social media sharing facilities. In this respect, it provides a halfway house between the personalisation of a Facebook newsfeed and features of digital editions.

But Apple News was not a new idea – Flipboard (flipboard.com), which works on both Android and iOS, launched five years earlier. Both platforms learn from user behaviour and an algorithm suggests content likely to appeal to the user.

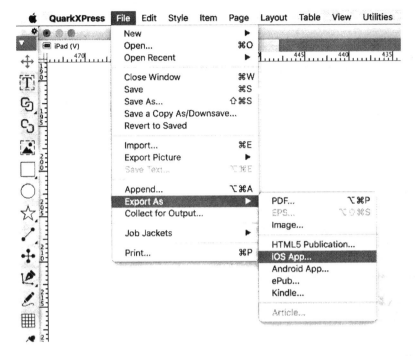

*Figure 9.4* QuarkXPress users can export their designs in Android, iOS and HTML5
         formats
By Quark Software

The Reuters Institute (2016) quoted an anonymous respondent:

> I usually go through Apple News. It gets a variety of things, like I'm interested
> in certain topics that I probably wouldn't find or I'd have to search for it
> myself so it's like a one stop shop of things that interest me.
>
> (18–34 year old, US Focus Group, *Digital News Report* 2016)

Yet the Reuters Institute found that uptake of news aggregator apps is very low,
with only 3 per cent of respondents to its survey in the UK using Apple News.
This suggests users prefer consuming news through other methods, such as social
media or dedicated news apps.

**Pros:** Personalised. The algorithm selects content that may interest users.
       Magazine pages look stunning on tablet devices.
**Cons:** Limited uptake. Costs are involved for publishers.

## Apps for wearables

It may be wise to be 'wary' of investing too much time in wearables. Uptake of smartwatches has been slower than many experts imagined. Similar to phones, the two biggest operating systems (OS) are made by Apple (WatchOS) and Google (Android Wear). The latter runs on watches made by LG, Asus and Fossil.

Academic Jeff Jarvis (2014) describes how it is important to look at use case scenarios – how people access news in their day-to-day lives. The use case for news on smartwatches seems a little dubious to us, when reading news on a phone or tablet feels pretty convenient.

However, smartwatch news alerts are popular. It pays to keep alerts simple and not cram too much information on the screen. WatchOS is famous for its system of 'cards' and 'glances' that contain just the essential information of a story.

There are two main types of smartwatch apps:

> **Companion** – that run on the companion smartphone, but send messages to and from the watch e.g. via Bluetooth.
>
> **Standalone** – these apps run on the watch itself, but use the phone to get a network connection. Watches are getting smarter and the latest version of the Apple Watch contains a SIM card meaning it can run autonomously without needing access to an iPhone.
>
> **Pros:** Great for short and snappy news alerts.
>
> **Cons:** Uptake has been disappointing.

## Conclusion

We are just at the start of the app revolution. There is likely to be growth in many new IoT devices, particular in cars where both Apple and Google have developed operating systems.

App design forces us as journalists to become more entrepreneurial. Taking into account 'use case scenarios', app design forces us to think about providing interactive services which play to the strengths and functionalities offered such as GPS, Bluetooth and APIs.

Take an experimental approach. We learn the most when we fail at something, even if it can be embarrassing and painful at the time. It is relatively straightforward to test ideas on these devices by creating prototypes with the basic functions using free design tools.

Apps are likely to form just one part of a publisher's distributive news strategy that also involves creating content for websites, social media, news aggregators or digital editions.

### Expert interview – Matthias Guenther

### Head of Desktop Publishing, Quark Software

*Figure* 9.5  Matthias Guenther

Quark offers two paths to digital publishing: App Studio and QuarkXPress (the desktop software). App Studio supports creating native apps and web apps (using HTML5) and works with InDesign and QuarkXPress. If you use QuarkXPress, all the functionality is provided within the program. If you want to use InDesign, you need to install a free plug-in first.

The way to work with App Studio is similar using either package – you design your layout and apply typography. You optionally add enrichments – e.g. slideshows, animations and videos. Content creation is really easy, as it hooks into standard functionality of InDesign or QuarkXPress. We have seen novice users create compelling content within hours.

Once you are happy with the design – layout and enrichments – you upload the content to the App Studio portal in the cloud where you configure the app and create a native app. You can then download the app and submit it to the app stores.

### Desktop Publishing

You can also use QuarkXPress without App Studio to create native apps, single apps for Android and iOS, and eBooks as ePub or Kindle.

The most attractive output format is probably HTML5 Publications. They give you app-like or PDF-like experiences, rich layout and typography, and powerful interaction. And you create them with a few mouse clicks. They are 100% HTML5 and you export them to your desktop, so you can host them on your own server. The learning curve is even lower with this option; we have seen users creating their first publication in under 5 minutes.

And since QuarkXPress offers IDML Import, you can even import your InDesign layouts and export them as HTML5 Publications using QuarkXPress.

Should publishers create an app or just have a responsive website?

This is not easy to answer without knowing the publisher, its audience and its intention.

To generalise, the huge difference between a web page and an app is the approach to storytelling – websites tend to throw information at users and require 'pull' requests. Apps are more suited to provide users with a linear storytelling experience, more like a TV programme or print magazine. However, I am sure we can find examples that contradict these generalisations.

## Further reading

Jarvis, J. (2014) *Geeks Bearing Gifts: Imagining New Futures for News*. Cuny journalism Press. Jeff Jarvis encourages an entrepreneurial approach to journalism.
White, C. (2013) *Idea to iPhone: The Essential Guide to Creating Your First App for the iPhone, iPad and iPod touch*. John Wiley & Sons.
Practical advice for app developers who lack coding skills.
The Swift Playground (apple.com/uk/swift/playgrounds/).
This iPad app is an excellent training tool to learn to code an iOS app and is a rival to MIT App Inventor for Android development.

## References

Anderson, C., and Wolff, M. (2010) The web is dead: long live the internet. *Wired*. Conde Nast. Available at: www.wired.com/2010/08/ff_webrip/all/1.
Apple (n.d.) App store review guidelines. Apple Developer. Available at: http://developer. apple.com/app-store/review/guidelines/.
Boyle, D. (2013) *Times* readers spend 30 minutes with the tablet versus five on the website. *Press Gazette*. Available at: www.pressgazette.co.uk/times-readers-spend-30-minutes-tablet-versus-five-website.
Breakingnews.com (2016) Statement from developers about closing of app. Cached at: webcache.googleusercontent.com/search?q=cache:7XkIxnZSuKwJ:tq1.me/WF3r0 N8G+&cd=3&hl=en&ct=clnk&gl=uk.

Costello, S. (2018) Charting the explosive growth of the app store. Lifewire. Available at: www.lifewire.com/how-many-apps-in-app-store-2000252.

Gov.uk (n.d.) Intellectual property and your work. Available at: www.gov.uk/intellectual-property-an-overview.

Greer, E (2017) The future of the internet will be decided in the next three weeks. NBCNews.com. Available at: www.nbcnews.com/think/opinion/ending-net-neutrality-will-destroy-everything-makes-internet-great-ncna823301.

Ha, A. (2017) BuzzFeed is getting into the smart appliance business with the Tasty One Top. TechCrunch. Available at: https://techcrunch.com/2017/07/27/buzzfeed-unveils-tasty-one-top/.

Ingram, M. (2014) Is the web dying, killed off by mobile apps? It's complicated. Mathew Ingram. Gigaom. Available at: https://gigaom.com/2014/11/17/is-the-web-dying-killed-off-by-mobile-apps-its-complicated/.

Jarvis, J. (2014) *Geeks Bearing Gifts: Imagining New Futures for News*. Cuny journalism Press.

Miller, C. (2016) Latest Gartner data shows iOS vs Android battle shaping up much like Mac vs Windows. 9to5Mac. Available at: https://9to5mac.com/2016/08/18/android-ios-smartphone-market-share.

*Radio Times* (2015) Media pack, immediate media. Available at: www.immediate.co.uk/wp-content/uploads/2015/09/RT-Media-Pack.pdf.

Reuters Institute for the Study of Journalism (2016) *Digital News Report 2016*. Reuters Institute for the Study of Journalism. Available at: http://reutersinstitute.politics.ox.ac.uk/our-research/digital-news-report-2016.

Sam, S. L. (2016) Nir Eyal: The psychology of building addictive products. Startup Grind. Available at: https://medium.com/startup-grind/nir-eyal-why-you-are-addicted-to-facebook-slack-pinterest-468a86eb562.

Statista (2017) App stores: number of apps in leading app stores 2017. Statista. Mar. Available at: www.statista.com/statistics/276623/number-of-apps-available-in-leading-app-stores/.

Systems analysis (2018) Available at: www.merriam-webster.com/dictionary/systems analysis.

Toor, A. (2016) Europe's net neutrality guidelines seen as a victory for the open web. The Verge. Available at: www.theverge.com/2016/8/30/12707590/eu-net-neutrality-rules-final-guidelines-berec.

*Washington Examiner* (2017) Sorry Netflix and Amazon: net neutrality regulation belongs in the trash folder. Available at: www.washingtonexaminer.com/why-ajit-pais-decision-killing-obamas-net-neutrality-fcc-regulation-is-good/article/2641528.

White, C. (2013) *Idea to iPhone: The Essential Guide to Creating your First App for the iPhone, iPad and iPod touch*. John Wiley & Sons.

Wired Media Group (2017) Media Kit 2017. Conde Nast. Available at: www.wired.com/wp-content/uploads/2015/03/WMG_Media_Kit_2017_v3.pdf.

# Index

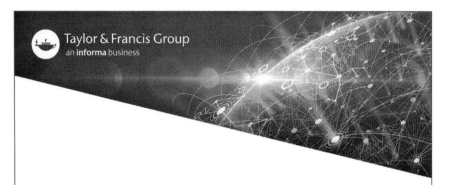